TECHNICAL ILLUSTRATION

TECHNICAL ILLUSTRATION

JAMES D. BETHUNE
Boston University
College of Engineering

John Wiley & Sons
New York   Chichester   Brisbane   Toronto   Singapore

Cover and Part Opening illustrations
by Mario Stasolla

Library of Congress Cataloging in Publication Data:

Bethune, James D., 1941–
  Technical illustration.

  Includes index.
  1. Technical illustration. I. Title.
T11.8.B47   1983   604.2′4   82-8529
ISBN 0-471-05308-2   AACR2

Printed in the United States of America

10 9 8 7 6 5 4 3 2 1

To KENDRA

PREFACE

This book has been written as both a teaching and a reference text. It introduces and explains the basic fundamentals of technical illustration to the beginner and offers the professional a quick reference for techniques and procedures.

Part One of the book deals with axonometric drawings and covers most of the basic construction procedures needed by illustrators to draw fasteners, intersections, and miscellaneous conventions. The intent is to use the isometric medium to explain the procedures that, once mastered, can easily be applied to the dimetric and trimetric axis systems.

Part Two discusses inking techniques, shows many of the tools used by illustrators, and explains different styles of shading and shadow casting. A brief explanation of the uses of computerized CAD/CAM systems as they relate to technical illustration is also included.

Part Three covers one-, two-, and three-point perspective drawings. The variations and uses of each type are explained and illustrated. How to create underlays for these perspectives is also demonstrated.

Part Four contains over a hundred Exercise Problems. These problems have been picked for their versatility. They can be used to teach isometric drawing, with or without shading and shadows, or to teach perspective drawing. Some suggested problems are listed at the end of each chapter, but these are only intended as suggestions. It may be helpful to draw the same figure in several different styles (isometic, perspective, with and without shadows) and to compare the results.

Some comments should be made about the level and the philosophical approach of this book. The book uses a simple step-by-step format. It has been my experience that students can easily skip over material that is too simple or obvious to them, but are stopped from learning material that is presented too rapidly or at too difficult a level. Since there is no way of predicting what material is too difficult or too advanced for each individual student, all the material must be presented in a slow, simple style.

The book is intended to be a foundation on which the student can build. No book can completely cover all aspects of technical illustration. The field is too broad with too many areas of specialty. This book covers the fundamentals and basic techniques in sufficient depth to allow students to gain entry-level industrial positions, and it can also serve as a reference guide throughout their careers.

Several people deserve special thanks: Professor Dave Paolino, my colleague at Wentworth Institute, who proofread and commented on the manuscript throughout its development; Loretta Moore, a good friend, who helped with the art work; Ms. Susan Weiss, my editor at Wiley, who sweated out my deadlines, and my wife, Kendra, who typed and edited the rough drafts. Special thanks to the following reviewers: Professor Patrick D. Murphy, The Williamsport Area Community College, Williamsport, PA; Mr. Paul Nordberg, Los Angeles Pierce College, Woodland Hills, CA; Mr. Bill Martin, Chesterland, OH; Mr. Frank Grady, Portland Community College, Portland, OR; Prof. Jam Mracek, El Camino College, Via Torrance, CA; Mr. Alvin A. Hanson, Grossmont College, El Cajon, CA; Mr. Norm Paul, Waubonsee Community College, Sugar Grove, IL; Mr. J. Lee Turpin, Oregon City, OR; Dr. Earl G. Yarbrough, Northeastern State University, Tahlequah, OK; Mr. Pete Larson, Cuyamaca College, El Cajon, CA; Prof. Leon G. Devlin, Northeast Missouri State University, Kirksville, MO; Mr. Clyde O. Craft, Richmond, KY; Prof. James E. O'Neal, Purdue University, West Lafayette, IN; Mr. James H. Earle, Texas A&M University, College Station, TX; Mr. Richard Cuozzo, Assabet Valley Regional Vocational School District, Marlboro, MA; and Mr. Stan Brodsky, Staten Island, N.Y. Thanks to each of you.

James D. Bethune
Boston University
College of Engineering
Boston, Massachusetts

CONTENTS

TECHNICAL ILLUSTRATION

CHAPTER 1

INTRODUCTION

1-1 INTRODUCTION

Simply stated, technical illustration is the pictorial presentation of technical information. Technical information is so specialized that only persons trained in the particular area can clearly understand it. Each technical area has its own symbols, language, and conventions that, to the untrained person, are meaningless.

It is the technical illustrator's job to translate the technical information into pictures that persons not trained in that particular technical area can understand. The pictures may be simple line drawings (Figure 1-1), exploded drawings (Figure 1-2), maintenance or assembly instructions (Figure 1-3), or cutaways (Figure 1-4). They may be drawn using either axonometric or perspective axis systems, provided the final results are accurate, clear, and easy to understand.

Technical illustrators must always be aware that the primary purpose of their work is to present information and not to create drawings that are necessarily beautiful to look at. This does not mean that the work should ever be shoddy, but it does mean that illustrators should avoid "showing off," and should instead concentrate on the meaning and message of their work. Unfortunately, if done properly, the drawings will go almost unnoticed and will serve only as a conduit for the information being presented.

1-2 TIME ESTIMATION

Whether working for a firm or on a freelance basis, illustrators are constantly asked, "How long will this job take?" An incorrect answer can be both embarrassing and costly (most freelancers use time as a way to estimate price). To help you learn to estimate "how long," it is suggested that you keep a record of how long each assignment takes. A simple pencil notation in the corner of the layout is sufficient. Before you start the assignment, estimate how long you think it will take (whole hours are sufficient); then list the actual time. Compare the estimate with the actual time, and readjust your estimate for the next assignment. See Figure 1-5.

This simple practice will teach you how to accurately estimate time requirements.

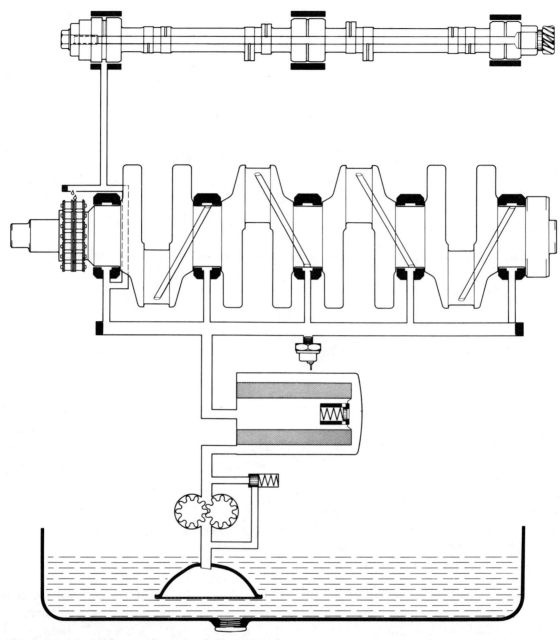

Figure 1-1 A simple two-dimensional illustration showing the operation of a four-cylinder engine with an overhead cam. Courtesy of Volkswagenwerk, Wolfsburg, Germany.

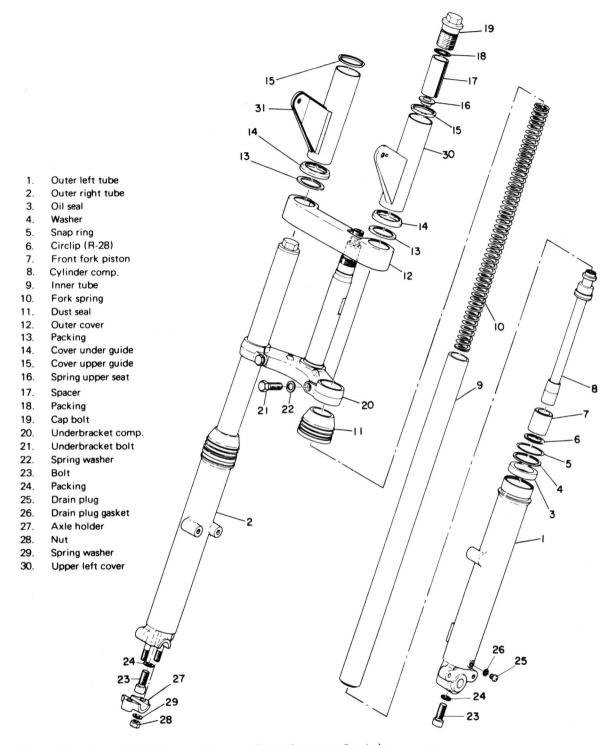

1. Outer left tube
2. Outer right tube
3. Oil seal
4. Washer
5. Snap ring
6. Circlip (R-28)
7. Front fork piston
8. Cylinder comp.
9. Inner tube
10. Fork spring
11. Dust seal
12. Outer cover
13. Packing
14. Cover under guide
15. Cover upper guide
16. Spring upper seat
17. Spacer
18. Packing
19. Cap bolt
20. Underbracket comp.
21. Underbracket bolt
22. Spring washer
23. Bolt
24. Packing
25. Drain plug
26. Drain plug gasket
27. Axle holder
28. Nut
29. Spring washer
30. Upper left cover

Figure 1-2   An exploded drawing. Courtesy of Yamaha Motor Co., Ltd.

FOAM DIE

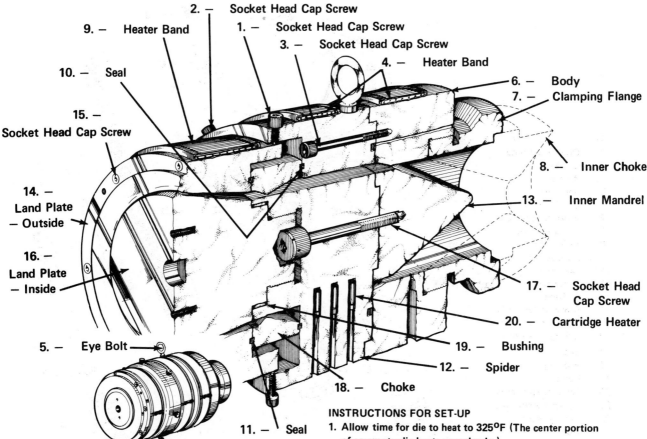

2. – Socket Head Cap Screw
9. – Heater Band
1. – Socket Head Cap Screw
3. – Socket Head Cap Screw
10. – Seal
4. – Heater Band
6. – Body
7. – Clamping Flange
15. – Socket Head Cap Screw
8. – Inner Choke
14. – Land Plate – Outside
13. – Inner Mandrel
16. – Land Plate – Inside
17. – Socket Head Cap Screw
20. – Cartridge Heater
5. – Eye Bolt
19. – Bushing
12. – Spider
18. – Choke
11. – Seal

TORQUE REQUIREMENTS
3 & 17 BOLTS

BOLT SIZE	TORQUE FOOT LBS $\pm$ 10 %
1/2	100
5/8	200
3/4	300

Gloucester Engineering Co.,Inc.
Blackburn Industrial Park/P.O. Box 900
Gloucester, Massachusetts 01930 U.S.A.
Telephone [617] 281-1800/Telex 940-333

European Subsidiary
Gloenco Limited
Berry Hill Industrial Estate
Droitwich, Worcestershire, England
Telephone 0905-7-3644 / Telex 338-484

Figure 1-3 Maintenance or assembly instruction. Courtesy of Gloucester Engineering Co., Gloucester, Mass.

INSTRUCTIONS FOR SET-UP

1. Allow time for die to heat to 325°F (The center portion of an empty die heats very slowly.)
2. Set die gap using brass shim stock or feeler gauge.
   a. Rotate center (No. 16) to alter overall gap.
   b. Bolts (No. 1) are used to correct variation in gap.
   c. Bolts (No. 2) are used only for minute adjustments and are far less sensitive than (No. 1) bolts (No. 2) bear on, and move only the choke ring. (No. 18)
   Readjustment of (No. 1) bolts is usually required when running since pressures & running temperatures tend to destort the flow.
3. Use a good brand of high temperature anti-seize compound such as "Silver Goop" made by the Crawford Co., Cleveland, Ohio on all bolt threads when needed. Use medium consistency Dow Corning 44 Silicone Grease on all teflon seals when needed
   These products are not needed for set-up of the die assembly. They are used during re-assembly.
4. Keep die clean. Take all precautions not to damage die lips. Use brass or copper for cleaning.

Give Lip Diameter and Key No. When Ordering Parts

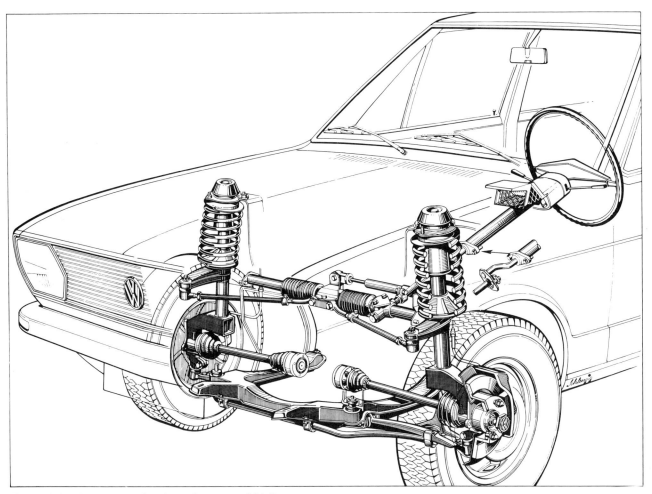

Figure 1-4 A cutaway drawing. Courtesy of Volkswagen-werk, Wolfsburg, Germany.

TIME ESTIMATES

EST: 3 HRS
ACT: 9|10 – 2 HRS
9|12 – 2 HRS
——————
4 HRS

Figure 1-5 A sample time estimate.

1-3 PORTFOLIO DEVELOPMENT

It is important that illustrators develop a portfolio of their work. Prospective employers will ask to see samples of work and will sometimes hire or not hire based on what is presented.

The portfolio should be as varied and complete as possible. Try to show both skill and versatility as an illustrator. If possible, include originals; but if this is not possible, include high-quality copies.

Student assignments may be included in portfolios. In fact, many of the assignments in this book would make a good starting point for your portfolio. Have your instructor grade in pencil so you can erase the marks. Save as much of your work as possible, and use the best for your portfolio.

PART ONE

AXONOMETRIC DRAWINGS

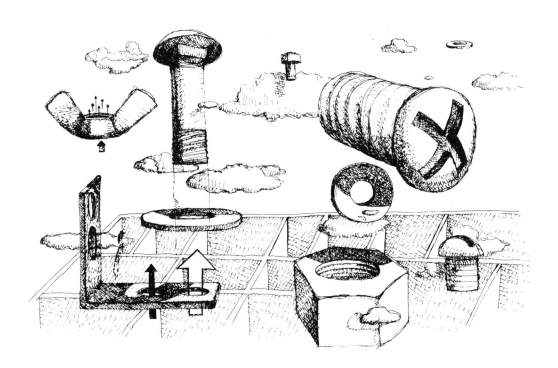

An *axonometric drawing* is a pictorial drawing whose receding lines remain parallel to infinite. This differs from what our eyes normally see—receding lines that converge toward the horizon.

Axonometric drawings are used extensively, despite their inherent visual distortions, because they are easier and faster to draw than drawings with converging receding lines, and because they can be drawn using conventional drafting equipment.

There are three principal types of axonometric drawings: *isometric*, *dimetric*, and *trimetric*. Each will be explained in detail in Part One of this book.

CHAPTER 2

FREEHAND SKETCHING

2-1 INTRODUCTION

The initial approach to most illustrations is to prepare a freehand sketch. A freehand sketch is a fast, easy way to start to put your ideas on paper. The initial sketches can serve as a starting point for discussion with an instructor or customer and can help to clarify any confusion or misunderstandings as to what the work should entail. Freehand sketches can easily be changed or disregarded, if incorrect, with little loss of time.

It is a good habit to make a fairly detailed freehand sketch of any potential illustration, and then check over the sketches for rough accuracy and visual effectiveness before starting finished drawings. It is much easier to redo a freehand sketch than a finished drawing. Figure 2-1 is an example of a technical freehand sketch.

2-2 STRAIGHT LINES

Straight lines are best sketched by using light, short lines, as shown in Figure 2-2. Graph paper or grid underlays are helpful in keeping the sketched lines straight. Grid pads with 4, 8, and 10 lines per inch are commercially available.

No one can draw perfectly straight freehand lines. However, with the help of graph paper, and by keeping the lines short and light, good results can be achieved. Turn the paper as you work so that your drawing stroke is as nearly uniform as possible, using the same length stroke and the same arm position.

Darken objects by going over the initial light short lines with darker, thicker, short lines. A soft lead, such as an H or HB, is excellent for this type of work. It is not necessary to erase the excess initial light lines. See Figure 2-3.

2-3 CIRCLES AND ELLIPSES

Circles and ellipses are sketched using the same basic technique. Sketch two perpendicular·lines. Mark off the circle or ellipse intersection with perpendicular lines, as shown in Figure 2-4. For circles, the marks are all equidistant from the centerpoint. For ellipses, the marks are in accordance with the proportions of the major and minor axes.

The final shapes are first lightly drawn through the marks; then darkened as necessary.

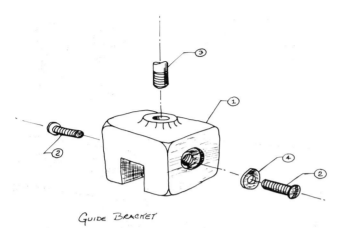

Figure 2-1   An example of a technical sketch.

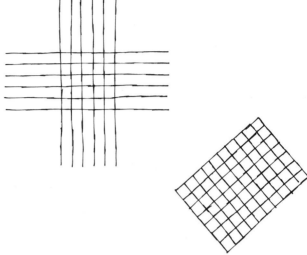

Figure 2-2   Sketch using short lines.

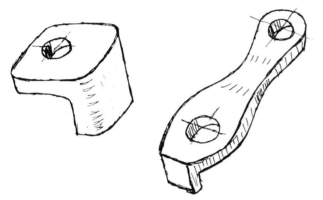

Figure 2-3   Sketch lightly at first; then use darker, heavier lines.

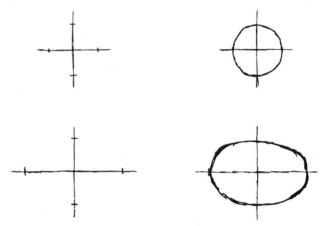

Figure 2-4   How to sketch a circle or an ellipse.

2-4 CURVES

Curved shapes can be sketched by first marking a series of key intersection points, and then by using light, short strokes, joining the points in a smooth, uninterrupted curve. After the basic shape has been defined, darken the curve as needed. Figure 2-5 illustrates the procedure.

2-5 LAYOUTS

When preparing sketches that involve more than one part, make an initial layout of all the parts. Sketch the parts as general geometric shapes (blocks, cylinders, etc.), and then add detail using thicker, darker lines.

The three parts of Figure 2-6 were first drawn lightly as basic geometric shapes, and then checked for positional and visual clarity—that is, to see if each part is easily seen and is located in the correct relative position. The parts are then darkened, shaded if desired, and labeled.

2-6 PROPORTIONS

An object's proportions can be sketched correctly by first sketching a background grid or other reference lines. If, for example, we wished to sketch a

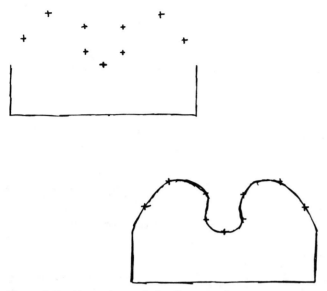

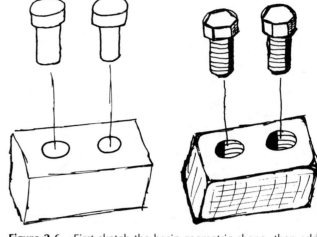

Figure 2-6 First sketch the basic geometric shape; then add the detail.

Figure 2-5 Use points to help align complex curves.

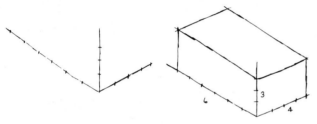

Figure 2-7 A proportional grid system.

block 3 × 4 × 6, we could set up a reference axis, as shown in Figure 2-7. Think of this procedure as first defining the bones, and then building the body around them.

CHAPTER 3

ISOMETRIC DRAWINGS OF NORMAL AND INCLINE SURFACES

3-1 INTRODUCTION

Isometric drawings are axonometric drawings based on an axis system that contains three 120° angles. They can be derived directly from orthographic views.

Figure 3-1-1 illustrates the orthographic views—front, top, and right side—of a 1.00 cube. In Figure 3-1-2 the top view is rotated 45°, changing the front and side view as shown.

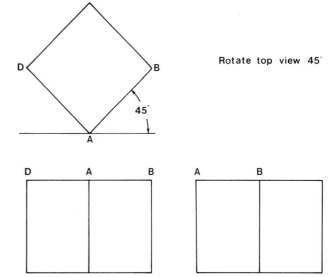

Rotate top view 45°

Figure 3-1-2

The front edge of the cube, AC, is now tilted back around point A, so that it matches the required 120° (30° from the horizontal) axis system, and the shortened distance AB is maintained. See Figure 3-1-3. The question is—What angle of rotation in the right side will match the isometric requirements?

Figure 3-1-4 shows the three equal sides of the cube, AB = AD = AC, positioned on an isometric axis. The side view of line AC is rotated until it

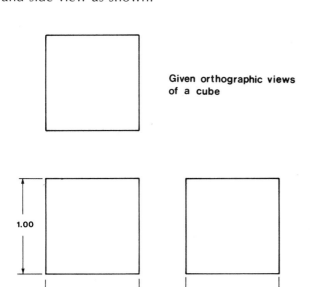

Given orthographic views of a cube

Figure 3-1-1

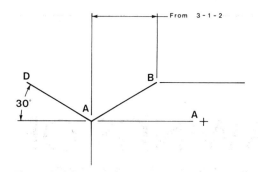

Figure 3-1-3

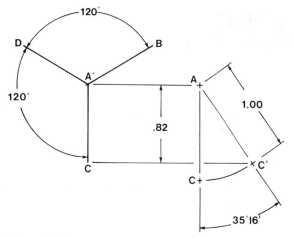

Figure 3-1-4

matches the distance AB that is generated in Figure 3-1-2. The matching angle is 35° 16′ and the resultant foreshortening factor is .82.

If the 35° 16′ rotation is applied, as shown in Figure 3-1-5, to the right-side view, the result will be a pictorial view of the cube that is slightly smaller (.82) than the original cube. By definition this is an isometric projection.

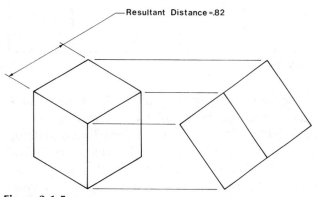

Figure 3-1-5
Figure 3-1 Derivation of an isometric projection.

3-2 ISOMETRIC DRAWINGS

Isometric drawings are pictorial drawings based on an isometric axis. An isometric axis consists of three lines, one of which is usually vertical, located 120° apart. Figure 3-2 illustrates.

An isometric axis may also be drawn, as shown in Figure 3-2, by using a T-square and a 30°−60°−90° triangle or drafting machine. Figure 3-2 also illustrates how a cube would be drawn on this type of isometric axis. Note that all lines are parallel to one of the three principal axis lines.

The intersections of the lines that define an isometric axis also define the three basic isometric planes: the base plane, the left-hand plane, and the right-hand plane. Figure 3-2 depicts these planes.

Figure 3-3 presents three orthographic views and an isometric drawing based on the orthographic views. The dimensions are exactly the same for both drawings even though it appears that the isometric drawing is larger. Dimensions may be directly transferred from orthographic views only to the axis lines or lines parallel to the axis lines. Angular dimensions or dimensions along nonisometric lines (lines not parallel to one of the isometric axis lines) may *not* be directly transferred.

The front view is generally located in the left-hand plane of the isometric drawing but may be varied according to the physical requirements of the object being drawn.

Illustrators transfer dimensions from orthographic views either by direct measurement or by using a compass, dividers, or proportional dividers. Dividers are much faster than using a scale and are therefore the preferred technique. If dividers are used, care should be taken to assure that all objects involved are drawn to the same scale. Figure 3-4 shows a set of proportional dividers.

3-3 FREEHAND ISOMETRIC SKETCHES

Given orthographic views, the first step in converting to isometric drawings is to prepare a freehand isometric sketch. Freehand sketches can be done quickly, corrected easily, and can serve as a guide when drawing the final isometric drawings. Sketches also provide a good way to visualize the

An Isometric Axis

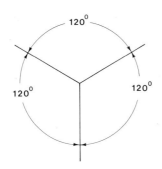

Can also be drawn

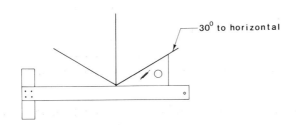

An Isometric Cube

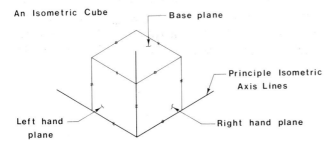

Lines marked //, ///, ∘ are parallel

Figure 3-2   An isometric axis.

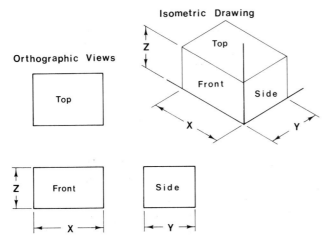

Figure 3-3   Orthographic views and an isometric drawing created from these views.

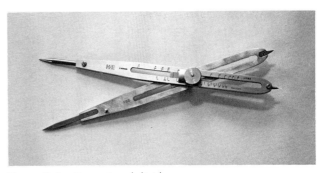

Figure 3-4   Proportional dividers.

objects to be drawn—that is, you can see the objects in three dimensions as opposed to the two, dimensions used in orthographic views.

To prepare a freehand isometric sketch, proceed as outlined here and as illustrated in Figure 3-5.

1. Sketch an isometric axis.
2. Mark off along the isometric axis the overall depth, height, and width and then sketch a box based on these dimensions.
3. Sketch in the detail of the object.
4. Darken the peripheral lines of the object and erase any construction lines that could cause confusion.

Figures 3-6 and 3-7 are further examples of freehand isometric sketches.

Illustrators usually prepare a complete set of sketches for most jobs and then go over the sketches with their customer or supervisor. This enables any changes or corrections to be made before a final isometric drawing is started, thereby saving drawing time.

3-4 NORMAL SURFACES

Normal surfaces are surfaces that are located 90° to each other and parallel to one of the principle planes. Figure 3-8 shows an object containing only normal surfaces. Both the orthographic views and an isometric drawing of the object have been included, and all corners have been numbered for reference purposes.

All surfaces of the object shown in Figure 3-8 are parallel to one of the three isometric planes. Planes 8-1-4-9 and 10-13-6-7 are parallel to the left-hand plane; planes 1-2-3-4 and 13-12-5-6 are parallel to the right-hand plane; and planes 10-13-12-11 and

Given Orthographic Views

STEP 1   Sketch an Isometric Axis

STEP 2   Add Overall Dimensions

STEP 3   Add Detail

STEP 4   Darken Appropriate Lines

Figure 3-5   Preparing an isometric sketch.

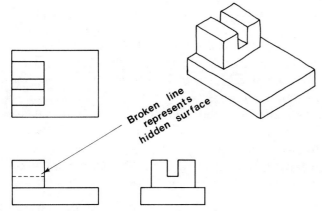

Broken line represents hidden surface

Figure 3-6   Hidden lines.

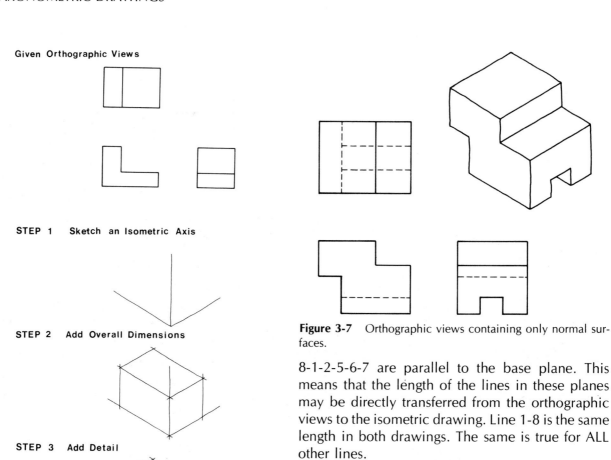

Figure 3-7   Orthographic views containing only normal surfaces.

8-1-2-5-6-7 are parallel to the base plane. This means that the length of the lines in these planes may be directly transferred from the orthographic views to the isometric drawing. Line 1-8 is the same length in both drawings. The same is true for ALL other lines.

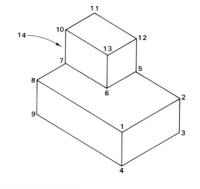

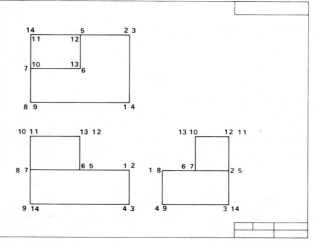

Figure 3-8   Compare the orthographic views with the isometric drawing.

Figure 3-9-1 shows orthographic views of another object, which contains only normal surfaces. In Figure 3-9-1 dimensions are included. To create an isometric drawing from these given views, the following procedure is used. See Figure 3-9-2.

1. Prepare a freehand isometric sketch of the object.
2. Draw, using light construction lines, an isometric axis.
3. Transfer the overall depth, height, and width from the orthographic views to the isometric axis and draw a box as shown.
4. Add specific detail as required.
5. Darken the lines that define the object and erase any excess construction lines. Most illustrators trace the final drawing from the layout created in step 4 to ensure a clean, neat, final drawing. When working in ink, the final drawing is usually traced from a layout.

Figure 3-10 is another example of how isometric drawings are created from orthographic views.

Note that hidden lines are not shown in isometric drawings. The only exception would be to call attention to some specific hidden feature.

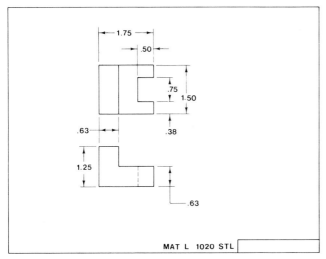

Figure 3-9-1 Given orthographic views.

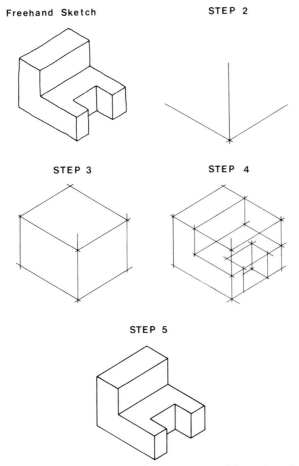

Figure 3-9-2 An isometric drawing prepared from the information given in Figure 3-9-1.

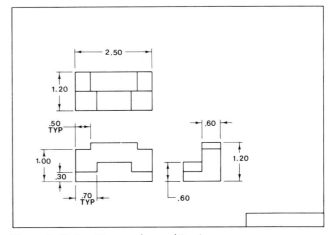

Figure 3-10-1 Given orthographic views.

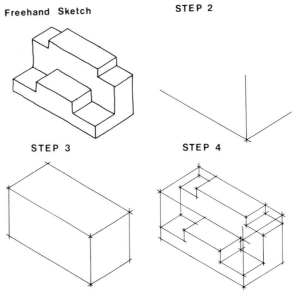

Figure 3-10-2 An isometric drawing prepared from the information given in Figure 3-10-1.

STEP 5

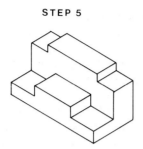

Figure 3-10-2 An isometric drawing prepared from the information given in Figure 3-10-1.

3-5 SLANTED SURFACES

More complex orthographic views that contain slanted surfaces can also be converted to isometric drawings. As with normal surfaces, the sequence of freehand sketch, layout, and final trace is used, but when working with slanted surfaces an additional step is required.

Figure 3-11 presents the orthographic views of an object that contains a slanted surface. The drafter has dimensioned the angle of the slant as 30°. This is called an *angular dimension.*

ANGULAR DIMENSIONS *CANNOT* BE DIRECTLY TRANSFERRED FROM ORTHOGRAPHIC VIEWS TO ISOMETRIC DRAWINGS.

They must first be converted to linear dimensions and then transferred. Figure 3-12 illustrates.

To convert the 30° angular dimension given in Figure 3-11, we must prepare a supplementary layout. Some illustrators simply add lines to given blueprints, but blueprints are not always accurate because of various reproduction processes. In Figure 3-11 the supplementary layout was created by redrawing the front view and then measuring the X and Y dimensions. X and Y are linear dimensions that are equivalent to the 30° angular dimension and may be transferred to the isometric axis.

Figure 3-12 shows the results of measuring an isometric drawing with a circular protractor.

Figure 3-13 is another example of an object that has slanted surfaces. Note that a supplementary layout was used to convert the given angular dimensions to linear dimensions and, in turn, the linear dimensions were transferred to the isometric axis to define the angle in the isometric drawing.

The problem of converting angular dimensions to linear dimensions can be simplified by using an isometric protractor. An isometric protractor makes it possible to measure angular dimensions directly onto an isometric drawing. However, it must be used carefully. It must be properly aligned in the correct position, and it should not be used when a high degree of accuracy is required. Figure 3-14 depicts an isometric protractor and illustrates how it is used.

Another method used to convert orthographic angular measurements to angles in an isometric drawing is to use a conversion table. Figure 3-15 shows a table that includes a list of orthographic angles and their equivalent isometric angles. The isometric angles specified in the table may be measured using a circular protractor.

Orthographic Views

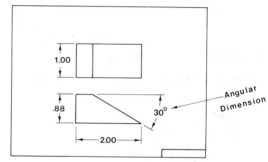

Supplementary Layout

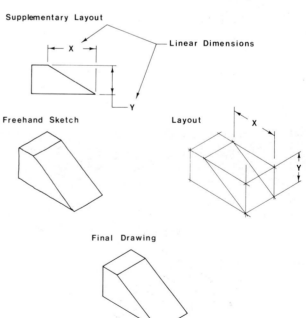

Figure 3-11 Supplementary layouts must be used to transfer angular dimensions to isometric drawings.

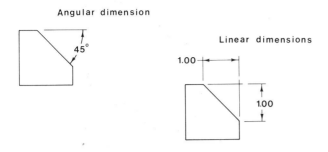

Angular dimension

Linear dimensions

1.00

1.00

Angular dimensions can not be transferred
to an isometric drawing using a protractor.
Only linear dimensions can be transferred.

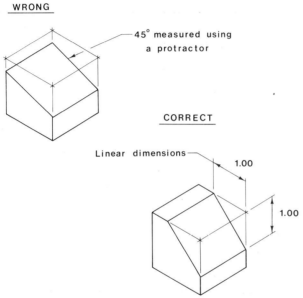

WRONG

45° measured using
a protractor

CORRECT

Linear dimensions

1.00

1.00

Figure 3-12 Do not use a circular protractor for measuring angles on isometric drawings.

Figure 3-16 shows a plot of isometric angles that can be used as an *underlay*—that is, to be placed under the drawing paper and traced. It is suggested that the student prepare an angle underlay using ink on a durable medium, such as mylar, and save the underlay for future use.

3-6 SCALED DRAWINGS

Because isometric drawings appear larger than orthographic views drawn at the same scale, illustrators sometimes prepare isometric drawings at a reduced scale. Figure 3-17 illustrates. A scale of ¾

to 1 produces results that appear most proportionally correct.

Working with different scales (orthographic views in one scale and isometric drawing in another scale) can be confusing and subject to conversion errors. The difficulty can be greatly reduced by using either a reduced scale or proportional dividers.

Figure 3-18 shows a reduced scale along with some sample measurements. Remember when using a reduced scale that the fractional divisions are to the left of the 0 mark. A dimension such as 2⅝ would be read on the ⅝ scale by reading the 2 to the right of the 0, and the ⅝ to the left.

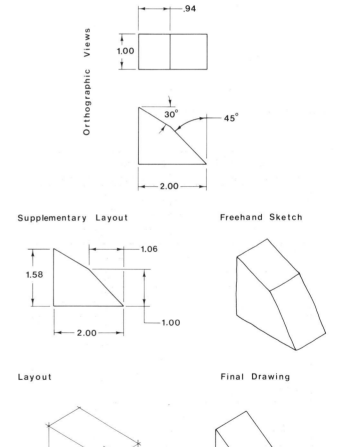

Figure 3-13 An object with slanted surfaces.

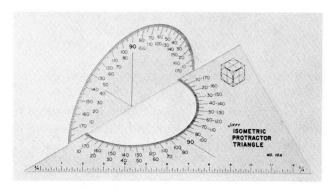

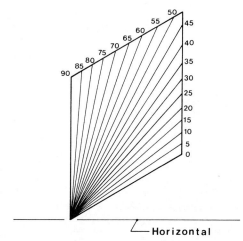

Figure 3-16 An isometric angle underlay.

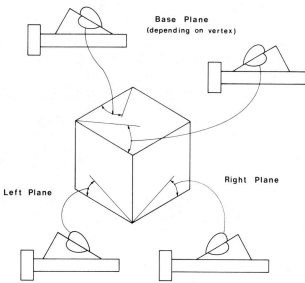

Figure 3-14 Using an isometric protractor.

Angle as specified on Orthographic views	Equivalent Angle on an Isometric Drawing
0	30.0
5	34.0
10	37.8
15	41.5
20	44.7
25	48.0
30	51.0
35	54.3
40	57.0
45	60.0
50	62.5
55	65.5
60	68.5
65	71.5
70	75.0
75	78.5
80	82.0
85	85.7
90	90.0

All angle measurements are in degrees as measured with a protractor from the horizontal.

Figure 3-15 Orthographic angles and their isometric equivalent.

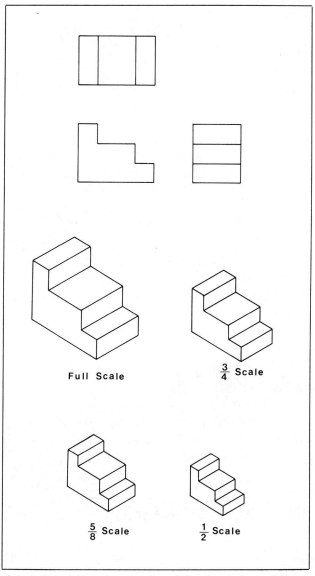

Figure 3-17 Drawing an isometric drawing at different scales.

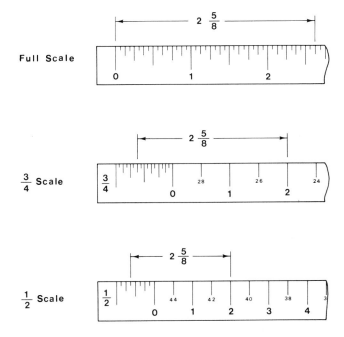

Figure 3-18 Different scales.

Figure 3-19 Creating an isometric scale.

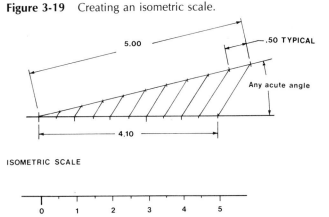

ISOMETRIC SCALE

Proportional dividers can be set to transfer measurements directly from one scale to another by adjusting the pivot screw. If, for example, we set the dividers to read $\frac{3}{4}$ to 1, we can open the longer legs to a certain dimension and know that the other legs, the shorter ones, will read $\frac{3}{4}$ of that dimension. Proportional dividers enable illustrators to work quickly with a high degree of accuracy and are therefore very popular. Figure 3-4 shows proportional dividers.

Figure 3-19 shows how to create an isometric axis. An isometric axis is .82 shorter than a full one-to-one axis system. It is suggested that students prepare their own isometric scale and then use it as an underlay when needed.

PROBLEMS

Prepare an isometric drawing for the following objects that appear in Part Four, Exercise Problems.

P-1	**P-7**
P-2	**P-8**
P-3	**P-9**
P-4	**P-10**
P-5	**P-11**
P-6	**P-12**

CHAPTER 4

HOLES AND ROUNDED SURFACES

4-1 HOLES

Holes can be drawn on isometric drawings by two methods: by using the four-center ellipse method, or by using templates. The word *hole,* as used here, is defined as a shape that appears as a perfect circle (constant radius) in orthographic views.

The four-center ellipse method is an approximation method that utilizes a compass. The procedure is as follows. See Figure 4-1.

1. Identify the plane on which the ellipse is to be drawn—either left, right, or base. The method is applied differently in each of the three planes.
2. Draw the centerlines for the hole and, after marking off the required radii on the centerlines, draw an isometric square through the radii marks.
3. Draw a diagonal line across the widest part (corner to corner) of the isometric square created in step 2. Define this line as AB. Draw lines DE and FG as shown, and label points J and K as shown.
4. Using points J and K as a center, draw an arc of radius JG or KD (they should be equal) from point G to L and from D to M. Then using points E and F as centers, draw arcs of radius EL or FG (they should be equal) from point G to M and point L to D.
5. Darken the appropriate lines. Be careful to ensure a smooth transition between the different radius arcs.

Holes may also be drawn in isometric drawings by using isometric ellipse templates. There are three size ranges of isometric ellipse templates: small, medium, and large.

The medium-sized template is the most commonly used and is pictured in Figure 4-2. The outside shape of the template is cut in a trapezoidal shape to permit quick and accurate alignment to whichever plane is required.

Each edge of the template is labeled for correct positioning. For example, LEFT-HAND PLANE. This means that this edge is placed against the T-square (horizontal line) to align the template correctly when drawing ellipses in the left-hand plane. The RIGHT-HAND and BASE edges are used in a similar manner. Figure 4-2 illustrates how the template is aligned in each of the three planes.

It should be pointed out that the three planes described refer not only to the frontal planes as shown, but also to all planes parallel to these planes. For example, all surfaces labeled A in Figure 4-3 are parallel to the BASE plane and, if ellipses are to be drawn in these surfaces, they would require the template to be aligned to the BASE edge.

Small ellipse templates are rectangular in shape

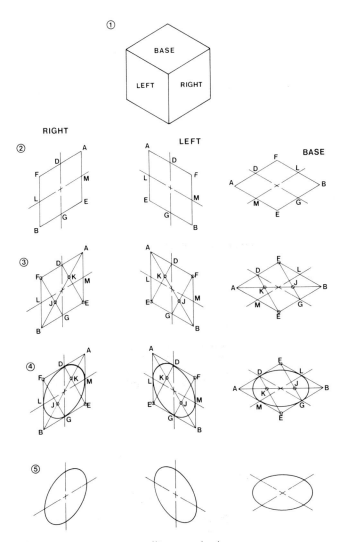

Figure 4-1 Four-center ellipse method.

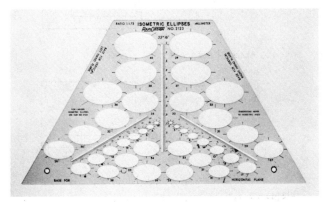

Figure 4-2-1 An isometric ellipse template.

and are rarely cut specifically for isometric shapes. To use them for isometric drawings, use only the holes labeled 35°, or whatever angle is closest to 35°, and align the template as shown in Figure 4-4. Note that just a T-square is needed for holes in the base plane, but a 30°-60°-90° triangle is needed in addition to the T-square or a drafting machine set at 30° for alignment in the right and left planes.

Large ellipse templates are the most difficult to use because a complete ellipse cannot be drawn in one positioning, but must be pieced together using different template positions. Figure 4-5 shows how to align the template when drawing ellipses in the left, right, and base planes. In each plane, at least two different alignments are required to draw a complete ellipse.

4-2 CYLINDERS

Isometric drawings of cylinders are based on the centerlines of the cylinder. This is somewhat different from other shapes where we used edge lines to transfer from orthographic views to an isometric drawing.

There are three centerlines used to define a cylinder: the two frontal centerlines and the longitudinal centerline. Figure 4-6 shows orthographic views of a cylinder and has the frontal and longitudinal centerlines labeled. To transfer the orthographic information to an isometric axis system, first draw the centerline as shown. Then, using either the four-center ellipse method or an isometric ellipse template, draw isometric ellipses at each end of the centerlines. Finally, draw tangency lines as shown, and darken in the appropriate lines. Tangency lines, in this example, are 30° lines drawn so they just touch the front and rear ellipse both on the top and on the bottom.

When preparing isometric drawings of cylindrically shaped objects, it is important to clearly define all centerlines involved. The locations of any point on the surface will require measurements from both the facial centerlines and the longitudinal centerlines. For example, to locate point A on an isometric drawing from the given orthographic information (Figure 4-7), we first locate the point on the frontal plane relative to the facial centerlines using dimensions X and Y. We then draw in the top

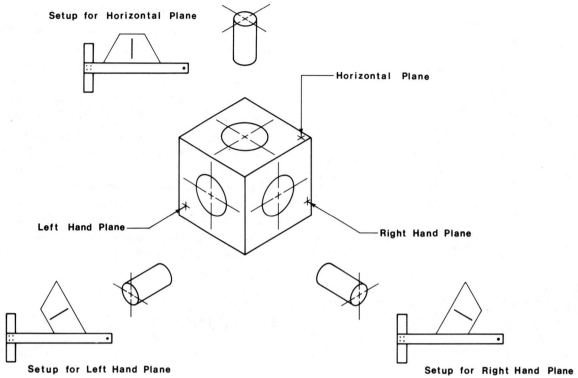

Figure 4-2-2 How to use an isometric ellipse template.

longitudinal centerline (not to be confused with rear tangency, which cannot be used for measurements) and measure off the dimension Z. Dimension Z is transferred to the projection of point A from the frontal plane by drawing a plane parallel to the frontal plane at a distance Z from the frontal plane. This is done by first defining the centerlines at distance Z, and then drawing an isometric ellipse equal in size to the base plane. Where this ellipse

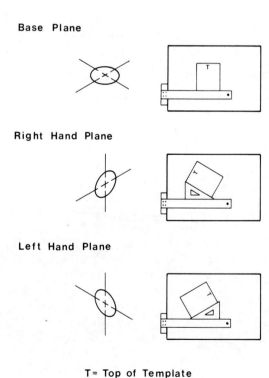

Figure 4-4-1 A small ellipse template.

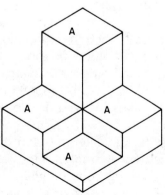

Figure 4-3 All surfaces labeled A are parallel to the base plane.

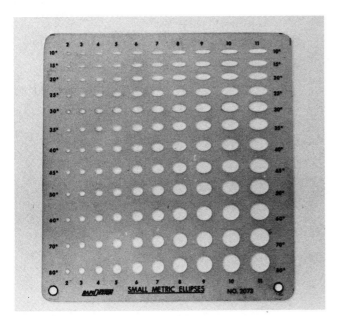

Figure 4-4-2 How to use a small ellipse template.

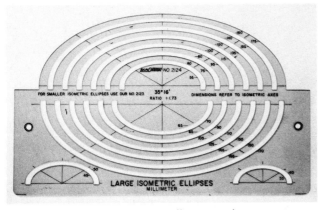

Figure 4-5-1 A large isometric ellipse template.

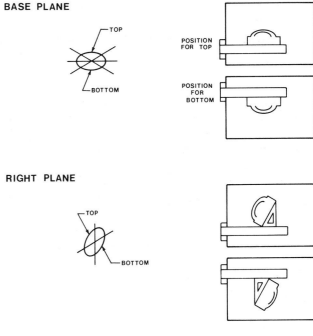

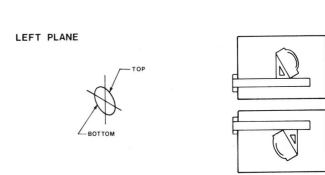

Figure 4-5-2 How to use a large isometric ellipse template.

intersects the projection line of point A from the base plane is the location of point A on the cylinder.

Cuts into cylinders either above or below the centerline are drawn in a similar manner. The only difference in surface cuts above or below the centerline is the effect the cuts have on the centerline, which represents the widest part of the cylinder. Cuts below the centerline have a width of less than the cylinder's major diameter, whereas cuts above the centerline also have a width of less than the cylinder's major diameter but also include the major diameter in the drawing. Figure 4-8-1 illustrates.

The isometric drawing shown in Figure 4-8-2 was created by using the procedure outlined above for locating a point on a cylinder's surface. Surface B on Figure 4-8-1 was drawn by first measuring a distance R along the centerline back from the frontal plane, and then by drawing a surface through the distance R parallel to the frontal plane. Distance Q is measured as shown.

The surface above the centerline is drawn using the same procedure. See Figure 4-8-2.

An isometric drawing of a cylinder that includes an inclined cut will require the development of a dimensional grid pattern. Figure 4-9 shows how this type of grid is developed. Here is the procedure.

1. Mark off a series of arbitrary points on the orthographic circular view of the cylinder.
2. Project these points onto the rectangular view.
3. Transfer the points defined in step 1 to the facial plane of the isometric drawing.
4. Project these points back into the cylinder.
5. Transfer the distances (E, F, G, and H) found in the orthographic rectangular view between the facial plane and the points on the inclined surface to the isometric drawing. The three-dimensional grid formed by the intersections of the projection lines of step 4 and the distances E, F, G, and H defines the shape of the inclined plane in the isometric drawing.
6. Draw in the inclined surface—using an irregular curve, snake, or ellipse template as a guide.

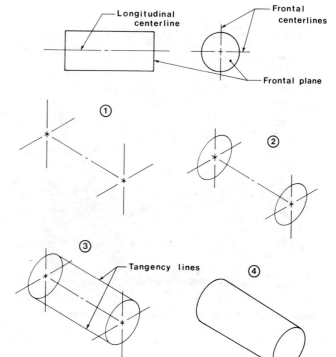

Figure 4-6   How to draw an isometric cylinder.

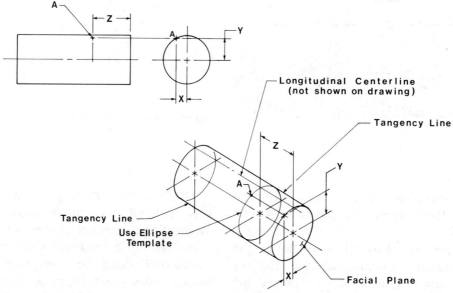

Figure 4-7   Locating a point on the surface of an isometric cylinder.

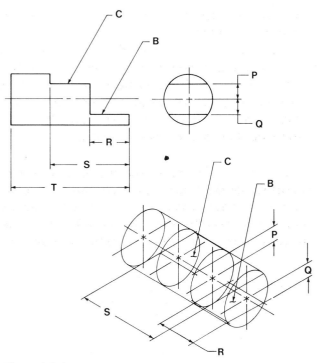

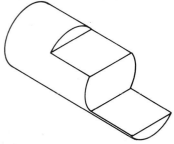

Figure 4-8-1

Figure 4-8-2

Figure 4-8 Preparing an isometric drawing of a cylinder from given orthographic views.

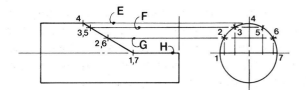

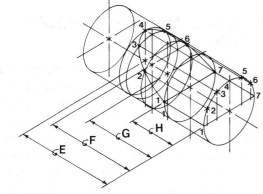

Figure 4-9-1

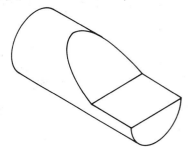

Figure 4-9-2

Figure 4-9 Preparing an isometric drawing of a cylinder with a slanted surface.

4-3 ROUNDED SURFACES AND EDGES

As with holes, rounded surfaces and edges may be drawn using either the four-center ellipse method or by using templates. Figure 4-10-1 shows an object with rounded corners. The procedure used is as follows.

1. Draw the object as if it were square—that is, as if it had no rounded corners.
2. Add the rounded corners. Use either the four-center ellipse method as shown, or an isometric ellipse template. Add both front and back corners.

3. Add tangency lines. Note that the tangency line is not the same as the square corner line.
4. Darken the object as required.
5. Add short, thin shading lines as necessary. These lines are usually evenly spaced, but could be spaced "by eye."

Variation 2 of Figure 4-10-2 shows an object drawn in a different orientation. The procedure used is exactly the same, although the location of the corner tangent lines is different.

4-4 BACK EDGE OF HOLES

Figure 4-11 shows an object where the large central hole is so large that the back edge will be seen in the final drawing. It is sometimes confusing to know when and how much of the back edge of a hole shows. This problem can easily be solved by drawing the complete back surface of the hole and seeing exactly how much can be seen. The final drawing is darkened in appropriately.

4-5 HOLES IN NONISOMETRIC SURFACES

Holes in nonisometric surfaces are difficult to draw because the shape of the ellipse will vary according to the angle of the surface and angle at which the hole (drill angle) penetrates the surface. The shape of the ellipse may be graphically determined by one of two methods, depending on whether the hole is perpendicular to an isometric plane or perpendicular to the slanted surface. Both methods require projection from the nonisometric plane, to

an isometric plane, and back again to the nonisometric plane.

Figure 4-12-1 shows the orthographic views of a vertical hole that penetrates a slanted surface. The centerline of the hole is a vertical line, meaning it is an isometric line. To determine the shape of the ellipse used to draw this hole correctly in an isometric drawing, proceed as follows.

1. Locate the hole on one of the known isometric planes. In this example, the base plane (top) was chosen. We cannot accurately draw the hole in this hypothetical plane based on the material presented in Section 4-1. The top orthographic

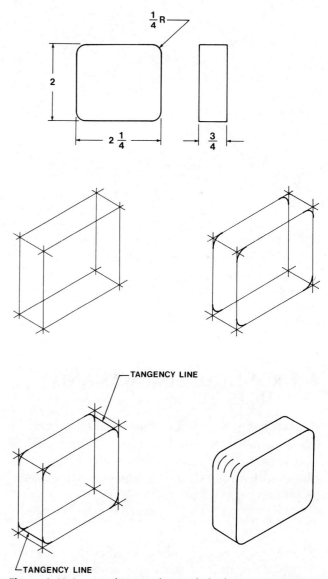

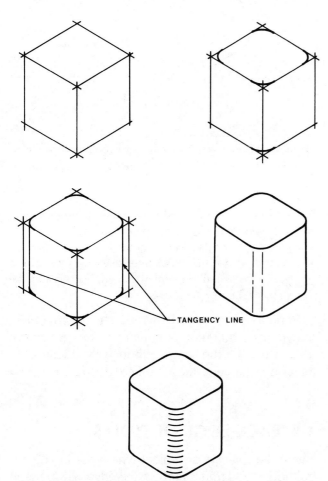

Figure 4-10-1 An object with rounded edges—variation 1.

Figure 4-10-2 An object with rounded edges—variation 2.

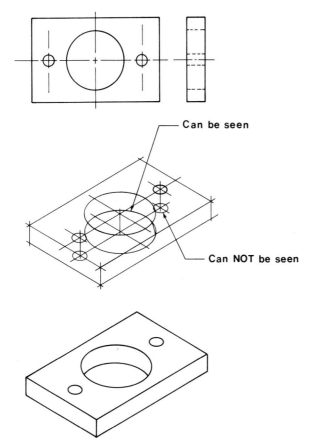

Can be seen

Can NOT be seen

Figure 4-11 Back edge of a hole.

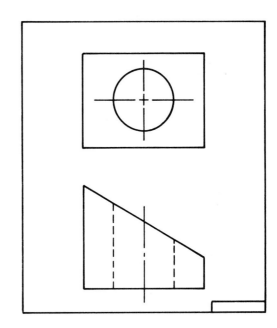

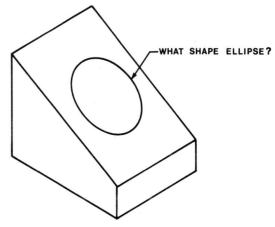

—WHAT SHAPE ELLIPSE?

Figure 4-12-1

view was used to determine the location of the hole. See Figure 4-12-2.

2. Determine the location of the hole's centerpoint and the direction of the centerlines on the slanted surface by projecting the intersection of the centerlines in the isometric plane with the edge of the isometric plane (labeled A) downward (vertical line), toward the edge of the slanted surface (E) and then across (30° line) the surface until it intersects a vertical line from the centerpoint on the isometric plane. The new centerpoint is labeled O. The inclined centerline on the slanted surface is determined by drawing a line in the isometric plane forward to the edge of the plane (point G), then down to the front edge of the slanted surface (point H), and finally from H through O to the back edge of the surface.

Theoretically, we have taken the given information and projected it by using *only* isometric lines and surfaces. For example, lines AE and GH are

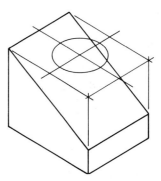

Figure 4-12-2

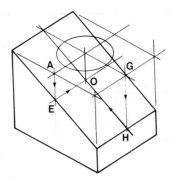

Figure 4-12-3

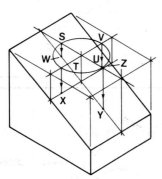

Figure 4-12-4

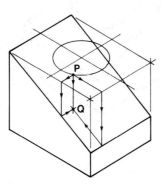

Figure 4-12-5

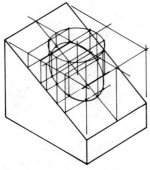

Figure 4-12-6

Figure 4-12   Drawing a hole in a nonisometric surface.

isometric lines in the left and right isometric planes, respectively, and can therefore be used for projection. Remember that accurate projection can *only* be done in isometric planes along isometric lines. See Figure 4-12-3.

3.   Project vertically the intersections of the isometric ellipse drawn in the base plane with the centerlines, points S, T, U, and V to the centerlines on the slanted surface. The equivalent points on the slanted surface are W, X, Y, and Z.

Once points W, X, Y, and Z are located, an experienced illustrator would then approximate the final shape of the ellipse. This is referred to as *approximating* and should not be used by students unless the hole is so small that further projection is not practical. See Figure 4-12-4.

4.   In order to get an accurate shape on the slanted surface, we can add more points to the isometric circle and project as shown. The more points added, the more accurate will be the final results—although too many points may cause more confusion than accuracy.

In the example shown, point P is shown individually for clarity. Any point added would be projected in the same manner. See Figure 4-12-5.

5.   Figure 4-12-6 shows the projection layout after eight additional points were added. The final elliptical shape is drawn by matching the points on the slanted surface with an elliptical template or by using an irregular curve. A set of ellipse templates is shown in Figure 4-13.

If the centerline of the hole is perpendicular to the slanted surface, a different procedure is used. In this method, an elliptical valve is calculated graphically. Figure 4-14 shows the method outlined as follows.

1.   Use the given orthographic views and prepare an isometric drawing including the centerline of the hole. See Figure 4-14-1.

2.   Define the lower right corner of the slanted surface as point O. Draw a 30° (isometric) line from point O as shown.

Using point O as the center, draw an isometric ellipse of any diameter using an isometric ellipse template as a guide. The ellipse should be set up in

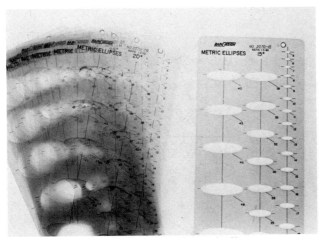

Figure 4-13 A set of ellipse templates.

the isometric plane profile ot the slanted surface—in this example, the RIGHT-HAND PLANE. See Figure 4-14-2.

3. Mark a point O' somewhere along the 30° line drawn in step 2. Draw a line through point O' perpendicular to the 30° line.

Draw two tangent lines, as shown, from the

isometric ellipse through the perpendicular line. Using O' as a center, draw a circle that just touches the tangent line, as shown in Figure 4-14-3.

4. Draw a vertical line from point O and label its intersection with the isometric ellipse V. Project V from the isometric ellipse to the circle and label the intersection V'. Draw a ray O'-V' beyond the circle. See Figure 4-14-4.

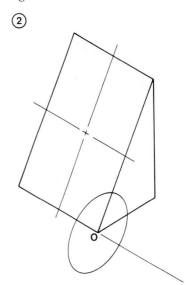

Figure 4-14-2

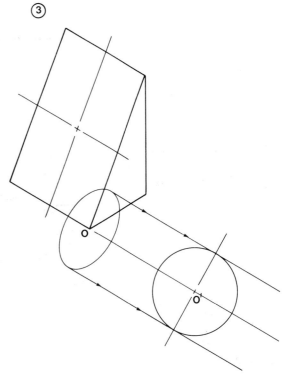

Figure 4-14-3

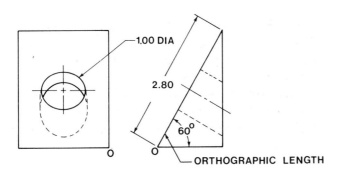

Figure 4-14-1

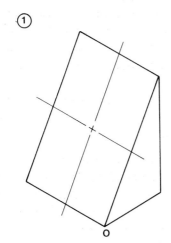

Figure 4-14 Drawing a hole in a nonisometric surface.

④

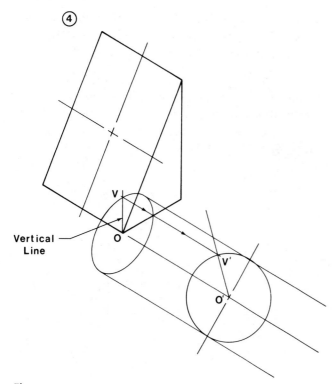

Figure 4-14-4

⑥

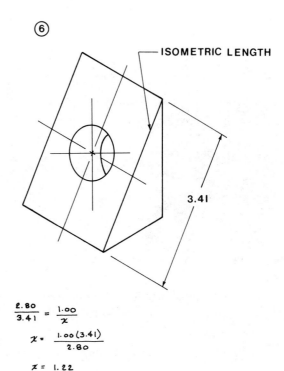

ISOMETRIC LENGTH

3.41

$$\frac{2.80}{3.41} = \frac{1.00}{x}$$

$$x = \frac{1.00(3.41)}{2.80}$$

$$x = 1.22$$

∴ HOLE DIA = 1.22

Figure 4-14-6

⑤

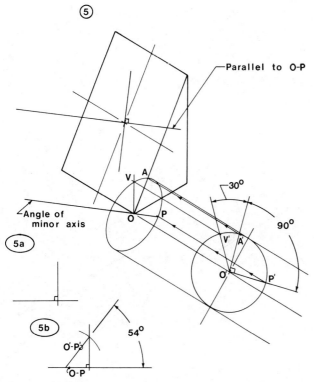

Parallel to O-P

30°

90°

Angle of minor axis

5a

5b

54°

O-P'

O-P

Figure 4-14-5

5. From the line O'-V', draw another line O'-A' that is 30° from O'-V'. Use a protractor for this measurement (30° because the surface is at a 30° slant from the vertical).

From line O'-A', draw another line O'-P' that is 90° from O'-A'. Project point P' from the circle back to the ellipse and label it point P. See Figure 4-14-5.

On a separate sheet of paper, lay out two perpendicular lines, as shown in Figure 4-14-5a. Mark off the distance O-P along the horizontal line and, using a compass, set the length O'-P', swinging an arc O'-P' as shown. Measure the angle. This angle will be the correct ellipse angle for the given slanted surface.

In this example 54° was measured, but 55° was used for the drawing since that is the nearest template size available.

6. Because isometric drawings pictorially "stretch" slanted surfaces, different size ellipses are used than are specified in the orthographic views. In this example, if a 1.00 inch 55° ellipse were used, it would appear undersized.

The correct size may be determined by the proportion

$$\frac{\text{ORTHOGRAPHIC LENGTH}}{\text{ISOMETRIC LENGTH}} = \frac{\text{ORTHOGRAPHIC DIAMETER}}{\text{ISOMETRIC DIAMETER}}$$

where ORTHOGRAPHIC LENGTH refers to the profile length of the slanted surface in the orthographic views, and the ISOMETRIC LENGTH refers to the profile length of the slanted surface in the isometric drawing.

ORTHOGRAPHIC DIAMETER is the given diameter of the hole, and ISOMETRIC DIAMETER is the diameter needed for the isometric drawing of the hole.

Figure 4-14-6 shows the appropriate calculations for this problem. Note the figures as shown are half-scale of the originals.

The ellipse used is therefore a 1.22 inch (rounded to 1.25) 55° ellipse. Note that in Figure 4-14-5 the angle of the derived line O-P indicates the angle of the minor axis of the required ellipse. A line drawn parallel to O-P through the centerpoint of the ellipse will define its orientation.

Figure 4-14-6 shows the final results.

PROBLEMS

Prepare an isometric drawing for the following objects that appear in Part Four, Exercise Problems.

P-14	**P-20**
P-15	**P-21**
P-16	**P-22**
P-17	**P-23**
P-18	**P-24**
P-19	**P-25**

CHAPTER 5

OBLIQUE AND IRREGULAR SURFACES

5-1 INTRODUCTION

Oblique surfaces are surfaces that are not parallel to any principal isometric surface. They are sometimes referred to as *compound* surfaces because they require two or more angles to define them.

To help understand the development of oblique surfaces, let us pretend we were actually trying to make one. Figure 5-1 shows orthographic views of an object that contains an oblique surface and a block from which we will make the object. It will require two cuts to make the surface—the first at 30°, the second at 45°.

The first cut is made at 30°, as shown in Figure 5-1, step 2, and will produce an object with a 30° slanted surface. The object is then cut at 45°, as shown in Figure 5-1, step 3. The final shape is shown in Figure 5-1, step 4.

The object is drawn in the same manner just described. We first lay out a 30° angle and then a 45° angle, as shown in Figure 5-2. Note that, as explained in Section 3-3, angular measurements cannot be directly used, but must be converted to their linear components.

Oblique surfaces are also shown in the examples of Figure 5-3. Oblique surfaces tend to be visually

confusing in isometric drawings, so some form of shading is usually included. Note how much clearer the shaded surfaces appear when compared to the nonshaded ones. The shading need not be intricate. Simple lines, drawn parallel to one of the edge lines of the surface, are usually sufficient. The choice of which edge line to use depends on the desired end results. Use thin lines—half as thick as the object's lines—for shading. Shading is covered in Chapter 15.

5-2 COMPOUND EDGES

If an object contains two slanted surfaces, the intersection of these surfaces will form a compound edge. Theoretically, a compound edge is a line that is not parallel to any principal plane line. Figure 5-4 shows an object with a compound edge.

The shape of a compound edge becomes more difficult to draw when one or both of the edges is curved. Figure 5-5 shows an object that has a circular surface C, and a slanted surface S. The two surfaces intersect along line AB.

To draw the exact shape of line AB, add points to

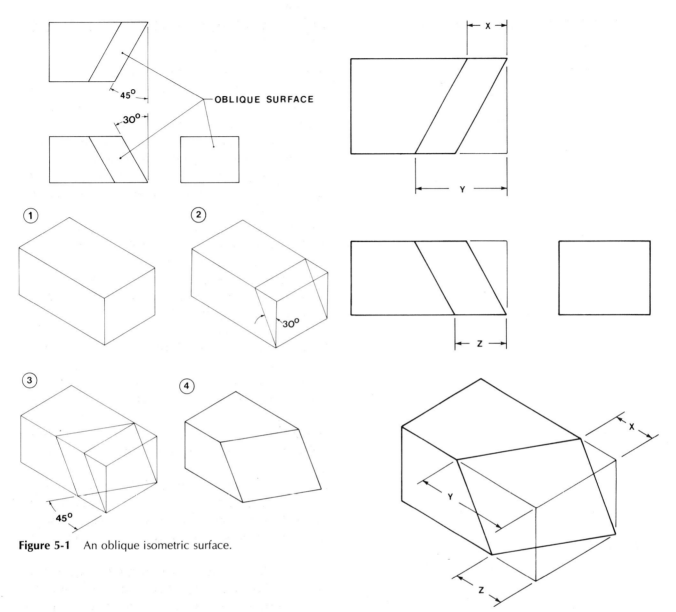

Figure 5-1 An oblique isometric surface.

Figure 5-2 Orthographic views containing an oblique surface and an isometric drawing of these views.

the object. These additional points will serve as reference points. The points are added to both surface C and S, but must be equally spaced from a common reference surface. In the example shown in Figure 5-5, two points, 1 and 2, were added. They are equidistant from the bottom surface. Points 1 and 2 are measured along isometric lines and projected along isometric planes to surfaces C and S. They are then projected along surfaces C and S until they intersect. A complete and accurate line A-B can now be drawn.

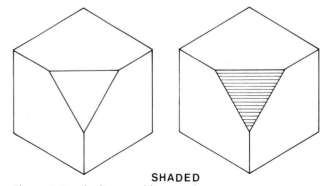

SHADED

Figure 5-3 Shading an oblique surface.

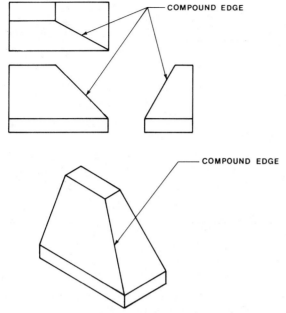

Figure 5-4 A compound edge.

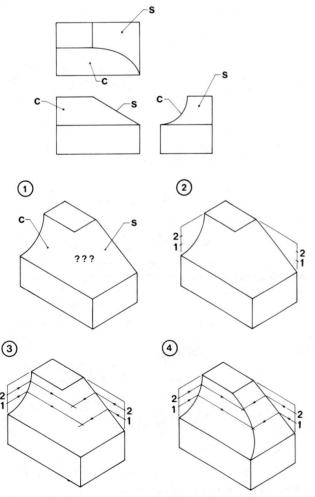

Figure 5-5 Drawing an irregular edge.

5-3 DIHEDRAL ANGLES OF OBLIQUE SURFACES

A *dihedral angle* is an angle between two planes. More simply stated, to an illustrator, it is the angle that defines the angle between oblique surfaces.

When working with dihedral angles, we must first define the surfaces in question by using linear components and then projecting known points on the surfaces to points of intersection, thereby defining the line between the surfaces (the vertex of the dihedral angle).

Figure 5-6 shows a V-block that has a 90° dihedral angle between two oblique surfaces. The isometric drawing of the V-block requires linear components of the given angle that must be obtained from accurately drawn orthographic views. If original drawings (not blueprints) are available, they may be scaled; but if they are not, the illustrator must accurately redraw the orthographic views (supplementary layout) in order to get accurate linear components for transfer.

As a rule, blueprints should never be scaled (measured). Even if the original drawings were accurately drawn, the reproduction process tends to distort the copies and thereby change the drawn distances. However, in actual practice and *only* for small distances, prints are scaled. If large distances are needed, or a high degree of accuracy is required, the distances should be calculated from the given dimensions or found by use of a supplementary layout.

Figure 5-7 shows a complicated object that contains dihedral angles. This isometric illustration was drawn by redefining the dihedral angle in terms of its linear components, and then by transferring each to the isometric axis. The intersection was then defined by projecting lines in the planes, as shown in Figure 5-5.

5-4 LOCATING A POINT ON AN OBLIQUE SURFACE

It is important for an illustrator to understand completely all surfaces being drawn so that any point on the surfaces can be accurately located. This is needed to locate hole centers, edge lines, and so on.

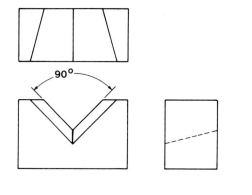

①

Figure 5-8 shows orthographic views that include one oblique surface. Point X is located on the orthographic views; however, the problem is to locate point X on the isometric drawing. The procedure is as follows.

1. Define the points in the orthographic views. This is done by adding lines to the orthographic views, as shown in Figure 5-8-1, and using the lines for measurements.

①

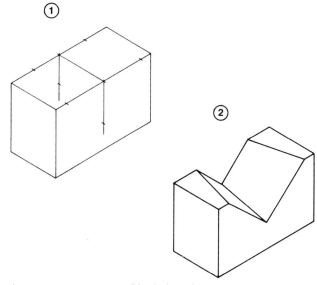

②

Figure 5-6 Drawing a dihedral angle.

②

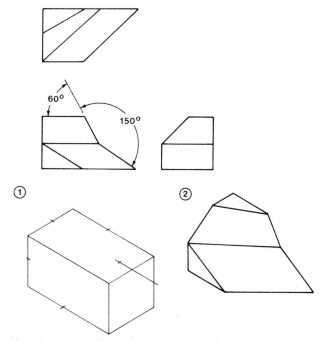

① ②

Figure 5-7 An object that contains a dihedral angle.

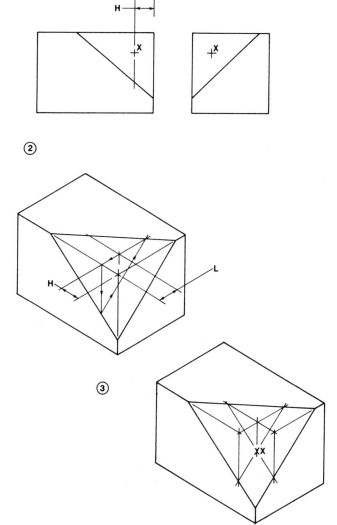

③

Figure 5-8 Locating a point on an oblique surface.

2. The added lines are then transferred to the isometric drawing. See Figure 5-8-2.

3. The points are then defined by the intersection of the lines. See Figure 5-8-3.

When projecting lines in isometric oblique surfaces, be careful that the line is really on the surface. It is very easy to draw a line that "looks" like it is on the surface but is really not. Study the works of M. C. Escher if you want to see spectacular results of how to confuse surface lines for visual effect.

5-5 HOLES IN OBLIQUE SURFACES

Holes in oblique surfaces are drawn using the two basic techniques described for holes in slanted surfaces; the method used depends on whether the hole centerline is perpendicular to the surface or on the isometric plane.

Figure 5-9 shows a hole with the centerline perpendicular to the top isometric plane. The hole is first redrawn in the top isometric plane and then projected onto the oblique surface as shown. An ellipse template, matched to the centerline intersection points, is then used as a guide to draw the hole on the oblique surface. If the hole is large, points should be added to the hole in the top isometric plane and then individually projected to the oblique surface, thereby defining the shape of the hole.

Figure 5-10 shows a hole with the centerline perpendicular to the oblique surface. To transfer the given orthographic information onto an isometric drawing, proceed as follows.

1. Label the hole center O in both orthographic views. Transfer the location of the centerpoint to the isometric views by using linear components as measured in the principal planes.

In the example shown in Figure 5-10, the front orthographic view was used for measurements. Distance H is the vertical distance of the centerpoint from the bottom surface. It is transferred to the rear vertical isometric line, then projected to the slanted surface R (use 30° line), and finally across the oblique surface. The projection line across the oblique line must be parallel to top and bottom surface lines as shown.

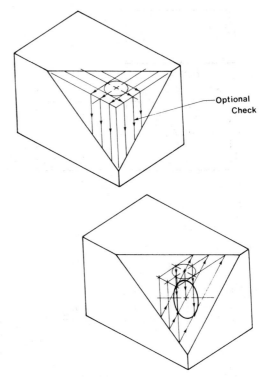

Figure 5-9 Drawing a hole in an oblique surface.

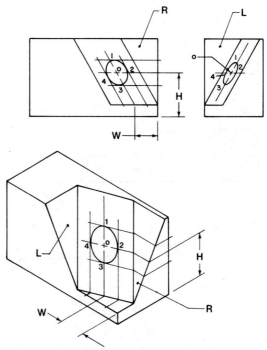

Figure 5-10 Drawing a hole in an oblique surface.

The horizontal distance W is projected in the same manner. The intersection of the two projection lines locates the centerpoint of the hole.

2. Label the four intersections of the hole centerlines with the periphery of the hole as points 1, 2, 3, and 4. Transfer points 1, 2, 3, and 4 from the orthographic views to the isometric drawing as outlined for the centerpoint in paragraph 1.

3. Match, as closely as possible, an ellipse template to points 1, 2, 3, and 4, and draw in the hole.

4. To draw the hole on the back surface, locate the hole of the orthographic views and transfer it to the back right surface of the isometric drawing. Define the four intersection points, as described for the front edge of the hole, and again using an ellipse template and the four projected points, draw in the back edge of the hole.

Darken only what can be seen through the front edge.

5-6 IRREGULAR SURFACES

Irregular surfaces are defined simply as surfaces that are not flat and are not round (of constant radius). Surface A in the orthographic views of Figure 5-11 is an example of an irregular surface.

To transfer an irregular surface from orthographic views to an isometric drawing, the basic idea is to define extra points and lines on the surface and to use those points for the transfer. More specifically, the procedure is as follows.

1. Study the given orthographic views and add points to the surface to define its shape. In this example (Figure 5-11), 3 points were added. The more points used, the more accurate the final shape will be, but too many points can be time consuming and give more accurate results than is necessary. See Figure 5-11-1.

2. From a defined reference point O, define the linear components of the added points. In this example, the lower right corner was chosen as the reference point. See Figure 5-11-1.

3. Transfer the linear component values to the isometric axis as shown. See Figure 5-11-2.

4. Draw in the irregular surface by connecting the transferred points using an irregular (French) curve. See Figure 5-11-3.

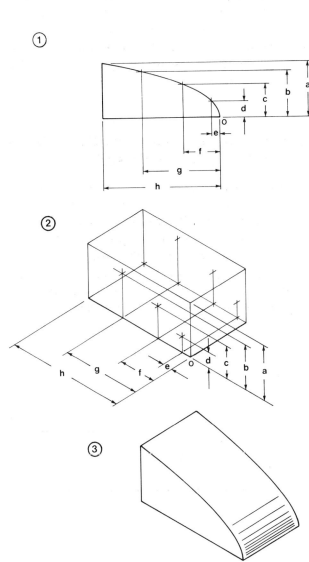

Figure 5-11   Drawing an irregular surface.

5-7 HOLES IN IRREGULAR SURFACES

If an irregular surface is pierced by a *small* hole, the procedure outlined in Section 5-6 can again be used. Figure 5-12 illustrates the procedure.

Figure 5-13 shows an example of a hole that penetrates perpendicular to the irregular surface. The same procedure is used here, but it should be pointed out that this type of hole creates an elliptical shape in the orthographic views as well as the

isometric views. Points can be added to the elliptical orthographic views as was done to the circular
views.

Very large holes must be projected by using
additional points. They do not appear as ellipses in
the isometric drawing (depending on the shape of
the irregular surface) and must be carefully plotted
and drawn by using a French curve or ellipse
segments guide. Figure 5-14 illustrates.

5-8 LOCATION OF A POINT ON AN IRREGULAR SURFACE

To locate any point (P) on any irregular surface,
define the location of the point in the orthographic
views (X and Y). Reference the location of the
points to lines parallel to the principal plane lines,
transfer the references to the isometric drawing,
and project them onto the irregular surface. Check
to make sure the projection lines really are on the
irregular surface. Figure 5-15 illustrates.

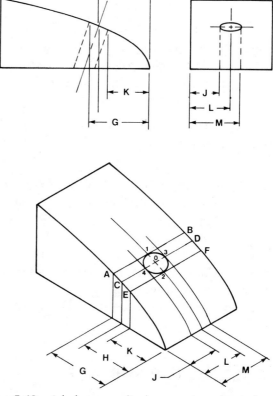

Figure 5-13　A hole perpendicular to an irregular surface.

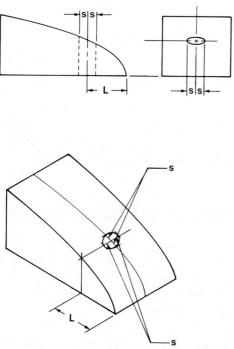

Figure 5-12　Drawing a hole in an irregular surface.

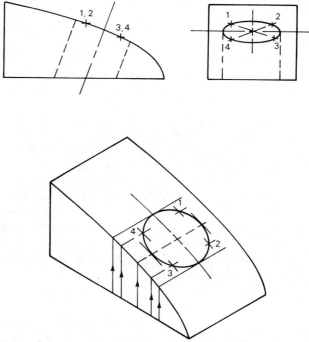

Figure 5-14　Drawing a large hole in an irregular surface.

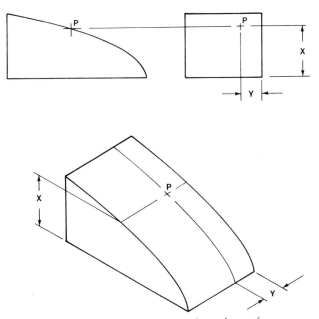

Figure 5-15   Locating a point on an irregular surface.

5-9 SPHERES

Spheres are drawn in isometric drawings as follows:

1. Draw an isometric axis as shown in Figure 5-16-1.
2. Using an isometric ellipse template as a guide, draw an isometric ellipse on each of the principal planes. The size of the ellipse should equal the diameter of the sphere. See Figure 5-16-2.
3. Using a compass or circle template with the point on the centerpoint of the isometric axis drawn in step 1, draw a circle that is tangent to the isometric ellipse, as shown in Figure 5-16-3.

Step 2 may be varied for effect. Not all three ellipses need be shown, depending on the final results desired and the shading. See Chapter 15 for a more detailed explanation of shading.

Slots, cuts and holes in spheres may be drawn by using the basic isometric axis for measurements. As with any type of isometric drawing, nonisometric measurements must be converted to their linear components before being transferred to an isometric axis. Figure 5-17 shows examples of spheres with slots and cuts.

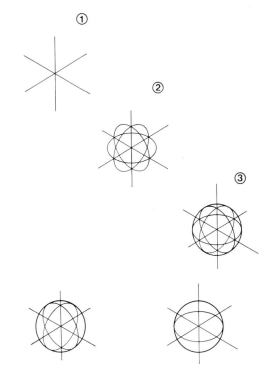

Figure 5-16   Drawing an isometric sphere.

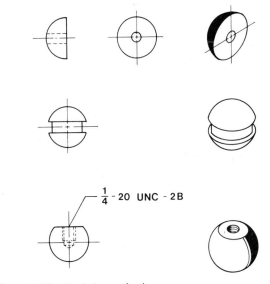

Figure 5-17   Variations of spheres.

CHAPTER 6

FASTENERS

6-1 INTRODUCTION

The term *fasteners* when used in technical illustration usually refers to mechanical fasteners such as bolts, machine screws, rivets, and so forth. This chapter will explain how to draw many of the most commonly used fasteners as well as nuts, washers, and pins.

6-2 THREAD NOTES

Drafters and engineers specify threads on a drawing by using a representation and a corresponding note. Figure 6-1 illustrates. The simplified, schematic, or detailed representation may be chosen, but in all cases the same type of thread note is used. Figure 6-2 explains how to interpret thread notes.

From an illustrator's standpoint, we need only know the thread diameter and length and an approximate idea of the number of threads per inch. UNF (Unified National Fine) threads should be drawn closer together than UNC (Unified National Coarse).

Figure 6-3 shows the metric version of the information shown in Figure 6-2. Metric threads are classified by a diameter pitch combination. The threads may be manufactured either coarse or fine. If the thread is a fine, the pitch must be specified. If it is a coarse, only the diameter need be given. The thread drawing representations are the same.

Most threads are cut with a chamfer on the end. The chamfer may or may not be drawn, depending on the amount of detail required, although for large diameter threads the chamfer is usually included. Figure 6-4 shows how to draw a chamfer.

If the exact size of the chamfer is not known, it may be approximated by choosing a slightly smaller ellipse on the isometric ellipse template and aligning, as shown in Figure 6-4.

6-3 THREAD REPRESENTATIONS

Most threaded fasteners are cut with either a Unified National Fine (UNF) or a Unified National Coarse (UNC) standard type thread, but there are many other types of threads that have specific applications (for example, buttress threads for jacks).

THREAD REPRESENTATIONS

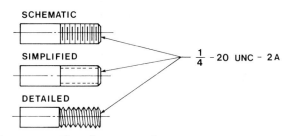

Figure 6-1   Thread representations.

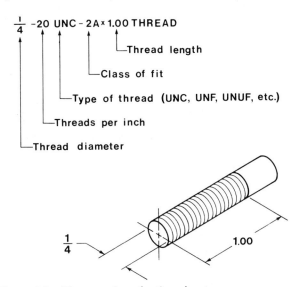

Figure 6-2   The meaning of a thread note.

UNF and UNC threads are represented on an isometric drawing by a series of evenly spaced ellipses, as shown in Figure 6-5. The lines representing the threads should be thinner than those representing the edge of the part. Shading may be added if desired.

The spacing of the thread lines must be uniform, with the distance between lines varied according to the thread diameter. Small diameter threads require the lines to be closer together; large diameter threads may be farther apart. In either case, draw thread lines that are not misleading—that is, not so close together as to appear crowded, and also not so far apart as to cause confusion.

Uniform thread line spacing may be achieved by measuring and marking off even spaces, as shown in Figure 6-5, or by putting a pencil mark on an isometric ellipse template, as shown in Figure 6-6, and then aligning the template with the mark for each successive thread line. Erase the marks off the template after use.

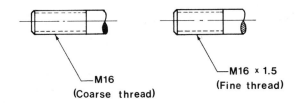

The thread diameter = 16/mm

Figure 6-3   Metric thread notes.

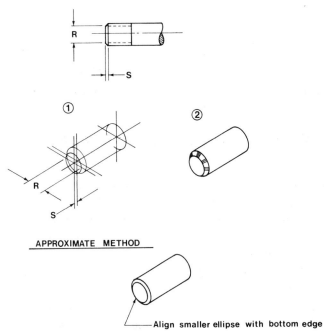

Figure 6-4   Drawing a thread chamfer.

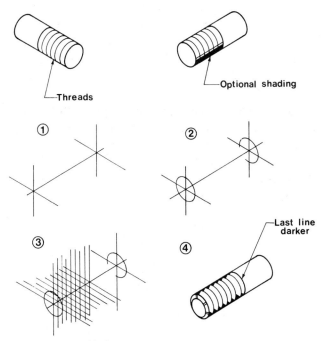

Figure 6-5   Drawing an isometric thread.

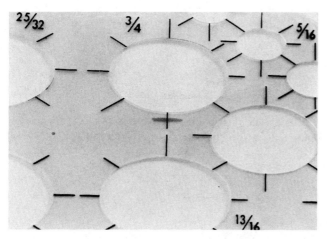

Figure 6-6 Marking an isometric ellipse template for drawing evenly spaced thread lines.

6-4 BOLTS AND MACHINE SCREWS

The term *bolt* refers to a threaded fastener that is joined to a nut. A threaded fastener that screws directly into a threaded hole is called a *cap* or *machine screw*. Both bolts and machine screws are made with different style heads—each of which is drawn differently.

An example of a drawing callout for bolts, caps, and machine screws is shown in Figure 6-7. The first part of the note specifies the thread information. The second part of the note specifies the head type.

The length of a bolt is measured from under the head. In other words, the head is not included in the length given in the drawing note. The only exception to this convention is flat head screws, which do include the head as part of the length. Figure 6-8 illustrates.

Figure 6-9 shows a cap screw in place. Note that the screw does not extend to the bottom of the hole. The threaded portion of the hole extends beyond the bottom of the screw, and the pilot hole (the unthreaded part of the hole) extends beyond the threads. The bottom of the hole is a 120° cone.

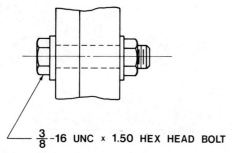

$\frac{3}{8}$ -16 UNC x 1.50 HEX HEAD BOLT

Figure 6-7 A bolt callout.

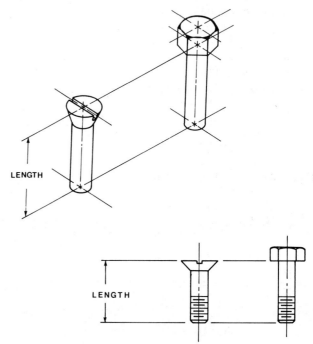

Figure 6-8 Bolt and screw lengths.

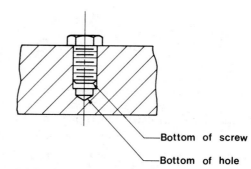

Bottom of screw
Bottom of hole

Figure 6-9 A cap screw in place.

6-5 HEXAGON SHAPES

Hexagon shapes are the most common head shapes for bolt and screw heads. They may be drawn in two different ways: by constructing around them an isometric ellipse or by using a template.

To construct a hexagon around an isometric ellipse, proceed as follows. See Figure 6-10.

1. Draw an isometric axis and an appropriate isometric ellipse, as shown in Figure 6-10-1.
2. Construct the hexagon by drawing 30° and 60° lines to the horizontal (use a 30°-60°-90° triangle and a T-square), as shown in Figure 6-10-2.
3. Add thickness by measuring along the isometric axis and repeat steps 1 and 2. See Figure 6-10-3.
4. Darken the appropriate lines. See Figure 6-10-4.

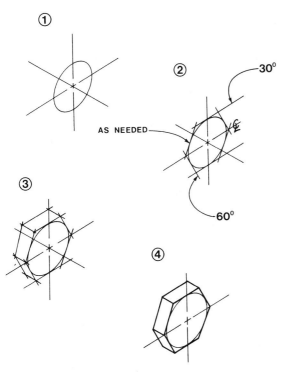

Figure 6-10 Drawing a hexagon-shaped head.

Figure 6-11 shows how to draw hexagons in the other two basic isometric planes.

To draw a hexagon-shaped head using an isometric hexagon template, proceed as follows. Figure 6-12 depicts an isometric hexagon template. Figure 6-13 illustrates the procedure.

1. Draw an appropriate isometric axis.
2. Draw an isometric ellipse equal in size to the distance across the flats of the hexagon.
3. Draw in the umbrella-shaped portion of the head by using the template as shown.
4. Slide the template along the isometric axis until the half-hexagon portion aligns with the umbrella portion and draw as shown.
5. Lay out the bolt length. Remember hex head bolt lengths are measured from under the head. Note in Figure 6-13-5 where the underside (back) of the head is located.
6. Add evenly spaced threads and darken the appropriate lines. Shading is optional.

Part 2 of Figure 6-13 shows the same procedure applied to drawing a hex nut.

Isometric hexagon templates may be used to draw hexagon heads oriented in either of the other two isometric planes. Be . careful to keep the umbrella-shaped portion of the head in proper perspective. Figure 6-14 illustrates.

6-6 NUTS AND BOLTS

Nuts and bolts can also be drawn using the two methods described in Section 6-5. A nut-bolt combination will have a common diameter and hex size. Figure 6-15 shows a nut-bolt combination.

The sizes of the bolt heads and nuts are determined according to the thread size of the bolt. Figure 6-16 gives some general rules of thumb for bolt and nut sizes. Exact sizes can be found in manufacturers' catalogs.

We see in Figure 6-16 that the height of the head is approximately $\frac{3}{4}$ D, and the head diameter is $1\frac{1}{2}$ D. If we apply these to a $\frac{3}{8}$-16 UNC threaded bolt, we have

Head height $= \frac{3}{4} D = \left(\frac{3}{4}\right)\left(\frac{3}{8}\right) = \frac{9}{32}$

Head diameter $= 1\frac{1}{2} D = \left(\frac{3}{2}\right)\left(\frac{3}{8}\right) = \frac{9}{16}$

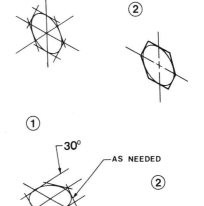

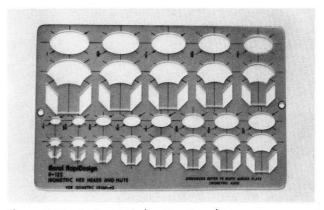

Figure 6-11 Drawing a hexagon in the base and left isometric planes.

Figure 6-12 An isometric hexagon template.

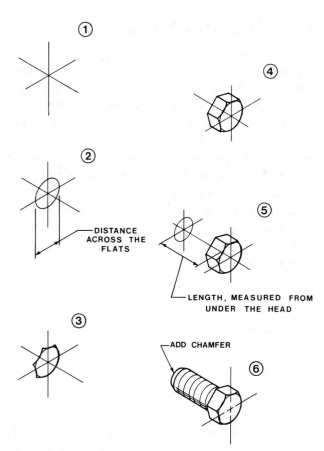

Figure 6-13 Part 1

If thread size is M10 × 1.5,

$$\text{Head height} = \frac{3}{4} D = (.75)\ (10) = 7.5 \text{ mm}$$

$$\text{Head diameter} = 1\frac{1}{2} D = (1.50)\ (10) = 15 \text{ mm}$$

Nut sizes are determined in a similar manner. The nut height is given as $\frac{7}{8}D$. Therefore, for the above examples,

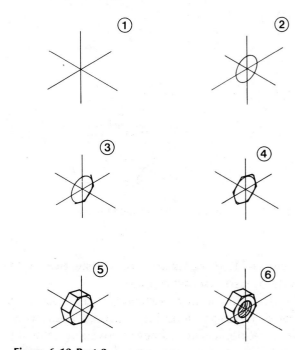

Figure 6-13 Part 2
Figure 6-13 Drawing an isometric nut and bolt.

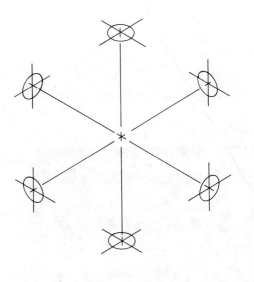

Figure 6-14 Variations of hexagon head orientations.

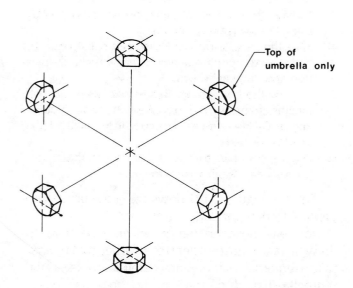

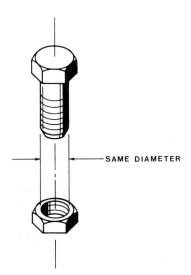

Figure 6-15 An isometric bolt and nut.

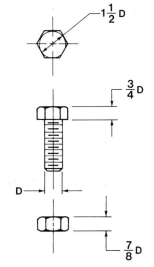

Figure 6-16 General sizes for bolts and nuts.

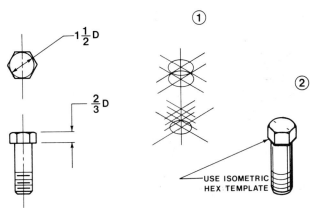

Figure 6-17 Cap screw.

Nut Height $= \frac{7}{8} D = \left(\frac{7}{8}\right)\left(\frac{3}{8}\right) = \frac{21}{64} \approx \frac{5}{16}$

or $\frac{7}{8} D = (.88)(10) = 8.8 \approx 9\,mm$

In all cases, some rounding off is permitted depending on the specfic drawing accuracy requirements.

6-7 CAP SCREWS

Cap screws refer to a group of machine screws that are differentiated by the head shape. Sizes are given in terms of diameters. For example, the height of the hex head shown in Figure 6-17 is specified as $\frac{2}{3}$ D. This means the height is $\frac{2}{3}$ times the screw diameter. If the screw were a $\frac{1}{4}$-20 UNC, the head height would be

$\frac{2}{3} D = \left(\frac{2}{3}\right)\left(\frac{1}{4}\right) = \frac{2}{12} \approx \frac{1}{6}$ or .17

When preparing isometric drawings of screws, the calculated sizes may be rounded off.

The following cap screws are shown in these figures.

Figure 6-18 Flat head
Figure 6-19 Round head
Figure 6-20 Fillister head
Figure 6-21 Hex socket head

6-8 HEADLESS SCREWS

Headless screws are, as the name implies, screws without heads. However, they do have recessed features such as slots and sockets. Figure 6-22 shows two common examples of headless screws.

6-9 MISCELLANEOUS FASTENERS

There are many types of fasteners other than those covered in this book. Many have very specialized usage and are used by only one industry. If an unfamiliar fastener is called for, ask for a print or request to actually see a sample so that an accurate representation can be created.

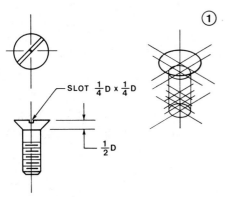

Figure 6-18 Flat head screw.

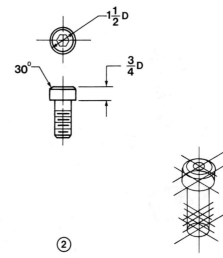

Figure 6-21 Hex socket screw.

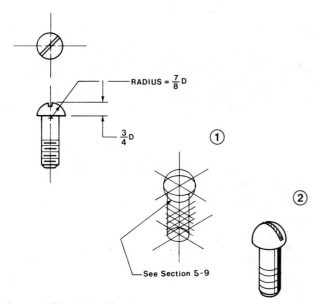

Figure 6-19 Round head screw.

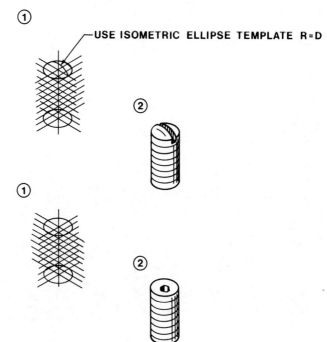

Figure 6-22 Headless screws.

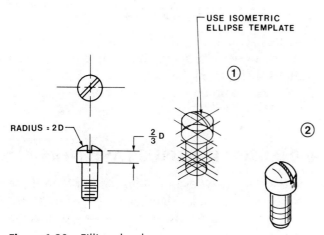

Figure 6-20 Fillister head screw.

DRAWING CALLOUT

$\frac{1}{16} \times \frac{3}{8} \times \frac{3}{4}$ WASHER

OR

.06 x .38 x .75 WASHER

MEANS

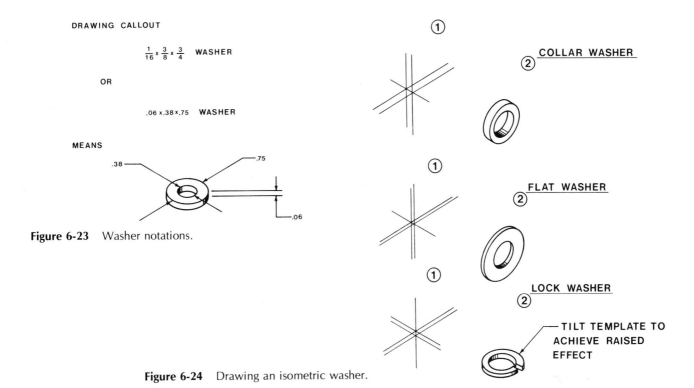

Figure 6-23 Washer notations.

Figure 6-24 Drawing an isometric washer.

6-10 WASHERS

Washers are often used in conjunction with fasteners. Their sizes are specified on drawings by listing the thickness, inside diameter (I.D.), and outside diameter (O.D.). Figure 6-23 illustrates the meaning of washer listings.

Washers can be drawn by using an isometric ellipse template as a guide in isometric planes or by using the appropriate ellipse templates in nonisometric planes. Figure 6-24 illustrates.

PROBLEMS

Prepare isometric drawings of the following problems listed in Part Four, Exercise Problems.

P-62	**P-67**
P-63	**P-68**
P-64	**P-69**
P-65	**P-70**
P-66	**P-71**

CHAPTER 7

CASTINGS

7-1 FILLETS AND ROUNDS

Cast objects are difficult to draw because they contain rounded edges called *fillets* and *rounds*. Figure 7-1 illustrates fillets and rounds: fillets are concave corners; rounds are convex. The sizes of fillets and rounds are usually specified by a note in terms of a radius.

To prepare an isometric drawing of a cast object, use this general procedure.

1. Draw the object as if all edges are square—that is, as if no fillets or rounds exist. See Figure 7-2-1.
2. Add rounded edges, as shown in Figure 7-2-2. Remember that fillet and round sizes are given in terms of R and, if drawn using an isometric ellipse template, must be referenced to the diameter dimension (two times the radius) because the template sizes are stated in terms of diameters.
3. Add quarter-circle shading, as shown in Figure 7-2-3. The shading is necessary to prevent confusion and to picture the rounded edges clearly. The shading lines should be evenly spaced and drawn thinner than the object lines.
4. Trace the final drawing from the layout created in step 3. See Figure 7-2-4

7-2 RUNOUTS

Because cast edges are rounded, they intersect by running together at tangency points. Figure 7-3 shows orthographic views where the corners of the front flange portion run into (become tangent to) the large cylinder portion. This is indicated on the drawing by a line curved on the end that is called a *runout*. Runouts sometimes cause confusion because they appear to be lines that stop in the middle of a surface. Remember that they are tangency points and do disappear (blend) into the surface.

Figure 7-4 shows another example of a cast object that includes runouts.

7-3 CAST CORNERS

Figure 7-5 shows some samples of how cast corners may be drawn. There are many different variations. When drawing cast corners and edges, the most important consideration is the visual integrity of the edge, and the corner pattern should, as near as possible, complement this.

ALL FILLETS AND ROUNDS = $\frac{3}{16}$ R

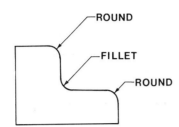

Figure 7-1 Fillets and rounds.

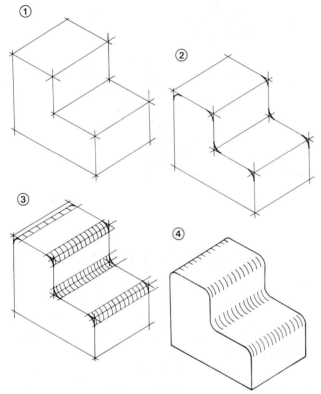

Figure 7-2 Drawing fillets and rounds in an isometric drawing.

7-4 MACHINE SURFACES

Cast surfaces are rough and often must be either in part or wholly machined. Machining is specified on a drawing by finish marks (see Chapter 9 for a further explanation).

Finish marks are located on the drawing either directly on the surface involved or on an extension line drawn from the surface. Figure 7-6 illustrates. The number refers to the quality of finish required. The smaller the number, the smoother the surface.

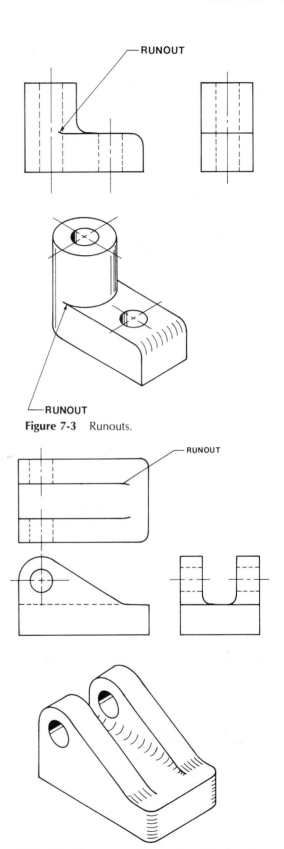

Figure 7-3 Runouts.

Figure 7-4 Drawing a runout in an isometric drawing.

From an illustrator's standpoint, cast surfaces are distinguished from machined surfaces by use of shading—more particularly, by use of a shading screen (see Chapter 16). Figure 7-6 shows how this contrast may be achieved. The shaded surfaces are cast; the unshaded are machined.

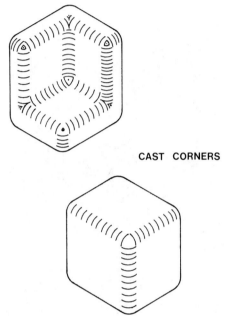

CAST CORNERS

Figure 7-5 Shading a cast object.

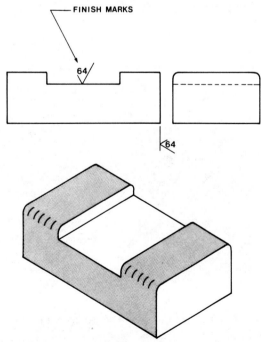

FINISH MARKS

Figure 7-6 Finish marks.

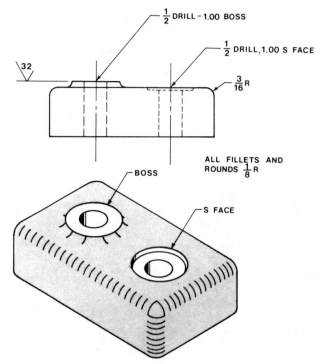

Figure 7-7 Bosses and spotfaces.

7-5 BOSSES AND SPOTFACES

Bosses and spotfaces are used in particular machining processes generally associated with castings. Figure 7-7 shows what each looks like in orthographic views. They are used to help minimize machining time.

A *boss* is a raised turret. It is above the cast surface and, therefore, it can be easily machined without machining the remainder of the cast surface. Boss sizes are specified by diameter, and the height is, if not otherwise specified, equal to the fillet and round radius. In the example in Figure 7-7, the boss height is .125. The actual height is somewhat less than this after machining, but .125 is close enough for illustration purposes.

A *spotface* is a circular cut made into a cast surface with a special tool. It also serves to minimize machining. A spotface is sized by a diameter but usually not a depth. The machinist cuts just deep enough to form a smooth surface. Because the depth is not specified, it can be drawn at any (shallow) depth. If a depth is specified, it must be drawn accurately.

PROBLEMS

Prepare isometric drawings of the following objects
listed in Part Four, Exercise Problems.

P-26	**P-35**
P-28	**P-36**
P-32	**P-37**
P-33	

CHAPTER 8

INTERSECTIONS

8-1 INTRODUCTION

This chapter explains how to draw intersections between different geometric shapes. In each example, orthographic views are used to define the intersections and isometric drawings are used to show the pictorial representations. The fundamental concepts explained are applicable to all types of pictorial drawings.

8-2 FUNDAMENTAL CONCEPTS

The key factor in analyzing any intersection is understanding the exact shape and location of all surfaces involved. This is not as easy as it may seem because of the visual distortions that occur in pictorial drawings—particularly those distortions associated with angular measurements.

There are two methods for developing intersections: one is exact; the other is an approximation. Figure 8-1 shows the exact method. In this example, a small rectangle intersects a larger rectangle. The procedure is as follows.

1. On an isometric axis, draw the centerline of the two intersecting pieces. See Figure 8-1-1.

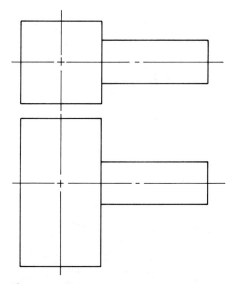

Figure 8-1 Part 1

2. Add the lengths, as shown in Figure 8-1-2, and add the appropriate centerlines.

3. Project surface 1-2-3-4 onto surface A-B-C-D by first establishing exactly where the intersection occurs. We can project lines from points 1, 2, 3, and 4 toward surface A-B-C-D, but the problem is to know where it intersects surface A-B-C-D. We can define the plane of intersection by projecting a line from the centerpoint of the larger square to surface

A-B-C-D. This point is labeled point X. Point X is then projected along surface A-B-C-D. Point Y is defined on the smaller square in a similar manner. The intersection of the projections of point X and Y (point Z) is on the plane of intersection. See Figure 8-1-3.

4. Draw an isometric line (30° line) through point Z so that it intersects the projection from point 1 and 2. Draw a vertical isometric line, as shown in Figure 8-1-4 to define point 4 on surface A-B-C-D.

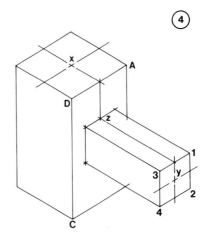

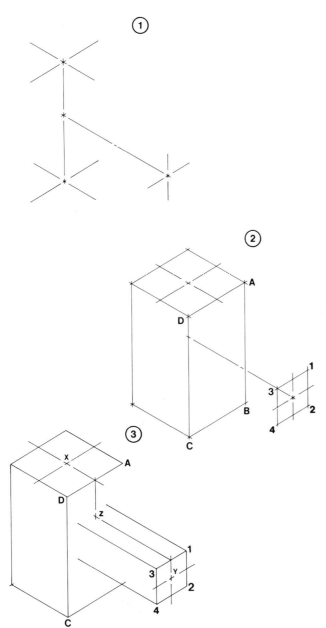

Figure 8-1 Part 2

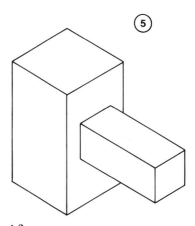

Figure 8-1 Part 3

Figure 8-1 Drawing an intersection between rectangular surfaces.

5. Darken the appropriate lines. Shade as desired. See Figure 8-1-5.

Figure 8-2 shows the above procedure applied to the intersection of two cylinders. As with any circle projection, we must add points to better define the shape and to help in projection.

Remember that the surfaces of cylinders are round. Therefore, in Figure 8-2-3, the projection of line 4-8 is a curved line. Line 4-8 is drawn on the larger cylinder by using the same template size that was used to draw the top and bottom surfaces of the larger cylinder.

Individual points, added to define the circle, are projected to the surface of the large cylinder, as shown in Figure 8-2-4, for point 2. The procedure used is as follows.

1. Project point 2 by drawing an isometric line (30°) from point 2 toward the intersecting surface location. We know the point of intersection is on this line, but don't know where.
2. Project point 2 by drawing a vertical line downward to line 4-8. Define point x. From point x, project a 30° line to line 4-8 on the larger cylinder. Where they intersect is defined as point y. Project a vertical line from point y upward until it intersects the project line of step 1. This intersection defines the location of point 2 on the surface on the larger cylinder.
3. Project all the added points as described for point 2 and darken the appropriate lines. Figure 8-2-5 illustrates.

Figure 8-3 shows a variation of the example shown in Figure 8-1. In this example the smaller square section is slanted upward 30°. The exact method, as described above, is used to define the intersection. Linear components marked off in the orthographic views and transferred to the isometric axis are used to define the front slanted surface.

Figure 8-4 shows another variation of the example shown in Figure 8-1. In this example, the orientation between the square sections has been changed so that the smaller section intersects the larger section on a corner. Figures 8-5 and 8-6 are further examples.

8-3 APPROXIMATION METHOD

When a problem is extremely difficult, such as the one shown in Figure 8-7, the approximate method is used to help develop the intersection. It is called *approximate* because it depends entirely on the accuracy of the given orthographic views. This usually means blueprints, which are not exact copies of the original drawings (blueprints tend to stretch about 2 percent beyond original size). However, for most drawing, the approximate method is sufficient.

The approximate method is as follows.

1. Draw an isometric axis marking off the top and bottom and centerline of intersection. See Figure 8-7-1.
2. Mark off, on the orthographic views, the linear components of the points necessary to define the centerline of the front surface of the intersecting

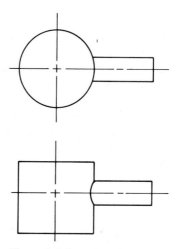

Figure 8-2 Part 1

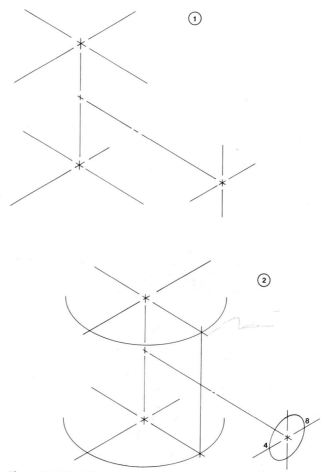

Figure 8-2 Part 2

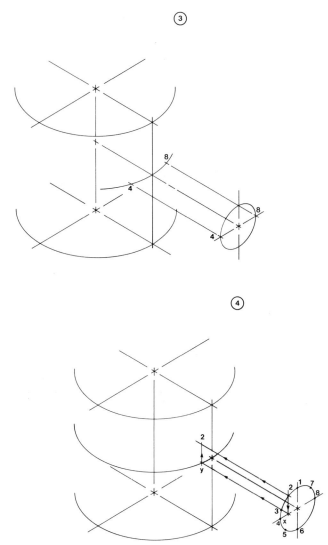

Figure 8-2 Part 3

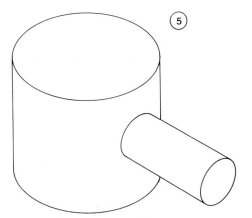

Figure 8-2 Part 4

Figure 8-2 Drawing an intersection between cylindrical surfaces.

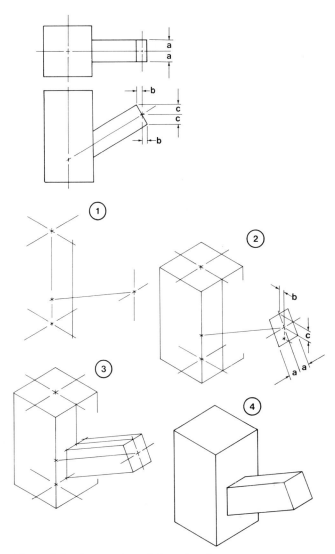

Figure 8-3 Intersection of slanted surfaces.

piece. Transfer the linear components to the isometric axis. See Figure 8-7-2.

3. Add the height of the intersection by using linear components, as shown in Figure 8-7-3.

4. Darken the appropriate lines. See Figure 8-7-4.

Again, it should be noted that this method is dependent on the accuracy of the orthographic views. If the orthographic views are not accurate, the isometric drawing will be in error.

8-4 OTHER VARIATIONS

Figures 8-8 and 8-9 are examples of other types of intersection problems. Each can be done by either the exact or approximate method.

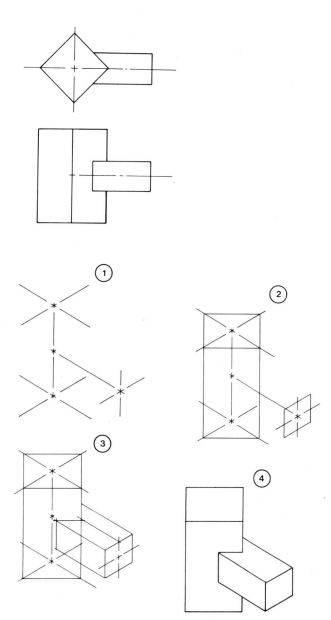

Figure 8-4   Intersection of a rotated surface.

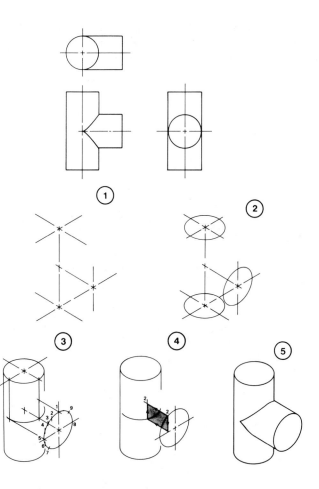

TYPICAL POINT PROJECTION

Figure 8-5   Intersection of equal-sized cylinders.

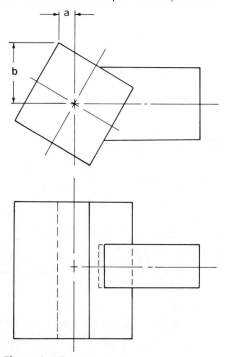

Figure 8-6 Part 1

8-5 PYRAMIDS

The development of intersections is made more difficult when one of the objects is a pyramid. The outside surfaces of a pyramid not only slant, but also taper toward the apex. This means that each point projected to the surfaces must be handled individually and with care to ensure accurate location.

The procedure for developing intersecting surfaces on pyramids is as follows. Figure 8-10 illustrates.

1. Draw an isometric axis system and lay out the appropriate centerlines. See Figure 8-10-1.
2. Project the centerlines onto the surface of the pyramids. The center of the pyramid surface is defined by a line drawn from the apex, through the centerline projection, to the midpoint of the baseline. Define the centerlines of the square on the pyramid surface, as shown in Figure 8-10-2.
3. Project points onto the pyramid surface, as shown in Figure 8-10-3. Note that the edge lines of the intersection are parallel to the centerlines drawn in step 2, NOT to the edges of the pyramid.
4. Darken the appropriate lines. Figure 8-10-4.

Figure 8-11 depicts another intersection problem that involves a pyramid.

8-6 CONES

The surfaces of cones not only slant and taper toward an apex, as do pyramids, they are also rounded. This means that each point must also include a circular reference in addition to the linear ones.

The procedure for developing intersections on conical surfaces is as follows. Figure 8-12 illustrates.

1. Draw an isometric axis and lay out the appropriate centerlines. See Figure 8-12-1.

Figure 8-6 Part 2

Figure 8-6 Part 3

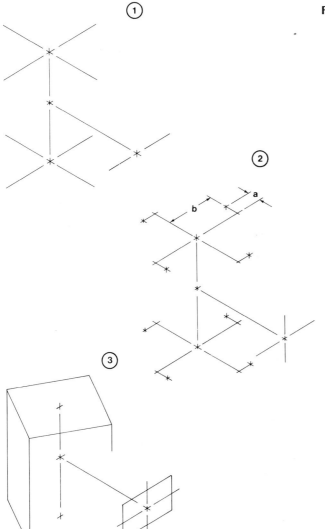

Figure 8-6 Intersection of irregularly rotated rectangular surfaces.

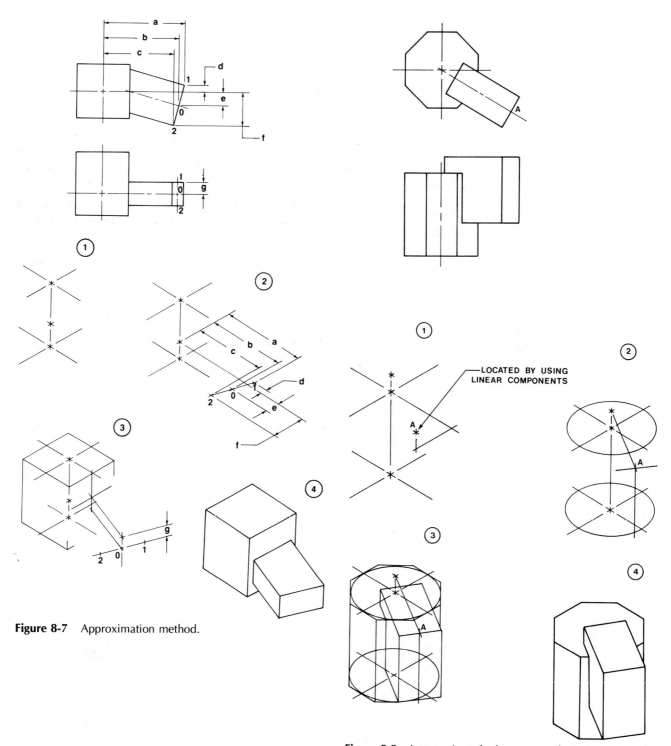

Figure 8-7 Approximation method.

Figure 8-8 Intersection of a hexagon surface.

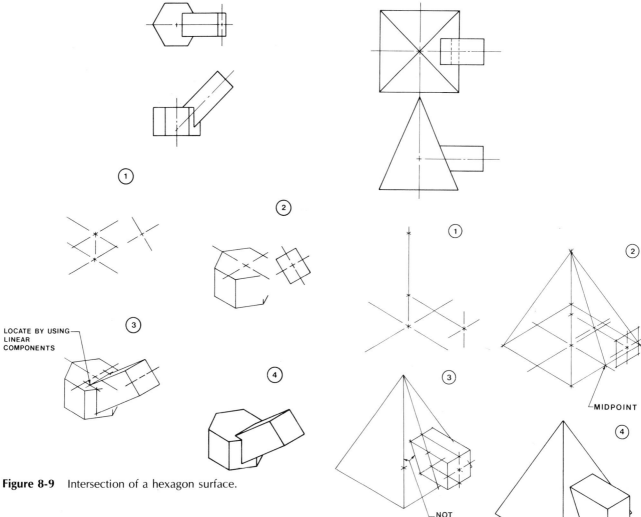

Figure 8-9 Intersection of a hexagon surface.

LOCATE BY USING
LINEAR
COMPONENTS

MIDPOINT

NOT
PARALLEL

Figure 8-10 Intersection of a pyramid surface.

2. Project the centerlines, as shown in Figure 8-12-2. Note that line intersection 4-2 on the cone is circular (drawn with an isometric ellipse template). The correct size ellipse is determined by aligning the template to the surface centerpoint and the edges of the cone.

3. Project the individual points by first referencing them to the vertical centerline, projecting this reference point (x in this example), to the centerline on the cone (point y), then drawing an ellipse through this point, and finally projecting the point directly onto this circular reference line. See Figure 8-12-4.

4. Project all points as outlined in step 3 and darken the appropriate lines. See Figure 8-12-4.

Figure 8-13 is an example involving the intersection of a hexagon and a square.

PROBLEMS

Prepare an isometric drawing of the following objects listed in Part Four, Exercise Problems.

P-87	**P-93**
P-88	**P-94**
P-89	**P-95**
P-90	**P-96**
P-91	**P-97**
P-92	

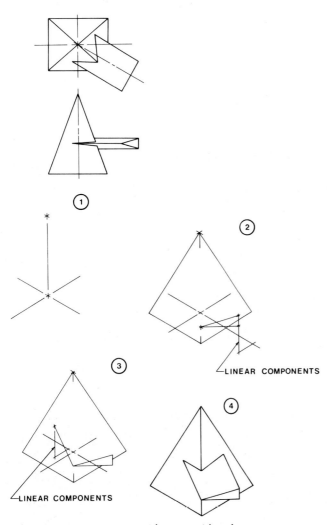

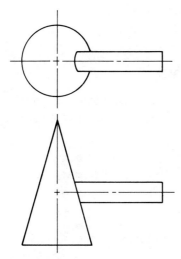

Figure 8-11 Intersection of a pyramid surface.

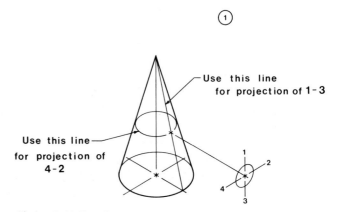

Figure 8-12 Part 2

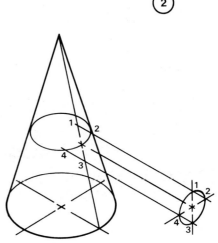

Figure 8-12 Part 3

Figure 8-12 Part 1

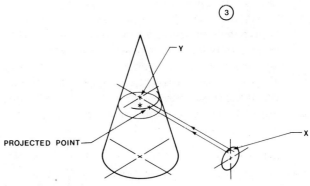

Figure 8-12 Part 4

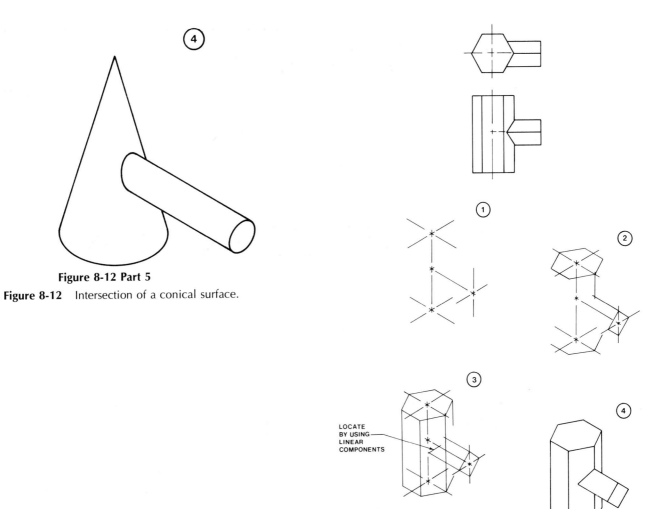

④

Figure 8-12 Part 5

Figure 8-12 Intersection of a conical surface.

①

②

③

LOCATE
BY USING
LINEAR
COMPONENTS

④

Figure 8-13 Intersection of a hexagon and a square surface.

CHAPTER 9

TERMS AND DEFINITIONS

9-1 INTRODUCTION

This chapter deals with a number of terms and definitions commonly used in the manufacturing industry. These terms will either appear on drawings or be used to refer to shapes or processes.

9-2 KEYS AND KEYWAYS

Keys are metal pieces used on shafts to transfer rotary motion. They fit into slots called keyways. There are four major shapes: square, woodruff, Prat and Wittney, and Gib. Key sizes are standardized and can be found in most engineering or company handbooks. See Figure 9-1.

9-3 DOVETAIL

A dovetail is a shape commonly used in manufacturing. Dovetailed parts slide together. See Figure 9-2.

9-4 COUNTERSINK

Countersinking is a manufacturing process that tapers the top of a hole. It is usually used to recess flat head screws. See Figure 9-3.

9-5 REAM

Reaming is a manufacturing process used to smooth the internal surface of a drilled hole. Reamed holes are closely toleranced—from an illustrator's standpoint, the nearest convenient dimension within the stated tolerance. For example, the notation

$$\begin{matrix} .5000 \\ .4999 \end{matrix} \quad \text{REAM}$$

would indicate that a half-inch hole should be drawn.

9-6 BUSHING

A bushing is a cylindrically shaped object used to reinforce the surface of a hole. If a hole is used to support a spinning shaft, a bushing would be mounted in the hole. After the bushing wears out, it is replaced. This saves replacing the entire object. See Figure 9-4.

9-7 COUNTERBORE

A counterbore is used when a larger diameter hole must be drilled along the same centerline as a

KEYS

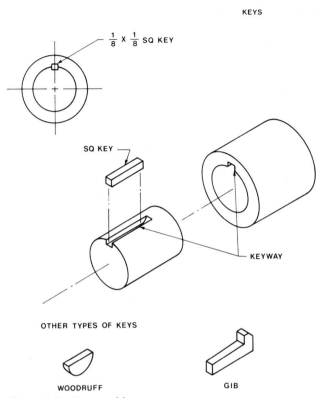

$\frac{1}{8}$ X $\frac{1}{8}$ SQ KEY

SQ KEY

KEYWAY

OTHER TYPES OF KEYS

WOODRUFF

GIB

Figure 9-1 Keys and keyways.

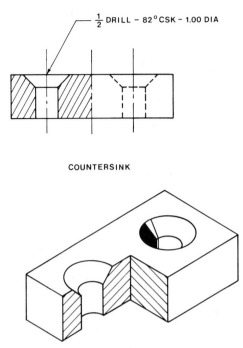

$\frac{1}{2}$ DRILL – 82° CSK – 1.00 DIA

COUNTERSINK

Figure 9-3 Countersink.

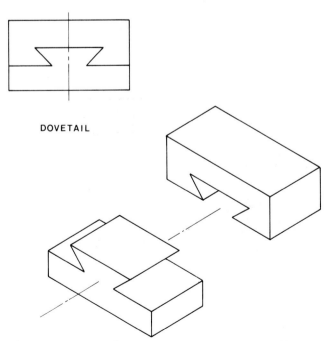

DOVETAIL

Figure 9-2 Dovetail.

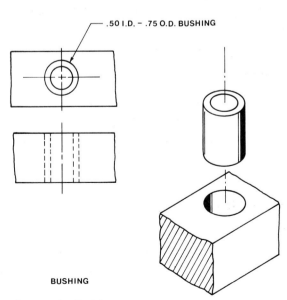

.50 I.D. – .75 O.D. BUSHING

BUSHING

Figure 9-4 Bushing.

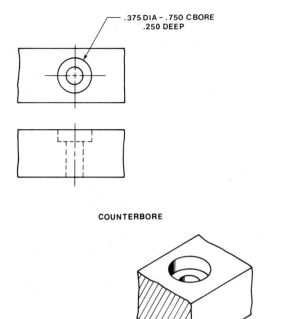

.375 DIA – .750 C BORE
.250 DEEP

COUNTERBORE

Figure 9-5 Counterbore.

smaller one. It has many design applications. See Figure 9-5.

9-8 SPEC and MIL SPEC

SPEC is the abbreviation for *specification* and MIL SPEC for *military specification*. A specification is a procedure or set of requirements that defines a certain manufacturing process or result. For example, the drawing note "Paint per SPEC 52" would mean that the object must be painted per the company specification number 52.

9-9 KNURL

Knurling is a manufacturing procedure that cuts either a diamond or straight pattern on a shaft. Knurling is usually used to allow the shaft to be gripped. See Figure 9-6.

9-10 WELDS

There are many different types of welds, including fillet, seam and so on. They are all identified by similar arrowlike notes, but with different symbols. The notes are interpreted as shown. See Figure 9-7.

9-11 CHAMFER

Chamfering is a machine process that removes corners. Chamfers are usually made at 45°. They serve to remove sharp corners or to help fit parts together. See Figure 9-8. (also see Section 6-2 for more information).

9-12 GEOMETRIC TOLERANCING

Geometric tolerancing is a system that uses standard symbols and numbers enclosed in a box. From an illustrator's standpoint, only *basic* dimensions are needed. These are the dimensions that are boxed individually. See Figure 9-9.

9-13 SURFACE FINISHES

Surface finishes are specified by a V-like symbol and a number. The larger the number, the rougher the finish. See Figure 9-10 (also see Section 7-4 for further information).

9-14 DRAWING ABBREVIATIONS

Most drawings include abbreviations along with the illustrated information. Figure 9-11 lists some common abbreviations along with their meanings.

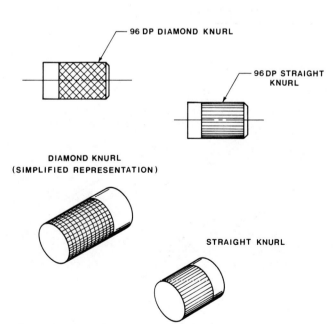

96 DP DIAMOND KNURL

96 DP STRAIGHT KNURL

DIAMOND KNURL
(SIMPLIFIED REPRESENTATION)

STRAIGHT KNURL

Figure 9-6 Knurls.

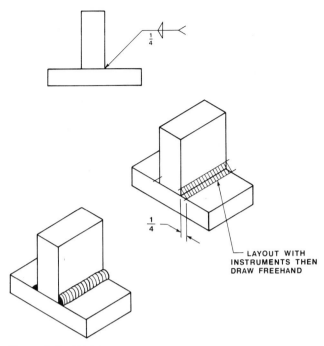

Figure 9-7 Welds.

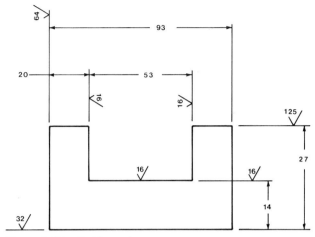

Figure 9-10 Finish marks.

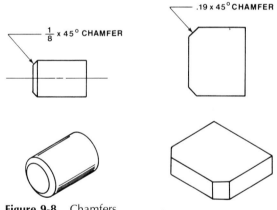

Figure 9-8 Chamfers.

DRAWING ABBREVIATIONS	
DIA	DIAMETER
∅	DIAMETER
TYP	TYPICAL
ST	STEEL
AL	ALUMINUM
R	RADIUS
SYM	SYMETRICAL
℄	CENTERLINE
CBORE	COUNTERBORE
CSK	COUNTERSINK
SFACE	SPOTFACE
ID	INSIDE DIAMETER
OD	OUTSIDE DIAMETER

Figure 9-11 Some abbreviations commonly used on engineering drawings.

9-15 GEARS

There are many different ways to draw gears pictorially. The simplest is to use underlays, as shown in Figure 9-12-1. The underlays are placed under the drawing paper and traced. It is suggested that pencil tracings be prepared first (rather than going directly to ink) and then saved for future use. The isometric gear underlay shown in Figure 9-12-1 can be used to draw different types of gears including the spur, worm, bevel, helical, and herringbone gear. Perspective drawings may also be prepared. Specific instructions are included with the underlays.

Gears are defined in terms of the number of teeth and the pitch (distance between teeth). The exact diameter, thickness, and so forth, is available from manufacturers catalogs.

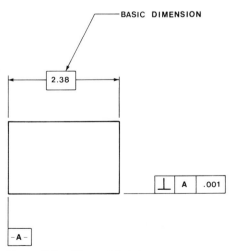

Figure 9-9 Geometric tolerances.

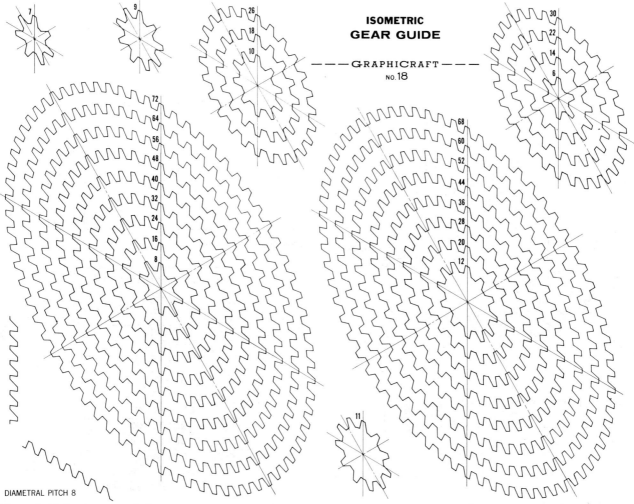

ISOMETRIC
GEAR GUIDE

——— GRAPHICRAFT ———
NO. 18

DIAMETRAL PITCH 8

Figure 9-12-1 A gear underlay.

20 TOOTH GEAR

Figure 9-12-2 An isometric drawing of a gear.

To use a gear underlay, trace the appropriate gear, slide the paper along the centerline until the correct thickness is reached. Again trace the gear, only drawing what can be seen, and connect the teeth corners.

Figure 9-12-2 is an isometric drawing of a gear.

9-16 SPRINGS

Springs are drawn using a template as a guide. Springs are classified as light, medium, or heavy, depending on the wire thickness used to make them, and as tension or compression, depending on their usage. See Figure 9-13.

To use an isometric spring template, proceed as follows:

1. Draw an isometric axis. See Figure 9-13-1.
2. Align the spring template with the isometric axis and draw a partial loop as shown. Depending on the wire thickness, align the appropriate corresponding loop of the template with the isometric axis line and the previously drawn loop, and draw the second loop. See Figure 9-13-2. It is important to keep the template aligned with the 30° isometric line. It is suggested that, in addition to the visual alignment with the isometric axis, a T-square and

30°-60°-90° triangle or a drafting machine set at 30° be used to reinforce the accuracy of the alignment.

3. Slide the template along the isometric axis and align the template with the open end of the loop. The larger and smaller loops are done separately. Note that the template is still aligned with the isometric axis. See Figure 9-13-3.

4. Continue step 3 until as many loops as needed are drawn: then darken the appropriate lines. See Figure 9-13-4.

9-17 SECTIONAL VIEWS

Sectional views are drawings that pictorially cut open objects to expose internal edges and surfaces not otherwise seen. In orthographic views, they appear as shown in Figure 9-14-1. The surfaces to be cut are defined by a heavy cutting plane line that is drawn across one of the regular orthographic views. The sectional view is located behind the arrows on the cutting plane line. All cut surfaces are identified by thin, equally spaced, crosshatching lines (sectioning lines).

Illustrators can also create sectional views. Pictorial sections can be drawn as full sections, half sections, or as random cutouts, as shown in Figure 9-14-2. In all cases, cut surfaces must be indicated by equally spaced crosshatching.

If two or more parts are shown in assembly, crosshatch each piece differently—either make the crosshatch lines closer together or change their angle for each part. See Figure 9-14-3.

ORTHOGRAPHIC REPRESENTATION

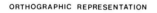

ISOMETRIC DRAWINGS

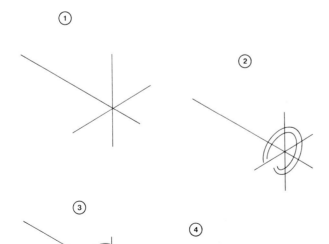

Figure 9-13-1 Springs

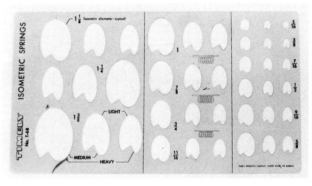

Figure 9-13-2

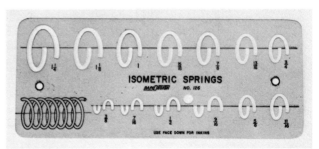

Figure 9-13-3
Figure 9-13 How to do an isometric drawing of a spring.

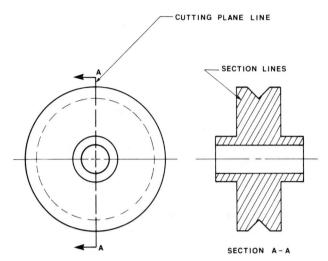

Figure 9-14-1

FULL SECTIONAL VIEW

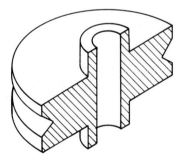

HALF SECTIONAL VIEW

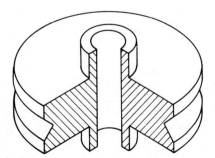

Figure 9-14-2

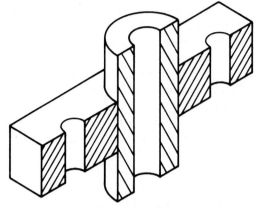

Figure 9-14-3 Two different parts

Figure 9-14 Sectional views.

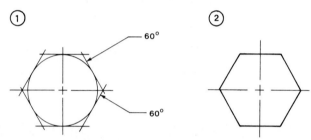

Figure 9-15 Geometric construction—hexagon.

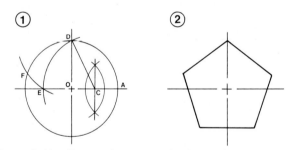

Figure 9-16 Geometric construction—pentagon.

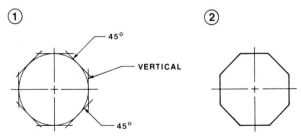

Figure 9-17 Geometric construction—octagon.

9-18 GEOMETRIC CONSTRUCTIONS

When drawing orthographic supplementary layouts, it is sometimes necessary to construct basic geometric shapes. These include hexagons, pentagons, and octagons, among others. Figures 9-15, 9-16, and 9-17 illustrate these shapes.

To construct a hexagon, draw a circle of a diameter equal to the distance across the flats or the required hexagon. *Across the flats* means from one side of the hexagon to the other—not along the edge of one side. See Figure 9-15. Add the 60° lines as shown and darken the appropriate lines.

To construct a pentagon, draw a circle of a diameter equal to the distance across the corners of the required pentagon. Figure 9-16 illustrates.

Bisect line 0-A and define point C. Using point C as a center, construct an arc radius C-D as shown. Define point E. Using point D as a center, construct an arc of radius D-E shown. Define point F. The distance D-F equals the length of one of the five required sides and can be marked off along the edge of the circle to complete the pentagon.

To construct an octagon, draw a circle of a diameter equal to the distance across the flats of the required octagon. See Figure 9-17. Add the 45° vertical and horizontal lines as shown and darken the appropriate lines.

Any of these finished constructions can be defined in terms of linear components and transferred to an isometric axis.

CHAPTER 10

EXPLODED DRAWINGS

10-1 GENERAL EXPLANATION

Exploded drawings are pictorial drawings in a series that show how parts fit together. They are most useful for maintenance and assembly instructions.

Figure 10-1 shows a simple exploded drawing. Note how the centerline is used to guide the viewer's eye and to define how the parts fit together.

Each part has also been assigned a simple number that has been defined in the included parts list. This is done because company part numbers are often very long (8 to 10 digits) and would tend to clutter and confuse the drawing.

Each part number used on the exploded drawing is enclosed in a circle. The same part would have the same number even if it is used several times. Each number uses a leader line to reference the appropriate part. Arrowheads are optional.

When possible, position the parts of an exploded drawing for maximum clarity (so that most surfaces are clearly visible). Internal parts and subassemblies may be drawn outside, as shown in Figure 10-2; then by using centerlines, they can be directed to the appropriate internal positions.

Small or confusing areas may be enlarged for better clarity. In the example shown in Figure 10-2, the small setscrew was enlarged by using a drawing detail. The scale of the enlargement is sometimes specified.

10-2 SHADING EXPLODED DRAWINGS

Shading may be used on exploded drawings, but shadows are rarely included since they tend to cover smaller parts. Shadows also add little to the overall understanding of the drawing.

10-3 COMPLICATED EXPLODED DRAWING TECHNIQUES

Large and complex exploded drawings are usually drawn in individual pieces and then traced, as needed, to complete the final exploded drawings. Most experienced illustrators keep a layout file of pieces frequently drawn so they won't have to redraw the pieces for each new drawing. Parts most often called for are screws, bolts, washers, fittings, and those parts commonly used on the customer's main product lines.

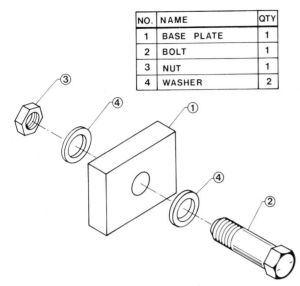

NO.	NAME	QTY
1	BASE PLATE	1
2	BOLT	1
3	NUT	1
4	WASHER	2

Figure 10-1 An exploded drawing.

The layout file should consist of the original layout drawings, not Xerox copies. Xerox copies are 2 to 3 percent smaller than originals and therefore are not in the same scale as the rest of the drawing. If reduced scale layouts are required, have them photographically reduced as needed (50 percent, 75 percent, etc.). Photographic size reduction is more expensive than Xeroxing, but it can be made true to scale.

Paste up is another technique frequently used to prepare exploded drawings. Paste ups are drawings that are prepared by cutting out various pieces from copies of previous work and pasting them, along with any new work required, together to form a new drawing. Figure 10-3 shows a paste up, and Figure 10-4 shows the resultant finished drawing. Note that the edges of the cutout pieces do not show in the final drawing.

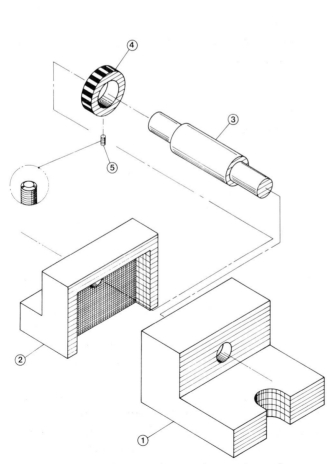

Figure 10-2 An exploded drawing showing internal parts.

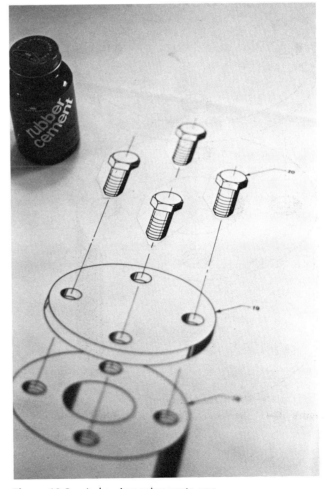

Figure 10-3 A drawing using paste ups.

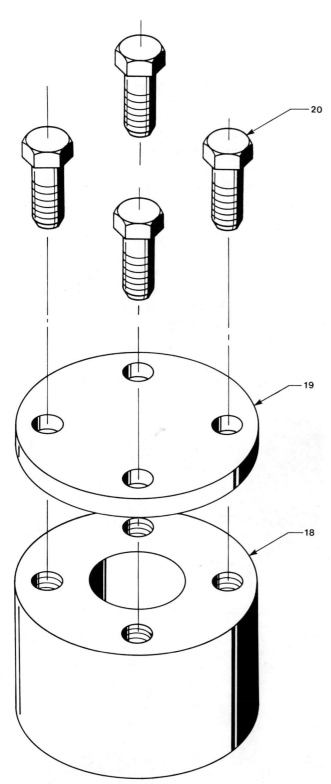

Figure 10-4 The results of reproducing Figure 10-3.

Students are encouraged to start their own reference file of drawings by saving their pencil layouts and by making and saving copies of all their work.

10-4 CUTAWAY EXPLODED DRAWINGS

Exploded drawings can be cutaway to expose internal parts. Figure 10-5 shows a cutaway exploded drawing.

The breaklines of a cutaway drawing are drawn freehand This will make them standout against the other lines of the drawing and add to their visual effectiveness.

10-5 NOTES ON EXPLODED DRAWINGS

Notes may be added to exploded drawings as necessary. If special emphasis is required, the note may be boxed or shaded or both, as shown in Figure 10-6. Keep notes far enough away from the main part of the drawing to prevent confusion and a cluttered appearance, but in the general area of where the note applies.

10-6 DETAIL AND ASSEMBLY DRAWINGS

There are two types of manufacturing drawings: details and assemblies. Detail drawings are drawings of only one part and contain all information necessary for the manufacture of that part. An assembly drawing is a drawing that shows how the parts are to be put together and includes only the information needed for assembly.

In technical illustration, assembly drawings translate into exploded drawings and detail drawings define the size and shape of the individual parts. Figure 10-7 shows how detail and assembly drawings are used to create an exploded drawing.

We see from the assembly drawing that the illustration includes a front and top view of the assembled pieces. Each part is labeled by a number and cross-referenced in the parts list (table in the lower right-hand corner of the drawing) to appropriate drawing numbers and size information. In this example, the LEFT BASE and RIGHT BASE are

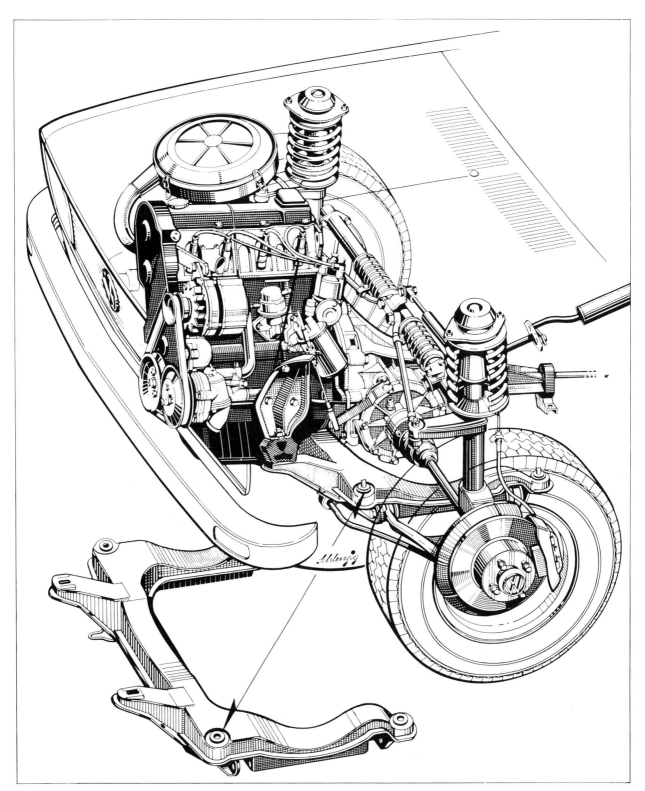

Figure 10-5 A cutaway drawing. Courtesy of Volkswagen-werk, Wolfsburg, Germany

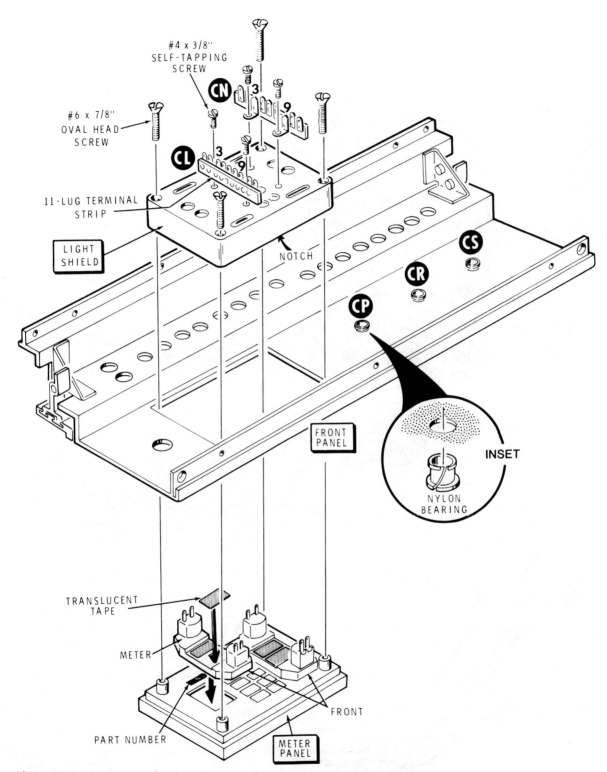

Figure 10-6 Notes on a drawing. Courtesy of Heath Company, Benton Harbor, Michigan.

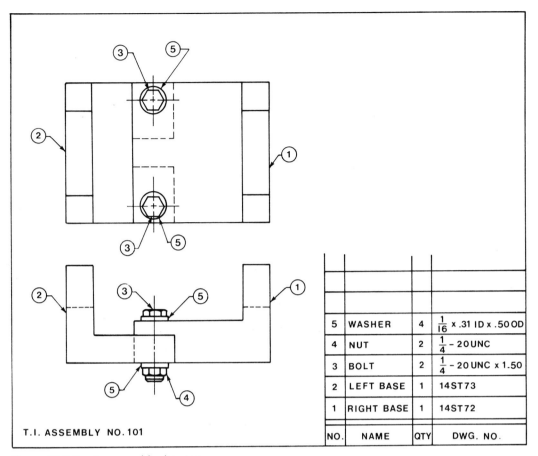

Figure 10-7-1 An assembly drawing.

5	WASHER	4	$\frac{1}{16}$ x .31 ID x .50 OD
4	NUT	2	$\frac{1}{4}$ – 20 UNC
3	BOLT	2	$\frac{1}{4}$ – 20 UNC x 1.50
2	LEFT BASE	1	14 ST 73
1	RIGHT BASE	1	14 ST 72
NO.	NAME	QTY	DWG. NO.

T.I. ASSEMBLY NO. 101

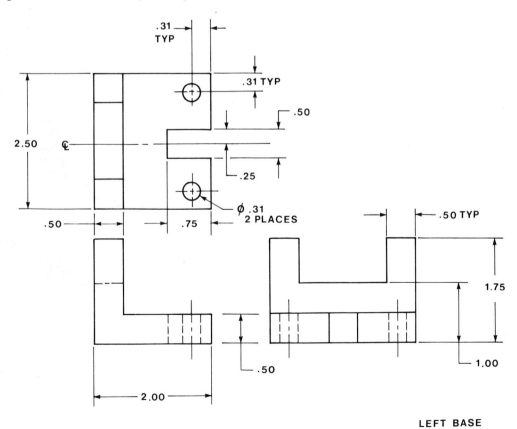

LEFT BASE
DWG. NO. 14 ST 73

Figure 10-7-2 A detail drawing.

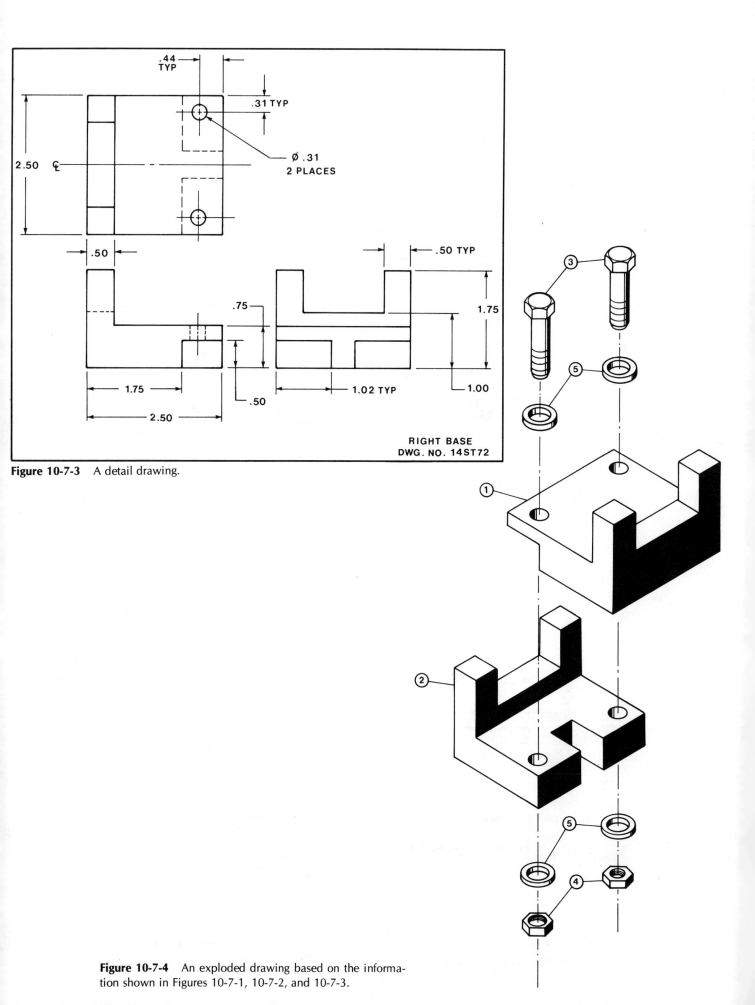

Figure 10-7-3 A detail drawing.

RIGHT BASE
DWG. NO. 14ST72

Figure 10-7-4 An exploded drawing based on the information shown in Figures 10-7-1, 10-7-2, and 10-7-3.

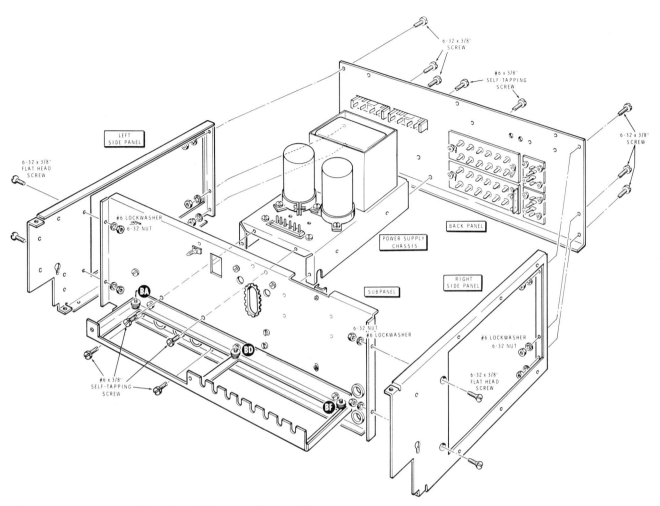

Figure 10-8 Courtesy of the Heath Company, Benton Harbor, Michigan.

referenced to drawing numbers 14ST73 and 14ST72, respectively. Drawings 14ST73 and 14ST72 are detail drawings and contain the manufacturing for the LEFT BASE AND RIGHT BASE.

Illustrators usually work from assembly drawings, but must have detail drawings for the dimensions of more complicated parts. Standard parts, such as bolts, nuts, and washers, do not normally have detail drawings, but are sized in the parts list of the assembly drawing. Chapter 5 contains information on how to interpret size notes for fasteners and washers.

Figures 10-8, 10-9, and 10-10 are further examples of exploded drawings.

PROBLEMS

Prepare an isometric exploded drawing for the following problems in Part Four.

P-77	P-82
P-78	P-83
P-79	P-84
P-80	p-85
P-81	p-86

Also consider these drawings.

P-72	P-75
P-73	P-76
P-74	

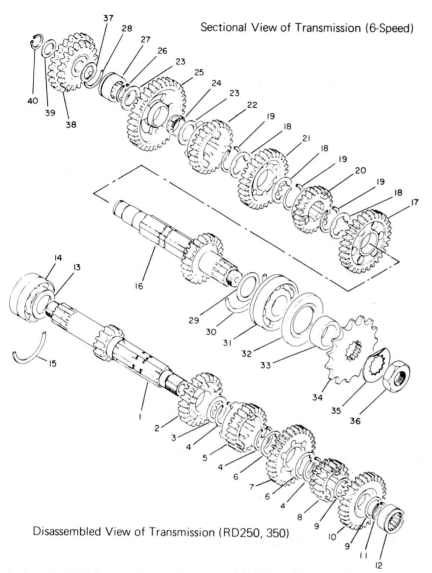

Sectional View of Transmission (6-Speed)

Disassembled View of Transmission (RD250, 350)

1. Main axle (14T)
2. 4th pinion gear (25T)
3. Gear hold 2 washer (25-32-1)
4. Circlip (25φ special)
5. 3rd pinion gear (22T)
6. Gear hold 1 washer
7. 6th pinion gear (28T)
8. 2nd pinion gear (18T)
9. Gear hold washer (**20-15-1**)
10. 5th pinion gear (27T)
11. Circlip (S-20)
12. Bearing (20-30-15)
13. Drive axle shim (25-34-0.3)
    Drive axle shim (25-34-0.5)
14. Bearing (25-52-20.6)
15. Circlip
16. Drive axle comp. (24T)
17. 2nd wheel gear (32T)
18. Gear hold 1 washer
19. Circlip (25φ special)
20. 6th wheel gear (22T)
21. 3rd wheel gear (29T)
22. 4th wheel gear (26T)
23. Gear hold washer (**23-30-1.0**)
24. Bearing (20-24-10)
25. 1st wheel gear (36T)
26. Circlip (S-20)
27. Bearing (20-33-15)
28. Circlip
29. Drive axle shim (25-34-0.5)
30. Circlip
31. Bearing (6305N special)
32. Oil seal (SD-35-62-6)
33. Distance collar (25-35-17.5)
34. Sprocket (14T)
    Sprocket (15T)
    Sprocket (16T)
35. Lock washer
36. Lock nut
37. Wave washer
38. Idler gear ass'y (22T & 27T)
39. Main axle shim (15.2-20-1)
40. Circlip (S-15)

Figure 10-9 Courtesy of the Yamaha International Corp., Buena Park, California.

CLUTCH ASSEMBLY

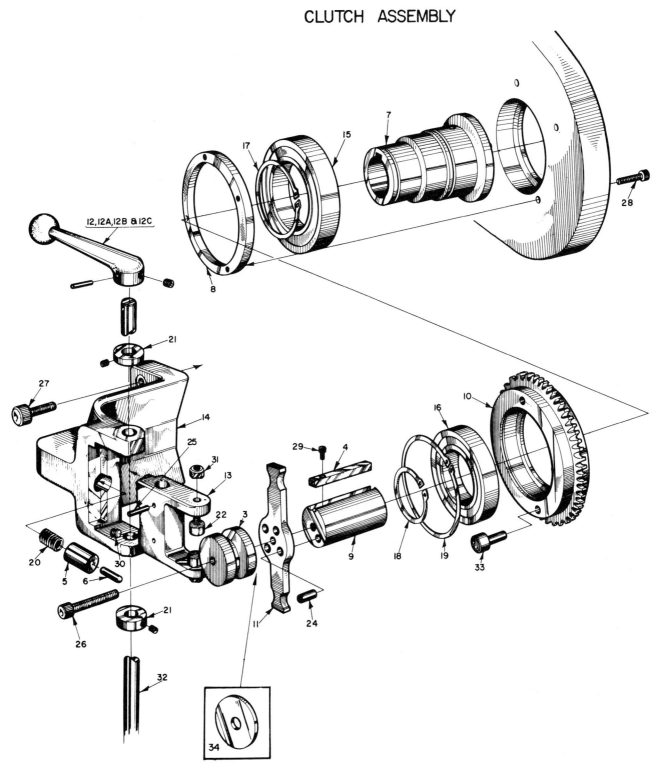

Figure 10-10 Courtesy of the Gloucester Engineering Corp., Gloucester, Massachusetts.

CHAPTER 11

DIMETRIC DRAWINGS

11-1 INTRODUCTION

Dimetric drawings are drawings based on an axis system that contains two equal angles. This is slightly different from isometric drawings because isometric drawings require an axis that contain three equal angles. When expressed in angles relative to the horizontal, isometric drawings use a 30° axis, whereas dimetric drawings use any two acute angles other than 30°. Figure 11-1 illustrates.

The 15° angle is the most popular choice for a dimetric axis. Most illustrations in this chapter are done using 15° angles.

Dimetric drawings done using a 15° axis system have less visual distortion than do isometric drawings. This is most evident when drawing large, flat objects. Note in Figure 11-2 how the rear corner of the isometric drawing appears distorted (seems to bend up), whereas the dimetric drawing appears more lifelike.

11-2 PREPARING A DIMETRIC DRAWING

As with isometric drawings, measurements may be transferred directly from orthographic views to a dimetric axis. If the dimetric drawing is created using the orthographic dimensions, it will appear larger than the orthographic views. Figure 11-3 illustrates. Use a scale of $\frac{3}{4} = 1$ to make dimetric drawings appear equal in size to their equivalent orthographic views.

The dimetric axis need not be drawn to equal

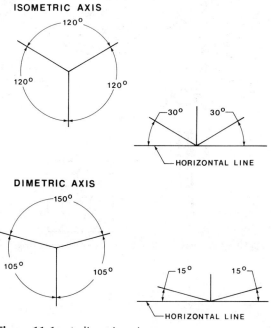

Figure 11-1 A dimetric axis.

ISOMETRIC

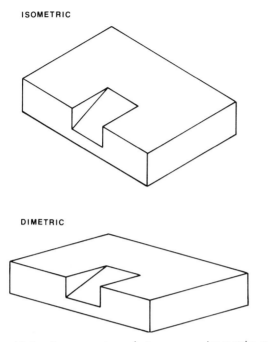

DIMETRIC

Figure 11-2 A comparison between an isometric and dimetric drawing.

scales. Figure 11-3-3 was drawn with the left-hand axis at half scale and the right-hand axis at full scale. Compare the results with Figures 11-3-1 and 11-3-2.

Figure 11-4 depicts an adjustable triangle. Adjustable triangles are helpful when preparing dimetric drawings because they can be set to any angle. Whatever angle is chosen for the dimetric axis, it can be set on the triangle, thereby eliminating the need for constant references to the axis lines.

Angular measurements may not be transferred directly from orthographic views to dimetric drawings. The angular measurements must be broken down into linear components and then transferred. Figure 11-5 illustrates.

Angular measurements may be directly measured in dimetric drawings by using a dimetric protractor. Dimetric protractors are available commercially, but it is very easy to draw your own and then use the drawing as an underlay.

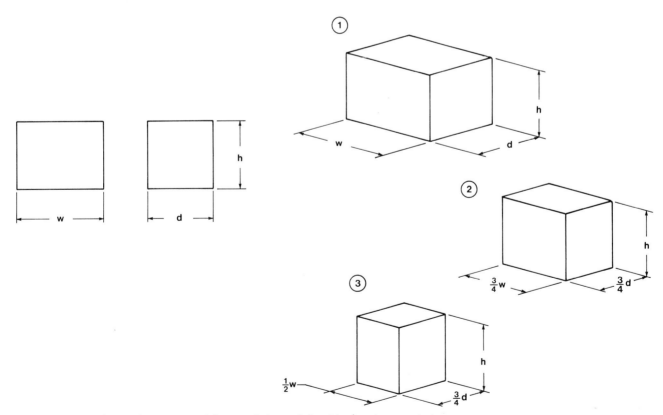

Figure 11-3 Orthographic views and three variations of dimetric drawings created from the orthographic views.

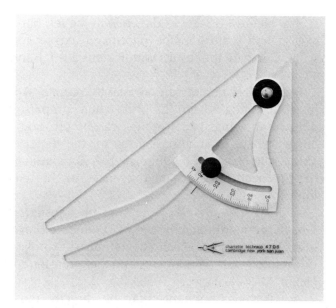

Figure 11-4 An adjustable triangle.

Figure 11-6 shows how to draw a dimetric protractor. The procedure is as follows.

1. Align an appropriate angled ellipse and a circle along a common vertical line, as shown in Figure 11-6-1. In this example, a 15° ellipse was used. The procedure is the same for any angle.

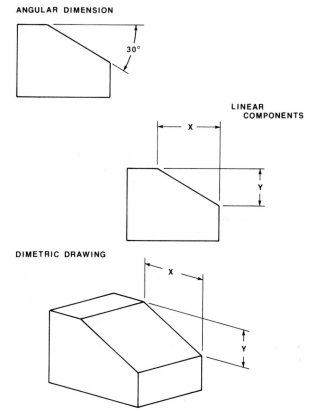

Figure 11-5 Angular measurements in dimetric drawings.

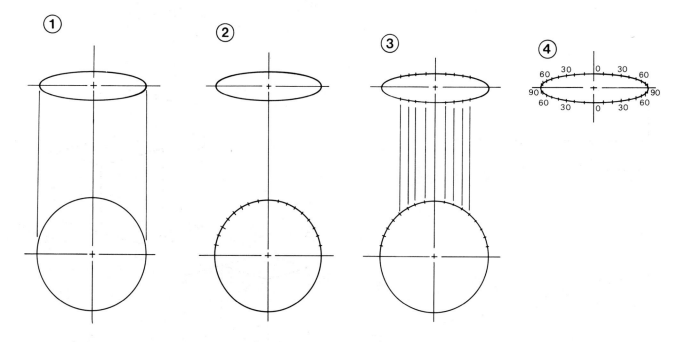

Figure 11-6 Creating a 15° dimetric protractor.

15° Protractor

2. Mark off equal angles on the circle (use a regular protractor) and project the distance onto the 15° ellipse. See Figures 11-6-2 and 11-6-3.
3. Darken the marks and label them with the value measured on the circle. See Figure 11-6-4. The 10° marks are usually accurate enough for most drawings.

11-3 CIRCULAR SHAPES

Circular shapes, such as curved surfaces and holes, are drawn as ellipses on dimetric drawings. The shape of the ellipse depends on the angles of the axis system. If, for example, the dimetric drawing uses a 15° axis, the left and right planes use a 45° ellipse and the base or top plane uses a 15° ellipse. Figure 11-7 illustrates.

The orientation of the ellipse template is determined by drawing 15° lines, as shown in Figure 11-8, for the left and right-hand planes and horizontal and vertical lines for the base plane. The orientation lines are matched to the reference marks on the template.

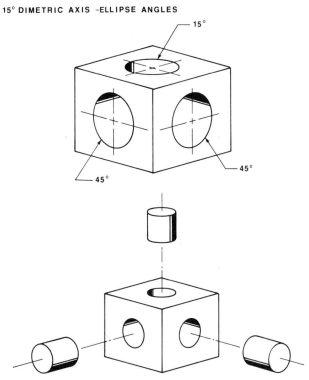

15° DIMETRIC AXIS –ELLIPSE ANGLES

Figure 11-7 Circular shapes in dimetric drawings.

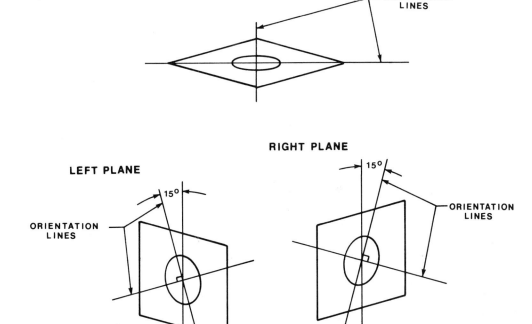

Figure 11-8 How to orient an ellipse for use on a dimetric drawing.

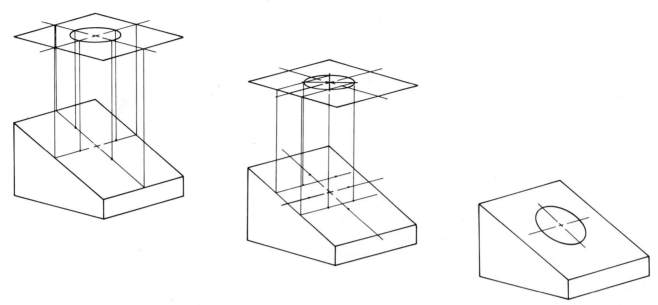

Figure 11-9 Holes in a slanted surface.

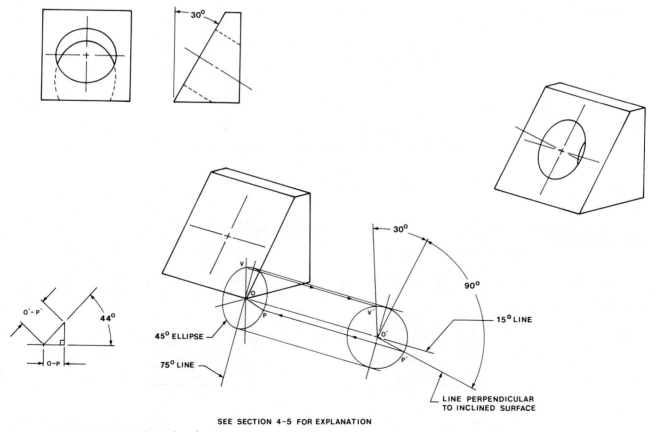

SEE SECTION 4-5 FOR EXPLANATION

Figure 11-10 Holes in a slanted surface.

The shape of holes in nondimetric planes is determined by one of three methods: by drawing the hole in one of the dimetric planes and then projecting the hole onto the nondimetric surface (Figure 11-9); by using the circle reference method (Figure 11-10); or by approximation (Figure 11-11).

The projection method shown in Figure 11-9 is the same as that explained for isometric drawings in Section 4-5. The only difference is the axis system and ellipse or shafts whose centerlines are perpendicular to one of the dimetric planes.

The circle reference method shown in Figure 11-10 was explained for isometric drawings in Section 4-5; however, for dimetric drawings the ellipse angle must match the axis angle. For a 15° axis, a 45° angle ellipse is used.

The approximation method shown in Figure 11-11 is done by first drawing the centerlines and then, in pencil, lightly sketching in the ellipse by eye. The approximated ellipse is then matched to an ellipse template and drawn in accurately.

11-4 FORESHORTENED AXIS

Dimetric drawings can be made more visually realistic by using a foreshortened axis. For a 15° axis system, the left- and right-hand axes measurements are foreshortened to a scale of $\frac{3}{4} = 1$; the vertical measurements remain full scale. Figure 11-12 illustrates. The amount of foreshortening depends on the axis angle.

It is important to consider the realistic qualities of a foreshortened dimetric drawing. Perspective drawings are the most lifelike, but are difficult to draw particularly when curved or irregular shapes are involved. Dimetric drawings are visually closer to perspective drawings than isometric drawings and, because their receding lines remain parallel to the basic axis system, are easier to draw. Templates may be used for all round surfaces, and irregular surfaces can be plotted.

Holes drawn on foreshortened planes must also be foreshortened. The amount of reduction is equal to the scale of the receding axis. For a 15° axis, this means all hole diameters are multiplied by $\frac{3}{4}$ (.75). Figure 11-13 shows a cube with 25-mm diameter holes in each surface, and the same cube drawn with a $\frac{3}{4}$, $\frac{3}{4}$, 1 foreshortened axis and then drawn

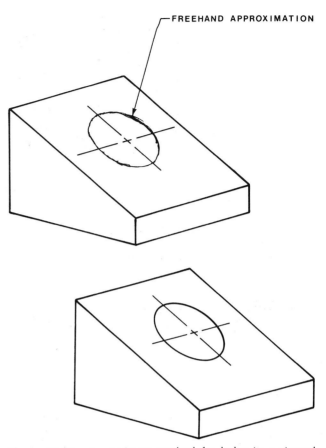

Figure 11-11 Approximate method for holes in a slanted surface.

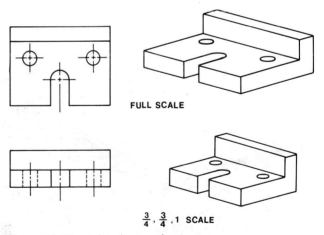

Figure 11-12 A foreshortened axis.

with the holes at $\frac{3}{4}$ scale. In other words, the 25-mm holes were drawn using 19-mm ellipses.

$$25 (.75) = 18.75 \quad \text{or} \quad 19 \text{ mm}$$

Most 15° dimetric drawings are drawn using a $\frac{3}{4}$, $\frac{3}{4}$, 1 foreshortened axis.

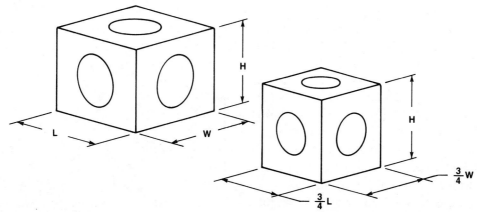

Figure 11-13 A foreshortened axis.

6 VARIATIONS OF 15° DIMETRIC AXIS

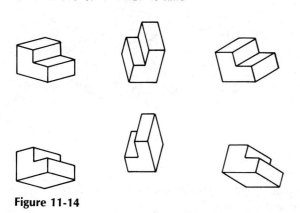

Figure 11-14

11-5 VARIATIONS

Dimetric drawings, by definition, must contain two equal angles in their axis system, but the orientation of the axis may be varied. Figure 11-14 shows six of the 144 possible variations that can be created using a 15° axis system.

The illustrator can take advantage of these variations to orient the object for maximum clarity and still maintain the advantage of a dimetric drawing.

Dimetric Drawing

15° Axis

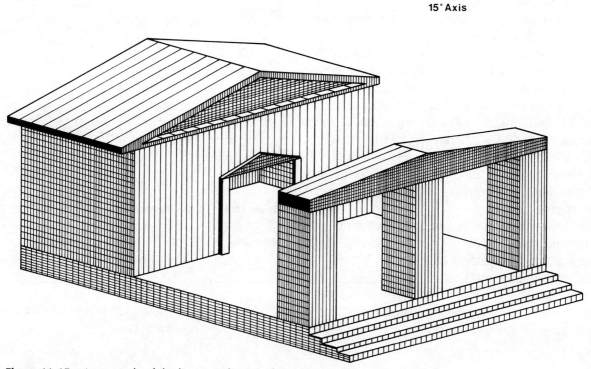

Figure 11-15 An example of shading on a dimetric drawing.

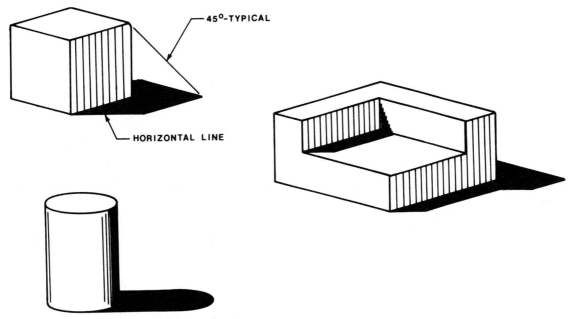

45°-TYPICAL

HORIZONTAL LINE

Figure 11-16 Shadows on a dimetric drawing.

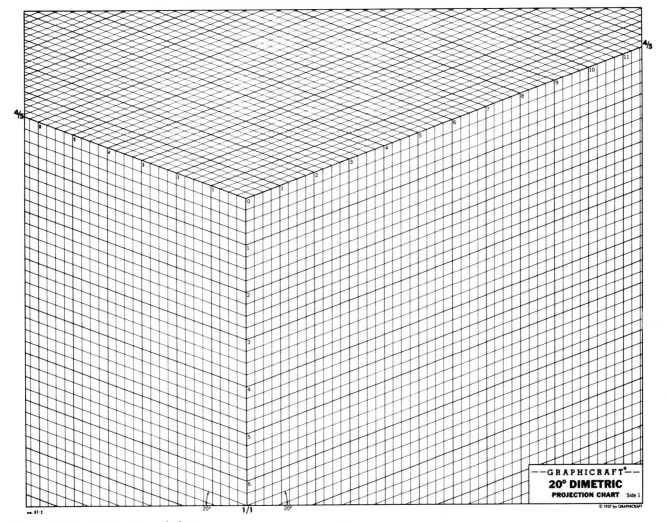

GRAPHICRAFT®
20° DIMETRIC
PROJECTION CHART Side 1

© 1957 by GRAPHICRAFT

Figure 11-17 A dimetric underlay.

11-6 SHADING AND SHADOWS

Shading and shadows can be applied to dimetric drawings as outlined in Chapter 12. Figures 11-15 and 11-16 give examples of shading and shadows on dimetric drawings.

11-7 DIMETRIC UNDERLAYS

An *underlay* is a predrawn pattern or shape that is placed under the drawing paper and then either traced or used as a guide. Dimetric underlays are predrawn grid patterns that are drawn according to a dimetric axis. Figure 11-17 shows one of the many different dimetric underlays commercially available.

Figure 11-18 shows how to prepare a dimetric underlay. It is suggested that the student prepare a dimetric underlay for future use. Use ink on mylar for durability. The procedure is as follows.

1. Lay out a dimetric axis. In this example, a 15° axis was used. See Figure 11-18.
2. Mark off the foreshortened axis distances. In this example, scales of ¾, ¾, and 1 were used. See Figure 11-8-2.
3. Draw in the reference lines and darken as shown. See Figure 11-18-3.

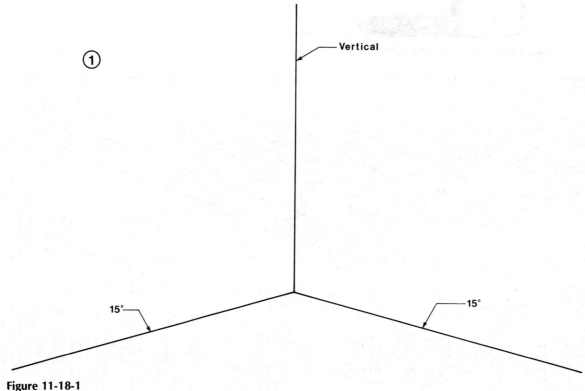

Figure 11-18-1

②

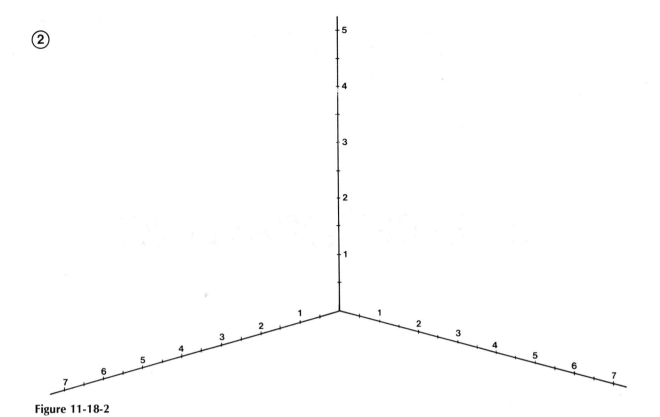

Figure 11-18-2

③

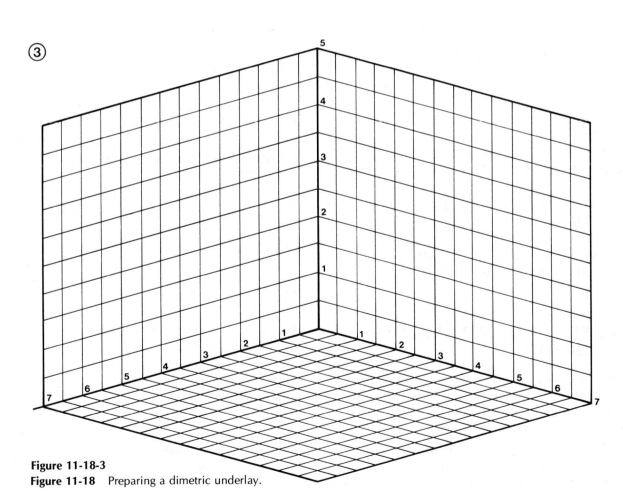

Figure 11-18-3
Figure 11-18 Preparing a dimetric underlay.

89

CHAPTER 12

TRIMETRIC DRAWINGS

12-1 INTRODUCTION

Trimetric drawings are axonometric drawings that have three unequal angles in their axes. Figure 12-1 compares isometric, dimetric, and trimetric axis systems and drawings.

Trimetric drawings permit the illustrator to rotate the object being drawn for maximum surface clarity. This means that an object with visual distortions when drawn on an isometric axis can be clarified by redrawing it on a trimetric axis. Figure 12-2 illustrates. Many trimetric drawings give the effect of looking down on the object, although this may be varied to best suit the individual requirements.

12-2 PREPARING A TRIMETRIC DRAWING

Most trimetric axes consist of a vertical line, one small angle (15° or less), and one large angle (30° or more). For purposes of discussion and illustration, an axis of 15° and 40° will be used.

Linear measurements may be transferred directly to a trimetric axis, as shown in Figure 12-3, but angular measurements must be converted to linear components, as shown in Figure 12-4, and then transferred to the trimetric axis.

An adjustable triangle (see Figure 11-4) is very helpful when preparing a trimetric drawing. It can be purchased in various sizes.

The most difficult part of preparing a trimetric drawing is knowing which angle ellipse to use and how much foreshortening is required. For an axis system of 15°, 40°, and vertical, ellipse angles of 25°, 30°, and 50° are used, as shown in Figure 12-5. The foreshortening factors are .86, .65, and .92 (also shown in Figure 12-5).

The correct orientation of the ellipse template is determined by reference to the given trimetric axis. The 25° ellipse shown on the 15°, 40°, vertical trimetric axis in Figure 12-6 is oriented to a vertical line, the 50° ellipse to a 40° line, and the 25° ellipse to a 15° line. In each case, the second orientation line is perpendicular to the first.

Figure 12-7 contains a listing of some of the more popular trimetric axis angles along with their ellipse angles and foreshortening factors. A sample, based on the given information, is also shown.

If an axis other than one of those presented in Figure 12-7 is required, an approximation should be used to determine the ellipse angles and fore-

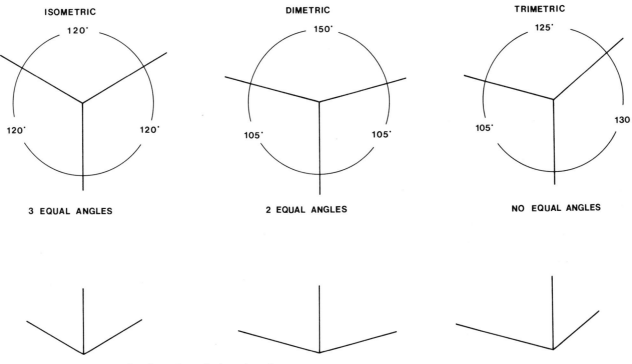

Figure 12-1 An isometric, dimetric and trimetric axis.

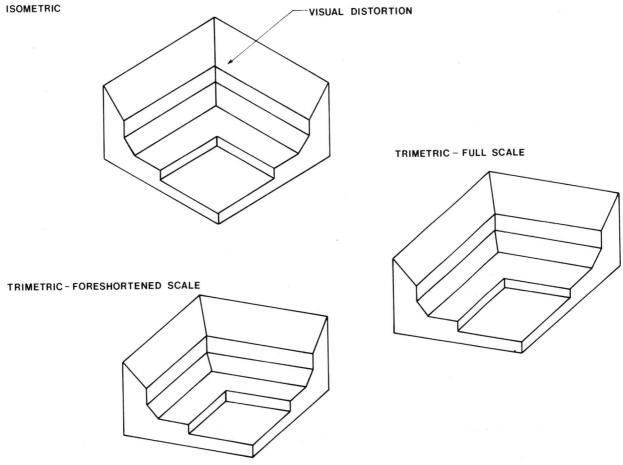

Figure 12-2 Examples of trimetric drawings.

ORTHOGRAPHIC VIEWS

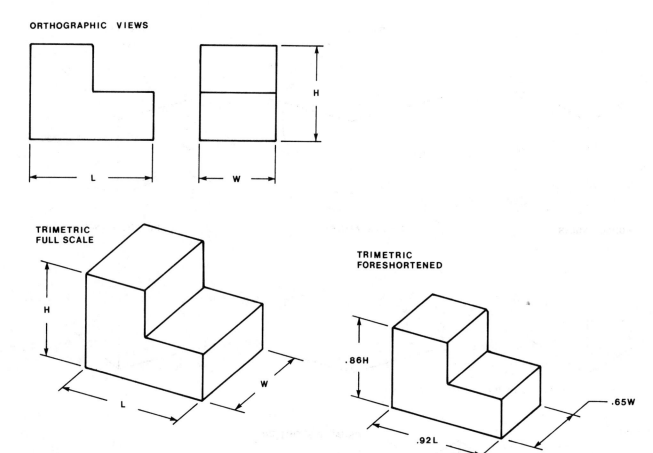

Figure 12-3 Orthographic views and two variations of trimetric drawings created from the orthographic views.

ANGULAR DIMENSION

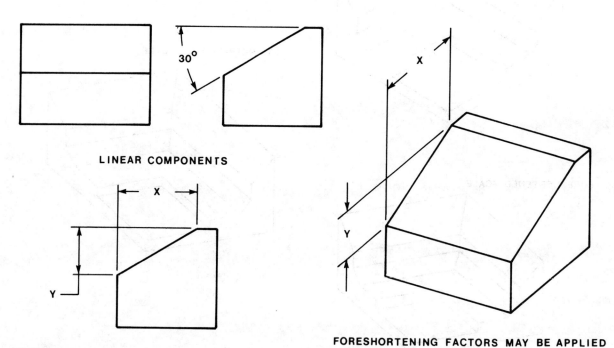

Figure 12-4 Angular measurements in trimetric drawings.

15, 40, 90 TRIMETRIC AXIS

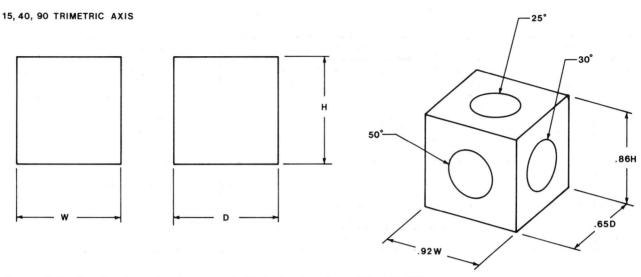

Figure 12-5 The foreshortening factors and elliptical values for a 15°, 40°, 90° trimetric drawing.

ELLIPSE ORIENTATION LINE FOR 15° 40° 90° TRIMETRIC AXIS

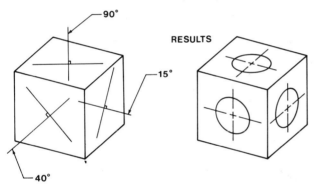

Figure 12-6 Elliptical orientation for trimetric drawings.

shortening factors. First draw the overall width, depth, and height of the object using the exact dimensions given. Then, by trial and error, foreshorten the dimensions. Once an acceptable size has been reached, divide the foreshortened distance by the true distance. The result is the foreshortening factor.

To approximate the ellipse angle, draw a freehand ellipse that looks visually correct; then match the approximate ellipse to one on the templates. Figure 12-8 illustrates.

12-3 SLANTED SURFACES

Holes in slanted surfaces can be determined by one of three methods: draw an ellipse on one of the trimetric planes and project it onto the slanted surface; use the circle projection method; or use the approximation method. These methods were discussed in Section 4-5, Figure 4-14, and may be applied to trimetric drawings provided the correct axis system and ellipse angles are used.

Figure 12-9 shows the circle projection method applied to a 15°, 40°, vertical trimetric axis system.

12-4 SHADING AND SHADOWS

Shading and shadows can be applied to trimetric drawings as outlined in Chapter 16. Figures 12-10 and 12-11 exhibit the use of shading and shadows on trimetric drawings.

12-5 TRIMETRIC UNDERLAYS

Trimetric underlays are grid patterns that match a trimetric axis. They are placed under the drawing paper and used as a reference for preparing trimetric drawings. They may be purchased commercially or drawn, as shown in Figure 12-12. The pattern developed in Figure 12-12 is based on a 15°, 40°, vertical trimetric axis, and the procedure used is as follows. This procedure may be used for any trimetric axis.

1. Lay out a trimetric axis. In this example, a 15°, 40°, vertical axis was used.

TRIMETRIC DRAWING DATA

LEFT PLANE			RIGHT PLANE			BASE PLANE		
ANGLE	ELLIPSE ANGLE	FORESHORTING FACTOR	ANGLE	ELLIPSE ANGLE	FORESHORTING FACTOR	ANGLE	ELLIPSE ANGLE	FORESHORTING FACTOR
10	55	.88	30	30	.58	90	15	.95
10	55	.94	50	20	.56	↑	25	.90
10	50	.96	60	15	.58		35	.86
15	50	.90	30	30	.63		25	.92
15	50	.92	40	30	.65		25	.86
15	50	.94	50	25	.65	↓	35	.82
15	45	.96	60	15	.65	90	40	.78

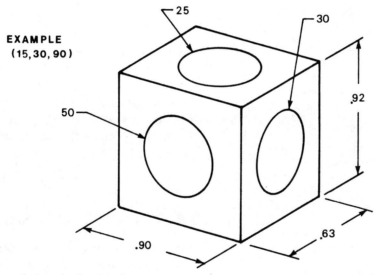

EXAMPLE
(15, 30, 90)

Figure 12-7 A listing of trimetric drawing data.

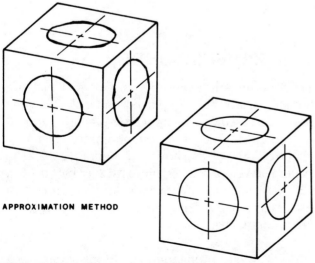

APPROXIMATION METHOD

Figure 12-8 Approximation method.

2. Mark off the foreshortened axis distances. This step could be difficult because trimetric fore-shortening factors are usually odd numbers such as .92, .86, etc. Figure 12-13 shows a simple way to handle the unusual factors. First, lay out the axis angle and then, from the same starting point, a line at any acute angle to the reference line. Mark off equal distances along the second line and measure the total length. (In this case, it is 5 inches.) Multiply the total length by the foreshortening factor and mark this distance on the axis line. Connect the two end points. Then connect the remaining points with lines parallel to the line that connects the end points. Use the projected points for the grid pattern development.

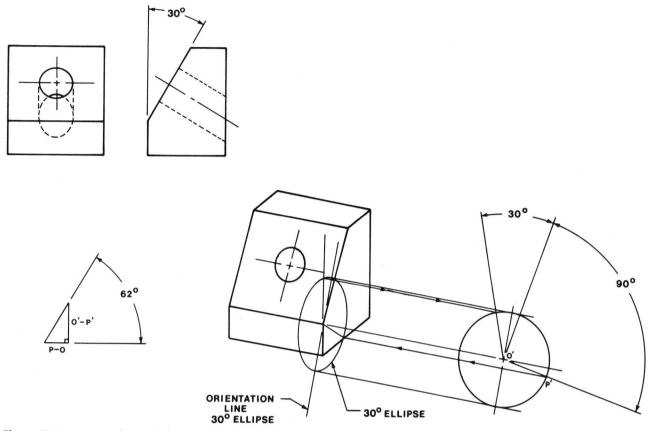

Figure 12-9 How to draw a hole in a slanted surface.

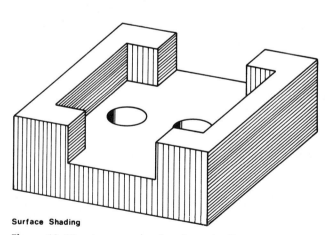

Surface Shading

Figure 12-10 An example of surface shading.

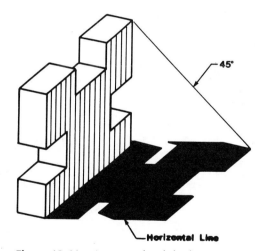

Figure 12-11 An example of shadow casting.

15, 40, 90, AXIS

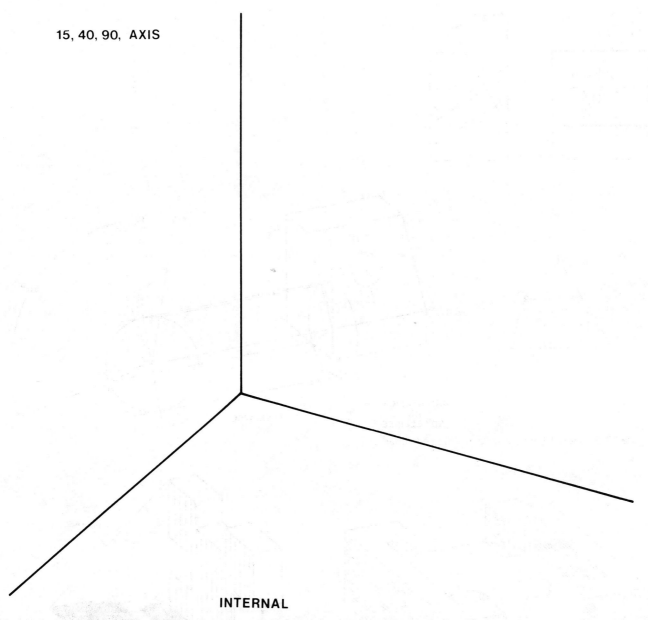

INTERNAL

Figure 12-12-1

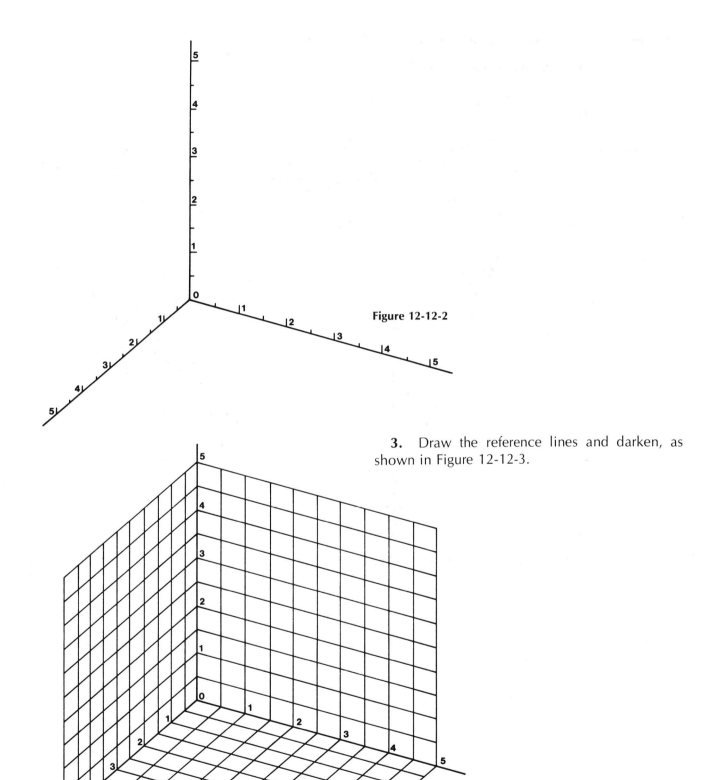

Figure 12-12-2

3. Draw the reference lines and darken, as shown in Figure 12-12-3.

Figure 12-12-3

Figure 12-12 Preparing a trimetric underlay.

DEVELOPMENT OF A 5″ x 5″ x 5″ (15, 40, 90) TRIMETRIC AXIS

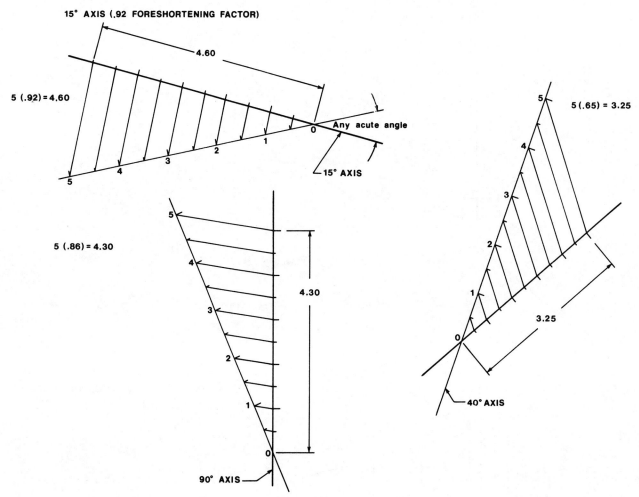

Figure 12-13 Foreshortened axis for the trimetric underlay of Figure 12-12.

CHAPTER 13

OBLIQUE DRAWINGS

13-1 INTRODUCTION

The oblique drawing is a specialized form of drawing. The three axis angles are unequal, but two of the angles are drawn 90° apart. The remaining receding axis can be drawn at any acute angle, although 30° is the most popular. Figure 13-1 illustrates an oblique axis.

Because of the 90° axis lines, the frontal plane, and all planes parallel to it, may be drawn both true size and true shape. More specifically, this means that in the frontal plane, round shapes can be drawn using a compass or circle template. The cylinder shown in Figure 13-2 was drawn using a compass, whereas the isometric required an isometric template.

Oblique drawings are the easiest type of pictorial drawing to draw, but also contain the most visual distortions. Note in Figure 13-3 that the oblique drawing of the cube does not look like a cube, but appears elongated. In some cases, the distortion is acceptable and does not distract from the meaning of the drawing. However, a more visually correct drawing can be created by drawing the receding axis measurements at half scale. This type of oblique drawing is called a *cabinet projection*. An oblique drawing done full scale is called a *cavalier*.

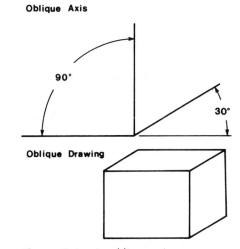

Figure 13-1   An oblique axis.

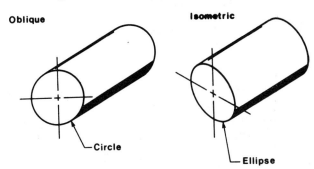

Figure 13-2   Position round shapes in the frontal plane of an oblique drawing.

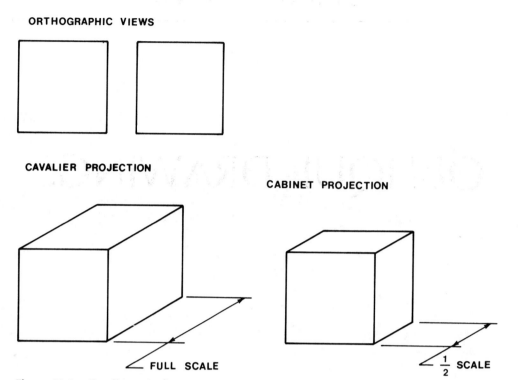

Figure 13-3 Cavalier and cabinet projections.

To take advantage of the special properties of oblique drawings, it is important to study the orientation of objects. The object shown in Figure 13-4 is easy to draw if oriented so that the round shapes are in the frontal plane. If not, the round surfaces become elliptical, negating any advantage in using an oblique drawing. Furthermore, if an object contains round surfaces in several different planes, there is no advantage to using an oblique drawing.

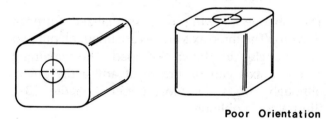

Poor Orientation

Figure 13-4 Position the circular shapes in the frontal plane.

13-2 HOW TO PREPARE AN OBLIQUE DRAWING

Oblique drawings are prepared as follows. Figure 13-5 illustrates.

1. Lay out an oblique axis. Select a receding axis (30° in this example).
2. Lay out the object using the given dimensions. Remember to reduce the distances along the receding axis to half scale if preparing a cabinet projection.
3. Darken the appropriate lines.

Figure 13-6 shows the procedure as it would apply to a cylindrically shaped object. Note that point B is the centerpoint for both the small and large circles.

Angular measurements may be transferred directly to the frontal plane but must be converted to linear components and then transferred for planes other than the frontal plane. Figure 13-7 illustrates. If possible, orient the object so that any angular measurements appear in the frontal plane.

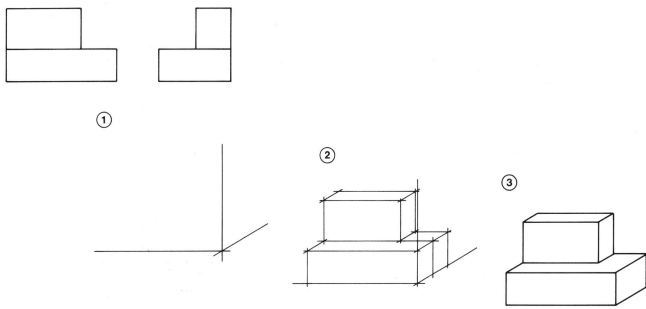

Figure 13-5 Orthographic views and an oblique drawing created from the orthographic views.

13-3 ROUND SURFACES

Round surfaces may be drawn as circles if they appear in the frontal plane or any plane parallel to the frontal plane, but round surfaces in the top and side receding planes must be drawn as ellipses. If a receding angle of 30° is used, the ellipse angles are 15° for the top plane and 30° for the right plane, as shown in Figure 13-8. Figure 13-9 shows how to locate the ellipse template to achieve the proper orientation. The perpendicular axis shown should align with the reference marks on the elliptical template.

Holes may be drawn in slanted surfaces in any one of three ways: draw the circle or ellipse in one of the oblique planes and project it onto the slanted surface (Figure 13-9); use the circle projection method (Figure 13-10); or use the approximation method (Section 11-3).

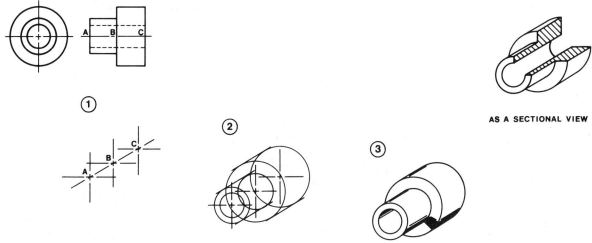

Figure 13-6 A cylindrically shaped object.

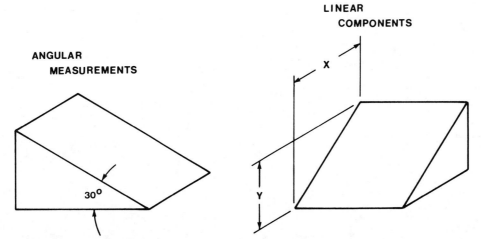

ANGULAR
MEASUREMENTS

30°

LINEAR
COMPONENTS

X

Y

Figure 13-7 Angular measurements on oblique drawings.

ORIENTATION ANGLES

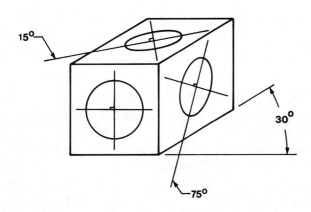

15°

30°

75°

Figure 13-8 How to orient an ellipse template on an oblique drawing.

CABINET PROJECTION

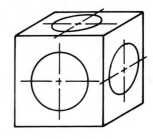

CAVALIER PROJECTION

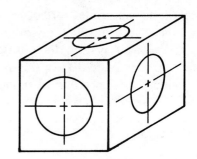

① ② ③

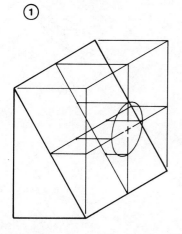

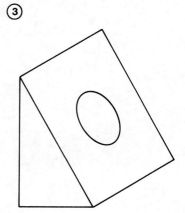

ADDITIONAL POINTS

Figure 13-9 A hole in a slanted surface.

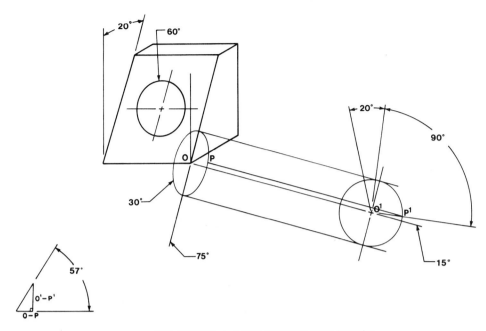

SEE SECTION 4-5 FOR FURTHER EXPLANATION

Figure 13-10   A hole in a slanted surface.

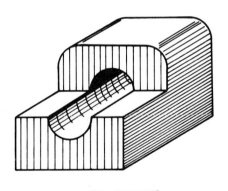

SURFACE SHADING

Figure 13-11   An example of surface shading.

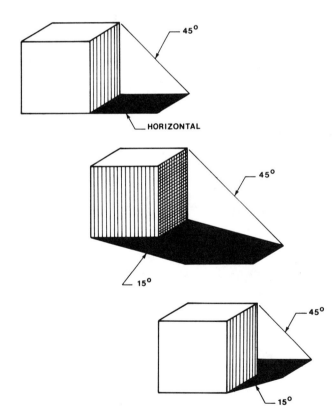

Figure 13-12   Variations of shadow casting on an oblique drawing.

13-4 SHADING AND SHADOWS

Shading and shadows can be applied to oblique drawings as outlined in Chapter 15. Figures 13-11 and 13-12 illustrate the use of shading and shadows on oblique drawings.

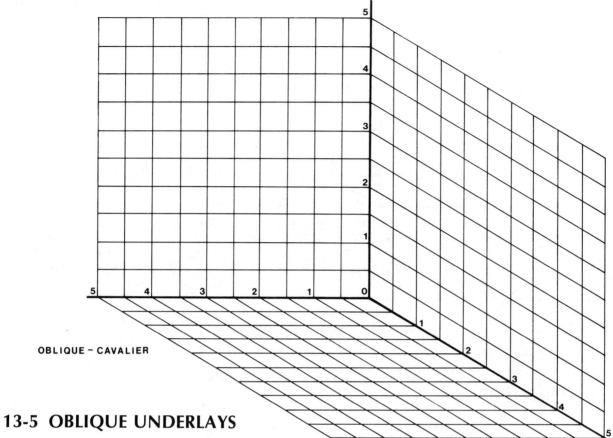

OBLIQUE - CAVALIER

Figure 13-13 A cavalier oblique underlay.

13-5 OBLIQUE UNDERLAYS

Figure 13-13 shows how to prepare a cavalier oblique underlay, and Figure 13-14 shows how to prepare a cabinet oblique underlay. Students should prepare oblique underlays in ink on mylar for future reference.

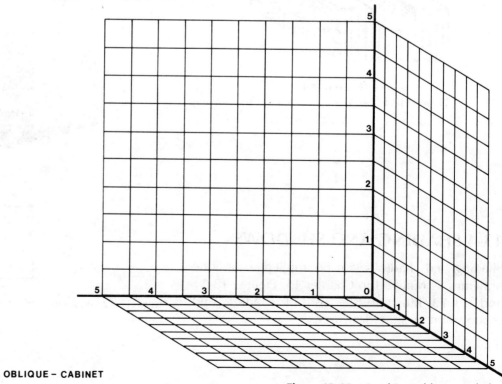

OBLIQUE - CABINET

Figure 13-14 A cabinet oblique underlay.

PART TWO

DRAWING TECHNIQUES

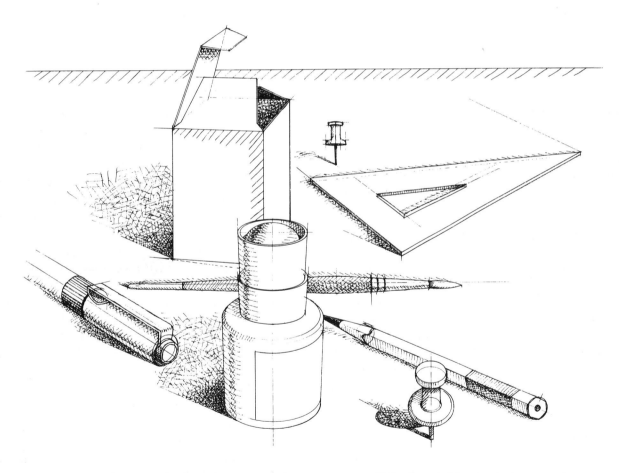

Part Two deals with drawing techniques. We will look at inking techniques, shading, and the use of shadows, as well as basic rendering techniques such as airbrushing and watercolor washes. Graphs and charts are also covered.

CHAPTER 14

INKING TECHNIQUES

14-1 INTRODUCTION

This chapter deals with the inking techniques used by technical illustrators. More specifically, it explains how to use a technical pen, which is the tool most often used for preparing inked drawings.

14-2 TECHNICAL DRAWING PENS

Technical pens have almost entirely replaced the ruling and detailing type pens because they are so much easier to use. Sometimes these technical pens are called by their brand names, for example, Rapidographs, Castels, Wricos, and so on.

Figure 14-1 shows a set of technical pens along with a disassembled one. Technical pens contain a cartridge to hold ink and are manufactured in different line-width sizes. Each pen will produce only one line width and cannot be adjusted for any other width.

Technical pens are manufactured in sizes 0000 to 7. The larger the number, the thicker the line width the pen produces. The pen labeled 0000 is the narrowest; 000 the next smallest; and so on.

Each pen is identified by number and a color code. Both the identifying number and color are located on both external and internal parts.

To use a technical pen, fill the cartridge with ink and hold the pen point down briefly. Then, test the pen on a piece of scrap paper to see if the ink is flowing. If leakage occurs, tighten all connections.

Once the pen flows smoothly, draw a few freehand lines to get the "feel" of the pen. A technical pen is used differently from a fountain or ballpoint type pen in that it does not operate with pressure. Once the ink starts to flow, the pen acts like a guide to direct the flow of ink. The pen is not pressed into the paper, but is pulled lightly over it.

If the pen clogs during use, shake it gently over a piece of scrap paper. This causes the internal plunger to free the ink passageways. (You should be able to hear the plunger rattling inside.) If shaking does not free the pen, disassemble it and clean all parts.

The pen should be cleaned after each day's use. The ink will eventually solidify and block all internal passageways if not cleaned properly.

It is a good practice to keep both a piece of scrap paper and a cloth handy while inking. See Figure 14-2. Before each usage, draw a few sample lines on the scrap paper to check the flow and to remove any excess ink (usually looks like a small bubble on the point of the pen). The cloth can be used to wipe excessive ink and to help clean the point.

Figure 14-1-1   A set of technical drawing pens.

Figure 14-1-2   A technical drawing pen.

A rubber plunger (see Figure 14-5) is used to blow air through the narrow internal passages. This discharges small particles of dried ink and dries the pen.

If parts become damaged or lost, they may be replaced. It is not necessary to buy a complete pen. Figure 14-6 shows a new point unit. Most distributors carry a supply of extra pen parts.

Figure 14-2   A setup for inking drawings.

14-3 CLEANING A TECHNICAL PEN

A technical pen may be cleaned by disassembling it and running warm water over each part. Each part must be dried thoroughly. Figure 14-3 shows a technical pen disassembled for cleaning.

If the ink has hardened, the pen should be soaked in a soapy solution overnight, rather than forced apart. Forcing could cause damage to the parts.

Cleaning kits are commercially available (see Figure 14-4) and contain small plastic jars for soaking pen parts. Cleaning kits also contain soaking baskets that fit into the jar and enable the user to easily lift parts in and out of the cleaning solution.

Figure 14-3   A disassembled technical pen.

Figure 14-4 A cleaning kit for technical pens.

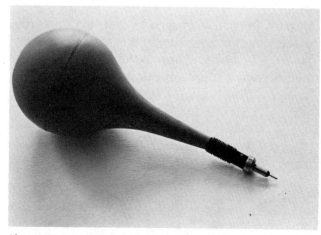

Figure 14-5 A plunger for cleaning technical pens.

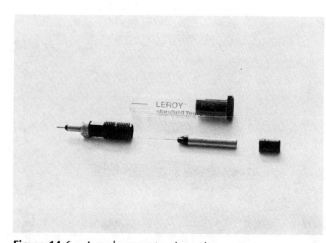

Figure 14-6 A replacement point unit.

14-4 DRAWING WITH A TECHNICAL PEN

Instruments used as guides for inking work must not be flush to the drawing paper, but must be slightly raised. If the instruments are not raised, the ink will flow under the instruments and smear the paper.

There are several ways to raise the edge of drawing instruments: use inking risers; use beveled-edge drawing instruments; or simply tape pennies to the instruments.

Figure 14-7 shows a card of inking risers. They are plastic pieces with glue on one side. They are stuck to the drawing instrument, as shown in Figure 14-8. It is recommended that inking risers be placed on the labeled side of templates, since this permits the template to lay flat during the pencil layout phase of the drawing.

Figure 14-9 shows a double-beveled edge. The double-beveled edges allow for a small airspace between the ink line and the flush edge of the triangle, thereby preventing ink from smearing.

Some templates are cut with a single bevel, as shown in Figure 14-10. When inking, flip the template over so the wider edge is on top. This creates the needed airspace.

Existing triangles may be adapted for inking by taping pennies to their undersurfaces. The tape should be changed periodically because it tends to gum with age.

Another technique that permits existing templates and triangles to be used for inking is to slide one template under another. Figure 14-11 illustrates. This technique also supplies the necessary airspace.

When drawing with a technical pen, keep the pen as near vertical as possible. See Figure 14-12. If the pen is used at too great an angle, the edge of the inked line will become jagged. This is different from pencil technique, which requires some slant and will take some practice to get used to. There are several practice exercises included in Part Four, Exercise Problems.

When drawing ink lines, be careful of how the line starts and ends. The pen must be pulled along the line at an equal tempo (speed) and pressure. Failure to do this will produce an uneven line and possible bubbles at each end. See Figure 14-13. Practice making lines smoothly by developing a steady constant motion applied throughout the entire length of the line.

Compasses can be adapted to ink by means of a compass adapter or by using a ruling pen point. Figure 14-14 shows a compass adapter for a technical pen, and Figure 14-15 shows it in place. Each

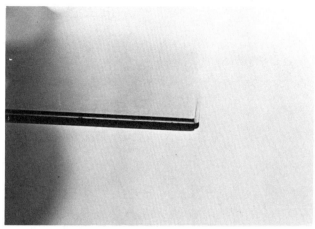

Figure 14-9 A double-develed triangel.

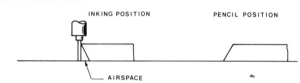

Figure 14-10 Using a beveled straightedge.

brand of compass is manufactured differently, so compass adapters may fit only one specific brand.

Figure 14-16 shows a compass fitted with a ruling pen point. The width of the line is controlled by the small screw on the side of the point. The tighter the screw, the narrower the line width.

To fill a ruling pen point, use the eyedropper that comes with the bottle of ink, and insert a small amount of ink into the pen from above the points (nibs). Figure 14-17 illustrates. The viscosity of the ink will hold it in place between the nibs. If too much ink is inserted, it will overflow, covering the outside of the nibs and producing a very heavy, uncontrollable line. If the pen clogs during use, draw a few lines on a scrap paper by angling the points to the side or by drawing a few short lines on your finger. Do NOT shake a ruling pen as you would a technical pen. Wipe the entire pen clean after each use.

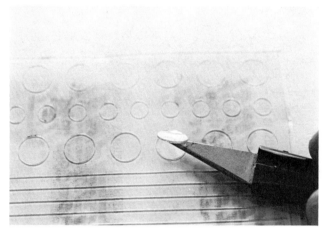

Figure 14-7 Inking risers.

Figure 14-8 Using inking risers.

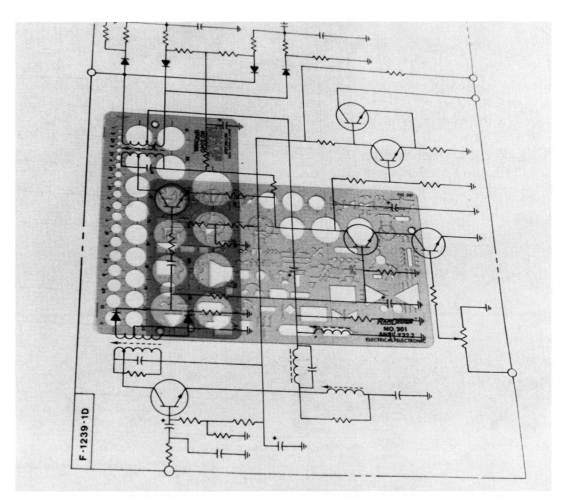

Figure 14-11 Sliding a triangle under another for inking purposes.

Figure 14-12 Using a technical drawing pen.

INCORRECT LINE

CORRECT LINE

KEEP PEN VERTICAL
Figure 14-13 Drawing inked lines.

14-5 LINE DRAWING SEQUENCE

Draw lines according to their difficulty, drawing the most difficult lines first. This usually means in the following sequence.

IRREGULAR CURVES
ARCS
CIRCLES
VERTICAL LINES
HORIZONTAL LINES

Also do thick lines before thinner ones. Therefore, centerlines and section lines would be inked after the object lines.

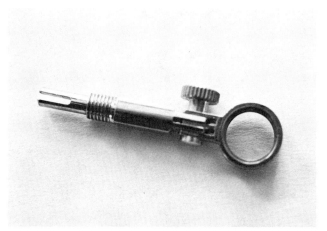

Figure 14-14 Compass adapter for a technical pen.

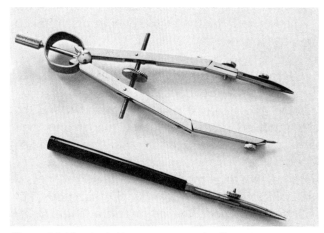

Figure 14-16 An inking compass and ruling pen.

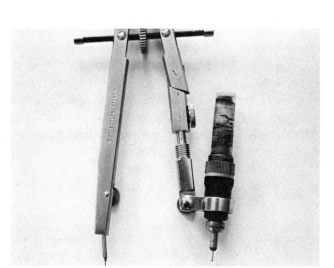

Figure 14-15 Using a compass adapter.

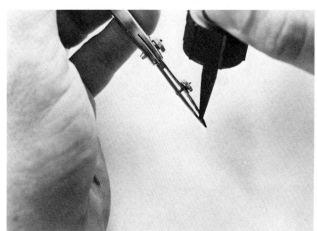

Figure 14-17 Filling a ruling pen or inking compass.

14-6 REMOVING INK LINES

Ink does not penetrate deeply into the drawing surface, but rather sits on top of the surface. This means that part of the line can be picked off by using an X-acto knife or other sharp instrument. See Figure 14-18. This method is risky because, if not done carefully, it can destroy the texture of the drawing surface causing the next inked line to blur.

Inked lines can be erased, but this must be done very carefully. If too much pressure is applied or too much speed (electric erasers), the drawing surface can be burned. Use a softer eraser after using an ink eraser to clean the surface before re-inking.

Another technique used to cover errors on inked drawings is to paint over them with the white corrective fluid used by typists. This technique is very limited and can only be used to cover errors. The area involved cannot be re-inked.

Large errors can be corrected by redrawing the area involved on nontransparent paper and then pasting the corrected area over the error. See Section 10-3. This technique can be used in conjunction with most modern reproduction processes and will produce a clean copy that does not distinguish between the original drawing surface and the pasteover. Figure 14-19 shows a drawing with a pasted over corner, and Figure 14-20 shows the final copy made from Figure 14-19.

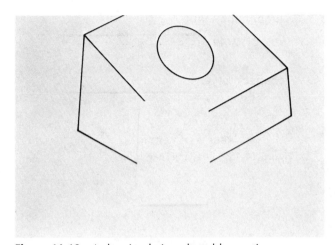

Figure 14-19 A drawing being altered by pasting on a new piece of paper and then redrawing.

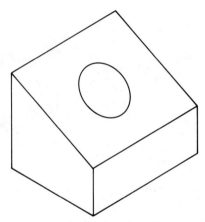

Figure 14-20 The results of Figure 14-19.

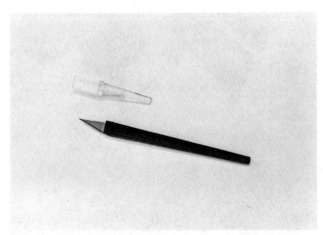

Figure 14-18 An X-acto knife.

14-7 LEROY LETTERING

Inked lettering is usually done by using a LEROY lettering set. Figure 14-21 illustrates.

The technical pen is placed in the LEROY scriber and then the scriber is placed in the LEROY template, so that the blunt rear peg fits into the long slot on the lower edge of the template and the other sharper peg fits into the appropriate letter guide. The scriber is then used to trace the letter on the template and to guide the pen in an identical shape. See Figure 14-21.

The slant of the letters is controlled by the adjustment of the scriber. This slant angle may be varied by releasing the holding screw and moving one of the scriber legs.

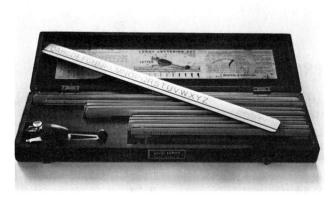

Figure 14-21-1

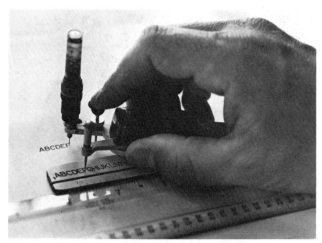

Figure 14-22 Using a LEROY lettering guide.

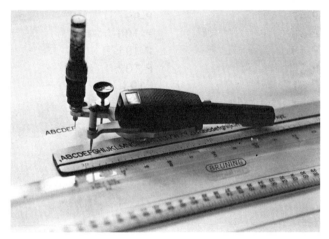

Figure 14-21-2
Figure 14-21 A LEROY lettering set.

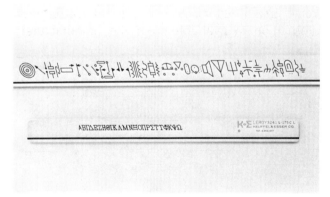

Figure 14-23 Examples of different LEROY lettering guides.

The LEROY template is aligned against a horizontal straightedge such as a T-square or drafting machine. The template is slid back and forth along the stationary horizontal straightedge as needed. The spacing between letters is done by eye; and the more practice that is done, the more even the spacing will become. Figure 14-22 shows how to use a LEROY lettering guide.

It should be noted that LEROYs are only set up for right-handed use. There is no way to turn them around, so a left-handed illustrator must adapt to using the right hand when using a LEROY.

LEROY guides are available for different size letters and for different technical shapes. Figure 14-23 shows LEROY guides for electronic symbols and for the Greek alphabet. Different sized scribers are also available. See Figure 14-24.

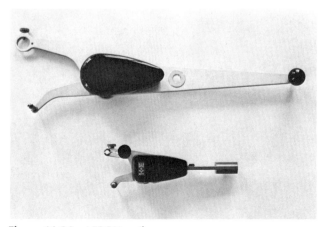

Figure 14-24 LEROY scribers.

Figure 14-25 A Varigraph headwriter. Courtesy of Varigraph, Inc.

A Varigraph headwriter can also be used to create inked letters. See Figure 14-25. Further information is available from the manufacturer, Varigraph, Inc., 1480 Martin Street, Madison, Wisconsin 53713.

PROBLEMS

To help develop inking techniques, start by tracing, in ink, a number of the pencil drawings already created. In addition, consider the following problems; see Part Four, Exercise Problems.

P-44	P-54
P-45	P-55
P-46	P-56
P-47	P-99
P-48	P-100
P-49	P-101
P-50	P-102
P-51	P103
P-52 (Difficult)	

CHAPTER 15

SHADING AND SHADOWS

15-1 INTRODUCTION

This chapter looks at shading and shadows. Of all the techniques and fundamentals covered in this book, shading and shadow casting is the area most open to individual interpretation. In other words, an illustrator can establish a personal style, in spite of the restrictions imposed by most other aspects of technical illustration, by the use of shading and shadows.

This chapter will explain the basic concepts used in shading and shadow casting and will present examples of each. Only general concepts are covered. Students are encouraged to first master these general concepts, and then to try to develop individual variations and styles.

15-2 SHADING

Shading, to technical illustrators, refers specifically to the shading of *surfaces*. It does not include shadows. There are several different techniques that can be used for shading, including line shading, crosshatching, shading screens, and airbrushing. Figure 15-1 compares the different types.

The choice of shading style depends on the desired end results. In general, the more black used in the shading, the bolder the results. Widely spaced crosshatch gives a more delicate look. Thus, an illustrator can take advantage of these results by shading dangerous or important parts with bold shading and breakable parts with delicate shading.

15-3 LINE SHADING

The simplest form of shading is line shading. This technique involves using an extra heavy line in outlining the periphery of an object. For example, if the object is drawn using an "0" pen, then the outside lines can be drawn using a "2" or "3." Figure 15-2 illustrates.

To draw line shading, first draw the complete object, including the peripheral lines; then widen the peripheral lines. Figure 15-3 shows two additional examples.

Line shading is well suited to thin-walled objects, such as an electronic chassis. Figures 15-4 and 15-5 illustrate.

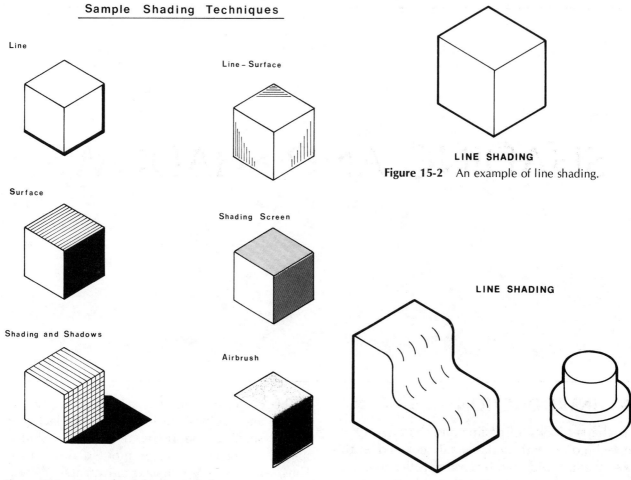

Sample Shading Techniques

Line

Line – Surface

Surface

Shading Screen

Shading and Shadows

Airbrush

Figure 15-1   A sample of shading techniques.

LINE SHADING
Figure 15-2   An example of line shading.

LINE SHADING

Figure 15-3   Examples of line shading.

15-4 SURFACE SHADING

Surface shading is a technique in which all surfaces in one of the isometric planes are shaded in a similar manner. (Can also be applied to other axonometric and perspective drawings.) In Figure 15-6 all surfaces in the left-hand plane are shaded using single parallel lines and in the right-hand plane using crosshatching; the base surfaces were left unshaded.

Figure 15-7 shows an example of surface shading done with a shading screen. See Chapter 16 for more information on shading screens.

Slanted or oblique surfaces are shaded by using a different shading pattern than that used for the principal planes. Figure 15-8 illustrates. The pattern used should help to visually define the direction of

the slanted surface. Parallel lines, aligned to the longest edge of the surface, usually achieve the desired results.

Figure 15-9 shows shading on several different geometric shapes. Round surfaces, or any other shaped surface that has transverse isometric planes, should have uneven shading. That is, it would be wrong to use uniform shading on a rounded surface where the amount of light on that surface varies. In Figure 15-9, object 1 shows a cylinder on which, as the surface approaches the back of the object, the shading becomes darker. The darker shading is achieved by using ever closer thin vertical lines starting at the midline.

In actual practice, uniform shading can be used on curved surfaces with satisfactory results. Figure

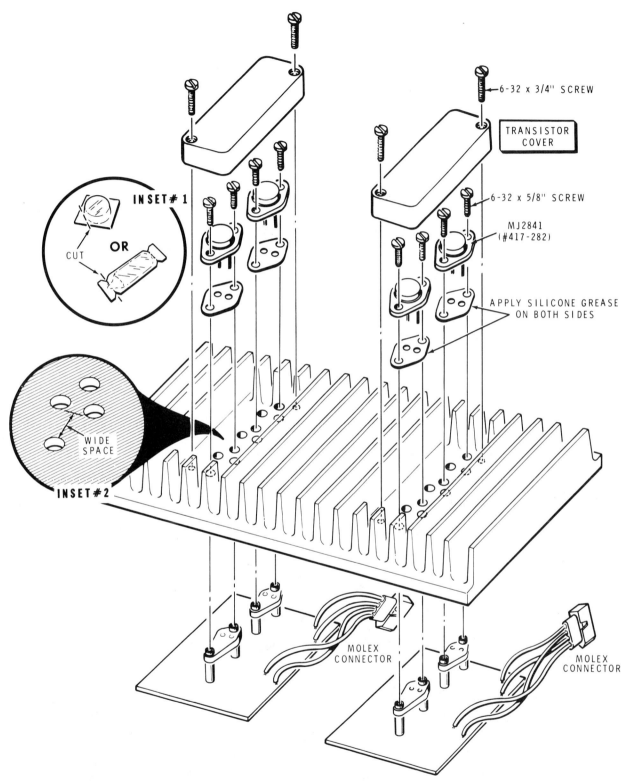

6-32 x 3/4" SCREW

TRANSISTOR COVER

6-32 x 5/8" SCREW

MJ2841 (#417-282)

APPLY SILICONE GREASE ON BOTH SIDES

INSET #1

CUT   OR

WIDE SPACE

INSET #2

MOLEX CONNECTOR

MOLEX CONNECTOR

Figure 15-4   Example of line shading. Courtesy of Heath Company, Benton Harbor, Michigan.

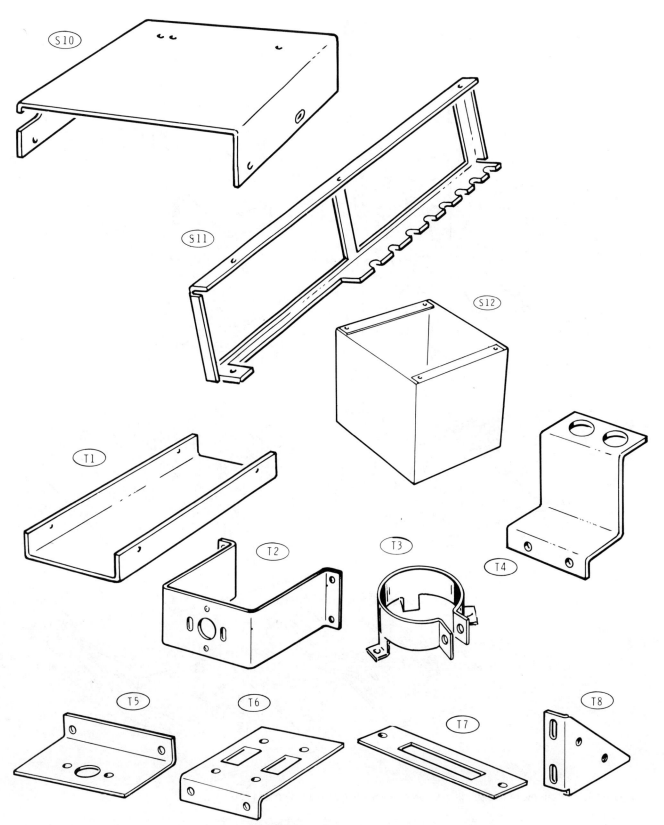

Figure 15-5 Example of line shading. Courtesy of Heath Company, Benton Harbor, Michigan.

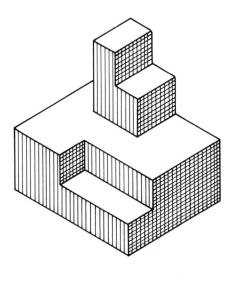

SURFACE SHADING – FREEHAND
Figure 15-6 Surface shading—freehand.

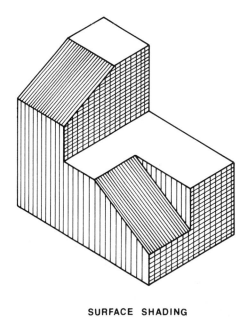

SURFACE SHADING
Figure 15-8 Surface shading—crosshatching.

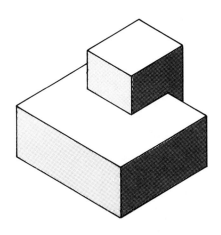

SURFACE SHADING – SHADING SCREEN
Figure 15-7 Surface shading—screening.

15-9, object 2, shows a cylinder uniformly shaded with a shading screen; compare the results with object 1. For most drawings, either method is acceptable.

Figure 15-10 is another example of surface shading.

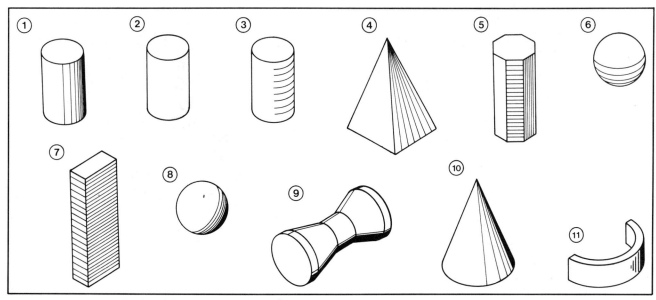

Figure 15-9 Surface shading for various geometric shapes.

119

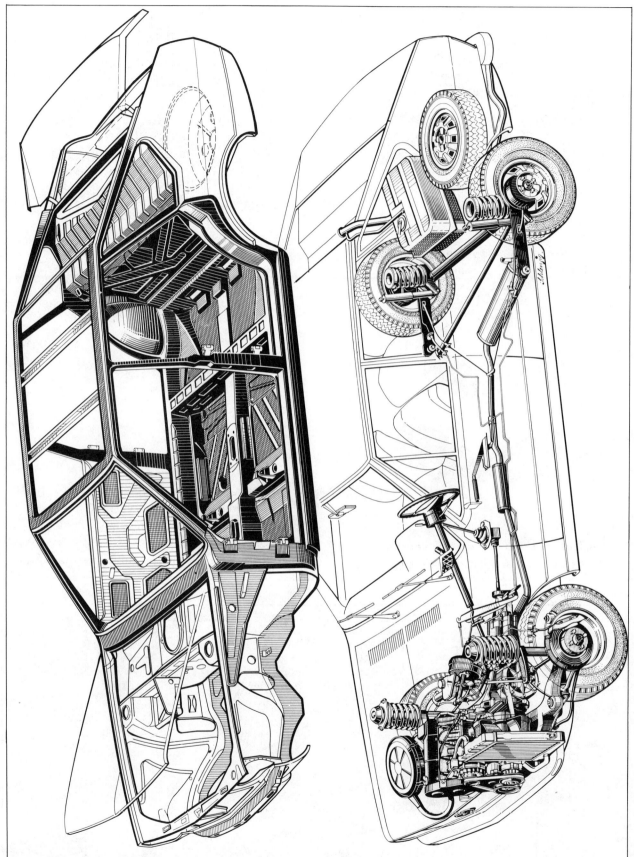

Figure 15-10 Courtesy of Volkswagenwerk, Wolfsburg, Germany.

15-5 SHADOWS

Shadows are usually not included on technical illustrations because the details of the individual parts could be covered and cause misinterpretation. However, sometimes certain drawings, such as those used for formal presentations, cover sheets, or renderings where appearance is very important, do use shadows.

Shadowcasting, as with shading, is very much a question of individual style. This section will explain several rigorous techniques that can be used on technical illustrations. There are many other styles, and the interested student is encouraged to experiment to develop a personal style.

Figure 15-11 is an isometric drawing of a cube along with the appropriate shading and shadowing. The shading follows the procedure outlined in Section 15-4, and the shadowing was created as follows.

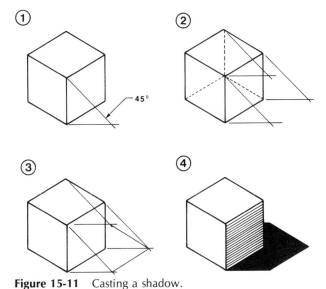

Figure 15-11   Casting a shadow.

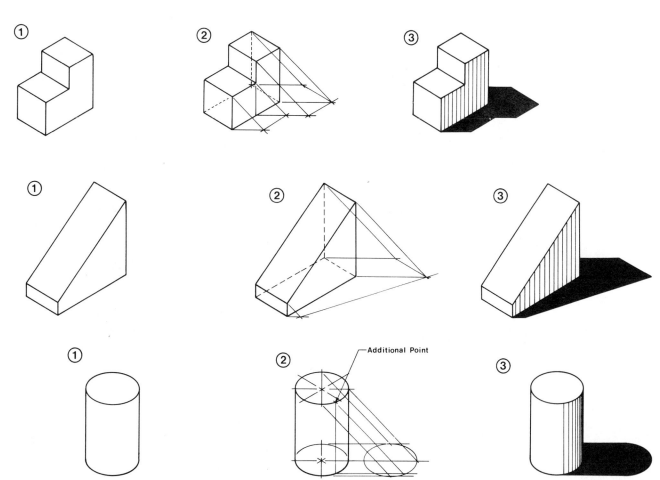

Figure 15-12   Casting a shadow for various shapes.

1. Draw a horizontal line to the right from the lower front corner of the cube. Draw a 45° line from the top front corner down to the right until it intersects the horizontal line.
2. Repeat step 1 for the back right corner and middle corner.
3. Draw 30° lines.
4. Erase the 45° lines and add the shadow.

The same technique may be used for any shape object. Figure 15-12 illustrates. Note that, for curved surfaces, several intermediate points must be defined and then used to plot the projected shape of the shadow.

Shadows for pyramids and cones may be developed by plotting the shadow of the apex and then drawing tangency lines back to the object. Note that for cones, the tangency lines do NOT intersect the midline. See Figures 15-13 and 15-14.

Shadows sometimes overlap or fall on uneven surfaces. In such cases, it should be remembered that the basic angle of light (45° in these examples) remains the same and that the total length of the shadow can never exceed the limits defined by this angle.

Figure 15-15 shows an object that casts a shadow on another surface within the same object. The shadow length was plotted as outlined above, but with some modifications.

Note the change in the shadow pattern as it crosses the different surface levels. The layout is also shown to illustrate how the shadow was plotted.

Figure 15-16 shows several variations of shadows cast onto or over different level surfaces.

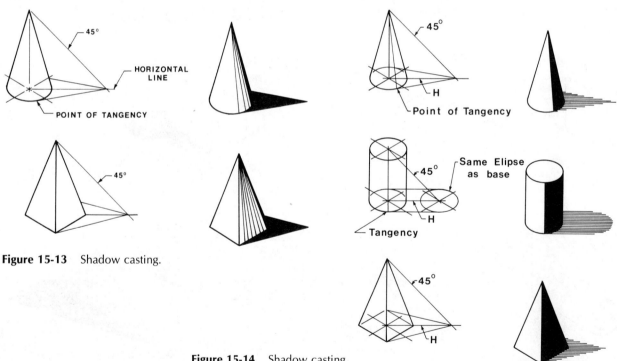

Figure 15-13 Shadow casting.

Figure 15-14 Shadow casting.

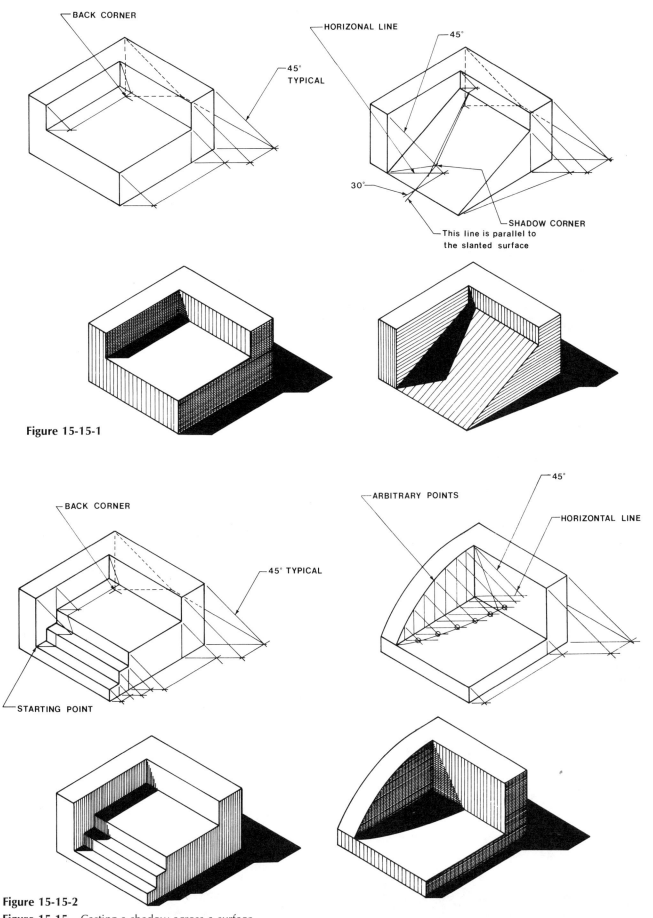

Figure 15-15-1

Figure 15-15-2

Figure 15-15 Casting a shadow across a surface.

123

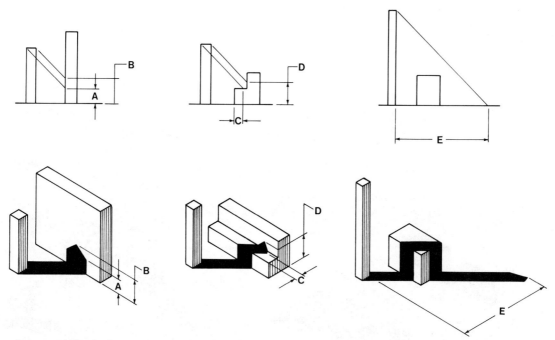

Figure 15-16 Shadow casting across other objects.

15-6 HIGHLIGHTS

Highlights are variations of light on the same surface. Usually they are the results of intense localized light and reflective surface materials. There are two ways to show highlights in technical illustrations: lightly crosshatch the surface and omit the crosshatching where the intense light occurs (Figure 15-17-1); use very limited crosshatching as a way to indicate bright light (Figure 15-17-2).

The crosshatch patterns used to represent highlights are done by eye. There is no rigorous way to plot the pattern. Study Figure 15-17; copy the patterns shown; then try to develop patterns of your own.

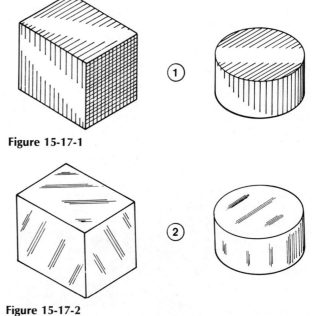

Figure 15-17-1

Figure 15-17-2
Figure 15-17 Examples of highlights.

CHAPTER 16

BASIC RENDERING TECHNIQUES

16-1 INTRODUCTION

This chapter explains how to use dry transfers, airbrushes, and color washes. Only the basic fundamentals of each has been included because the advanced applications are dependent on individual style and ability. It is recommended that the interested student consult books on rendering and then practice to develop good technique and style.

16-2 DRY TRANSFERS

Dry transfers are numbers, symbols, or shading screens printed on plastic film whose backside has been treated with adhesive. Figure 16-1 shows a sheet of dry transfer letters. Chartpak is a commercial brand name.

Dry transfer sheets are available for many different style letters and symbols (bolts and nuts for example) and for various densities of shading screens. There are many different brand names such as Normatype, Letraset, and Chartpak. It is recommended that students thumb through a few manufacturers' catalogs to see what is available.

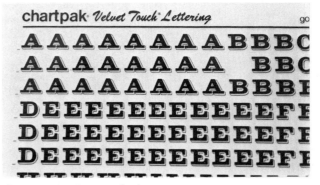

Figure 16-1   Dry transfer letters.

16-3 HOW TO APPLY DRY TRANSFERS

Figure 16-2 shows some of the equipment needed to apply dry transfers. These include a burnishing pen, an X-acto knife, a steel straightedge, and a nonreproducible blue pencil.

Dry transfer letters are applied to a drawing by aligning the letter to the drawing, sticky side down, and rubbing it with a burnishing pen. Figure 16-3 illustrates.

Figure 16-2   Equipment for dry transfers.

Figure 16-3   Applying dry transfer letters.

Figure 16-4   Nonreproducible blue guideline.

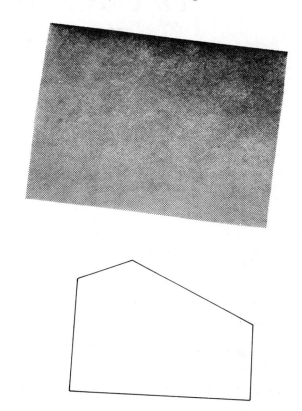

Figure 16-5   Applying dry transfer shading screen placement.

Dry transfer letters can be aligned by either sliding a grid pattern under the drawing paper and using the pattern as a guideline, or by drawing guidelines on the drawing with a nonreproducible blue pencil. The blue lines will not show after reproduction. Figure 16-4 illustrates. The guideline is blue and would not show in normal reproduction.

A shading screen is applied to a drawing by cutting a piece of screening slightly larger than needed. See Figure 16-5. Then peel off the back layer and gently place the screening over the desired area. (Do not rub it since it may need to be moved.) Smooth out any air bubbles. See Figure 16-6.

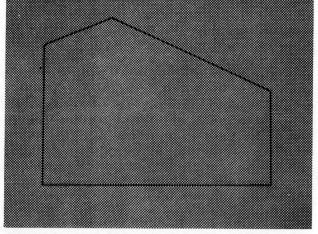

Figure 16-6   Applying dry transfer shading screen.

Trim the shading screen to the exact shape required by using a sharp X-acto knife and a steel straightedge. Figure 16-7 shows the shading screen being trimmed. Do not use plastic straightedges such as drawing triangles or T-squares. The X-acto knife will cut into and damage the plastic edges. Only gentle pressure is required to cut through the screening.

After the screening is trimmed, rub it firmly with the broad end of the burnishing pen. Be sure to remove all air bubbles. Figure 16-8 shows the final results. Figure 16-9 shows another example of how the shading screen can be used.

Figure 16-7 Applying dry transfer shading screen.

Figure 16-8 Applying dry transfer shading screen.

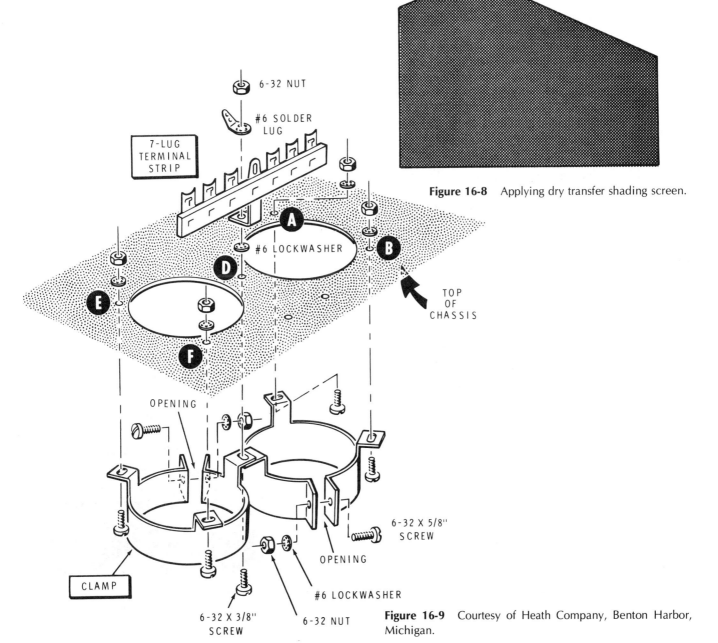

6-32 NUT

#6 SOLDER LUG

7-LUG TERMINAL STRIP

#6 LOCKWASHER

TOP OF CHASSIS

OPENING

CLAMP

6-32 X 5/8" SCREW

OPENING

#6 LOCKWASHER

6-32 X 3/8" SCREW

6-32 NUT

Figure 16-9 Courtesy of Heath Company, Benton Harbor, Michigan.

16-4 AIRBRUSHING

An airbrush is a device that sprays ink. The airbrush unit consists of the airbrush itself, an ink jar or cup that attaches to the airbrush, and a compressor along with the appropriate hoses. Figure 16-10-1 shows a typical airbrush unit.

To operate an airbrush, fill the ink jar with ink and attach the jar to the main body of the airbrush. Attach the airhose to the compressor and to the airbrush and turn on the compressor. See Figure 16-10-2.

The ink spray is activated by pressing the air valve with the forefinger, as shown in Figure 16-11-1. The density of the spray is controlled by turning the adjusting screw at the rear of the airbrush. See Figure 16-11-2. If a thinner spray is needed, the ink may be diluted with water.

The basic spray pattern of an airbrush is circular. See Figure 16-12. Areas are covered by moving the airbrush back and forth in an even motion. An uneven motion will result in an uneven pattern; that is, the density will not be uniform.

The spray pattern has an inherent unevenness in that the outside edges are lighter than the center portion. See Figure 16-12. This makes it difficult to shade defined areas uniformly from center to edges. To overcome this difficulty, illustrators use a masking technique. For example, say we wish to shade the cube shown in Figure 16-13 so that the shadow is very dark, the right-hand plane moderately dark, and the other two surfaces clear.

The first objective would be to shade the shadow, or darkest part of the drawing. Take the pencil layout or a Xerox copy of the object (remember Xerox copies are slightly larger than originals) and cut out the shape of the shadow, as shown in Figure 16-14. Tape the cutout directly over the drawing, as shown in Figure 16-15. Airbrush the exposed shadow portion of the drawing. See Figure 16-16.

Next cut out the right-hand plane so that the overlay now exposes both the shadow and right-hand plane. See Figure 16-17. Airbrush the exposed area. This will darken the right-hand plane and further darken the shadow. Figure 16-18 shows the results.

The air from an airbrush sometimes blows the edges of the cutout, which results in shading be-

Figure 16-10-1   An airbrush.

Figure 16-10-2   An airbrush.

Figure 16-11-1   Operating an airbrush.

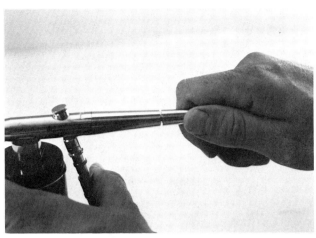

Figure 16-11-2   Adjusting an airbrush.

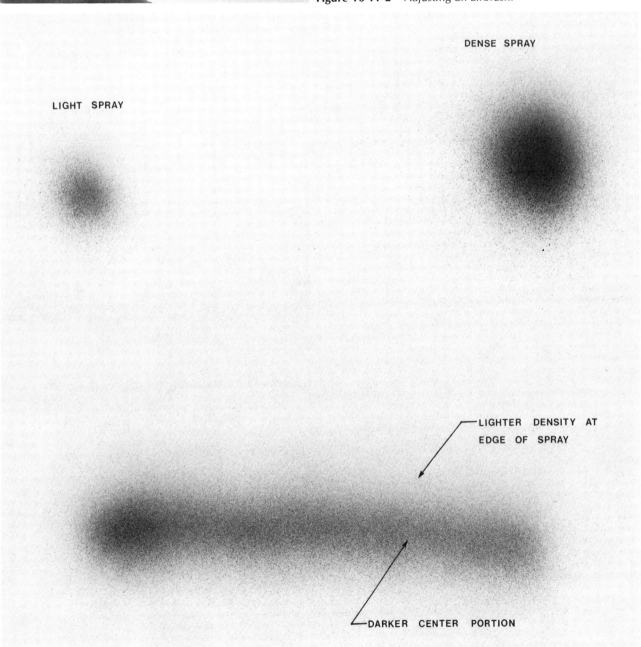

DENSE SPRAY

LIGHT SPRAY

LIGHTER DENSITY AT
EDGE OF SPRAY

DARKER CENTER PORTION

Figure 16-12   Airbrush spray patterns.

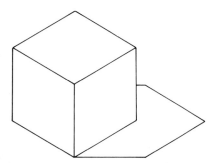

Figure 16-13 A cube and shadow prior to airbrushing.

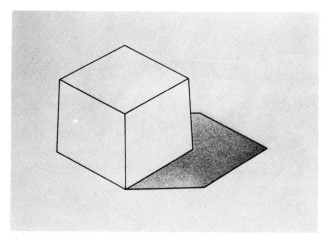

Figure 16-16 Shadow airbrushed.

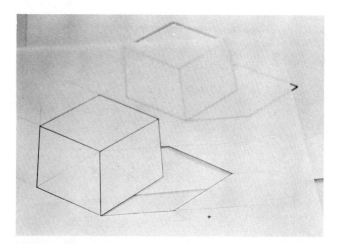

Figure 16-14 Shadow removed from pencil layout.

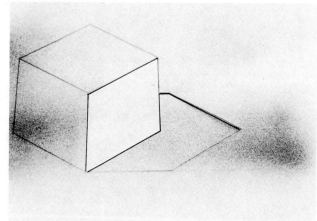

Figure 16-17 Right surface cut out and placed over Figure 16-13.

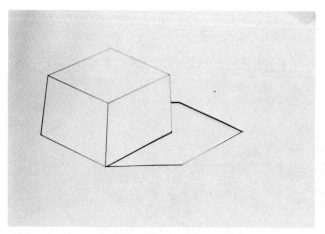

Figure 16-15 Cutout placed over Figure 16-13.

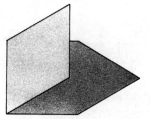

Figure 16-18 The airbrush results of Figure 16-13.

yond the edges of the exposed area. If this happens, tape down the edges of the cutout with either double-sided tape, folded over masking tape, or light paste. Slight overruns can be erased with an ink eraser.

An airbrush can also be used to create different density shading within a given area. Figure 16-19 shows a cutout of a circle. By shading the area unevenly (see Figure 16-20), an illusion of depth can be created, as in the sphere shown in Figure 16-21.

The airbrush is a very useful tool and when used by a skilled artist, the results can be spectacular. See Figure 16-22.

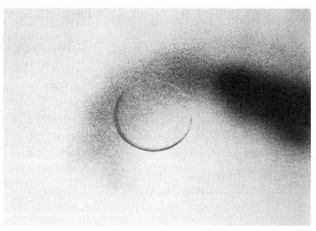

Figure 16-20   The cutout airbrushed.

Figure 16-19   A circle cutout.

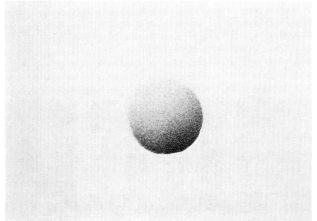

Figure 16-21   A sphere created by airbrushing the circle cutout of Figure 16-19.

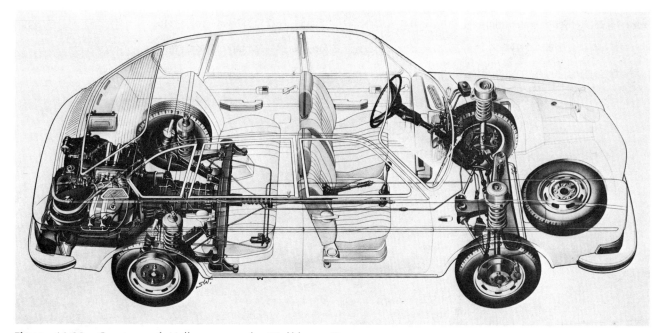

Figure 16-22   Courtesy of Volkswagenwerk, Wolfsburg, Germany.

16-5 WATERCOLOR WASHES

Another technique used to shade surfaces is the watercolor wash. Watercolors come in many colors. Figure 16-23 shows a six-color beginner's set available at most art supply stores.

To prepare a watercolor wash, you need good quality brushes (ones that hold their shape when wet), as shown in Figure 16-24. Also needed is paper suitable to watercolors, such as the Strathmore 400 series watercolor paper, a blotter, a bowl of clear water, and a bowl of each color needed. Figure 16-25 shows a typical watercolor setup.

When applying watercolors, a bubble or ridge of thicker color is formed and then guided across the area to be shaded. See Figure 16-26. The excess color is then blotted up at the end of the wash. Gentle blotting is sufficient.

Different densities with the same color may be created by applying several light washes over the same area. Figure 16-27 shows a single wash in the left-hand rectangle, a second wash in the center rectangle, and a third wash in the right-hand rectangle.

Figure 16-28 shows how this technique is applied to shading an object. First, a pencil drawing is prepared. Then, the entire object is shaded. Next, the right-hand plane and shadow are given a second wash. Finally, just the shadow is given a third wash. The results are as shown.

Figure 16-29 shows a professionally finished illustration with a watercolor wash, used for shading.

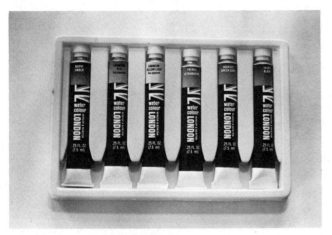

Figure 16-23   A set of watercolors.

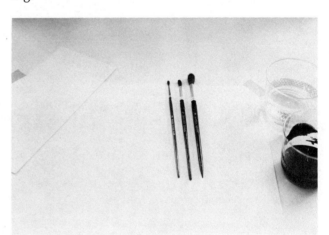

Figure 16-25   A watercolor setup.

Figure 16-24   Watercolor brushes.

Figure 16-26-1   Applying watercolor.

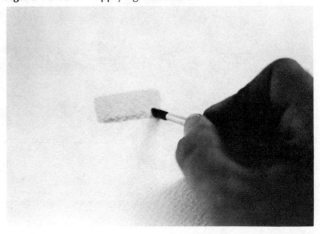

Figure 16-26-2   Watercolor bubble in lower right of area.

Figure 16-27   Different shades are created by multiple washes.

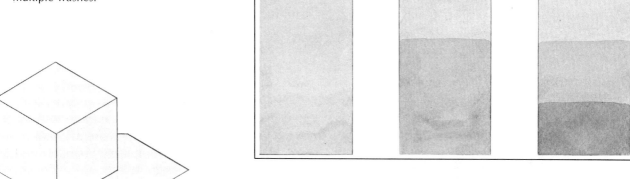

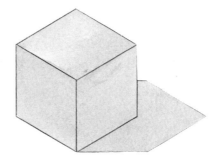

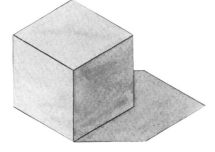

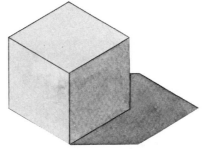

Figure 16-28   An object shaded by a water-color wash.

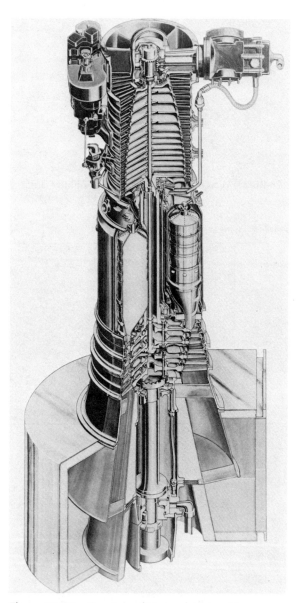

Figure 16-29 Courtesy of General Motors Corp.

16-6 COMPUTER-AIDED ILLUSTRATIONS

Recent advances in computer graphics have made it possible to use computer-plotter combinations to produce illustrations. Several companies manufacture computer graphic equipment; others produce only plotters that can be used with several different standard computers; while others produce entire systems.

Some systems produce hardcopy (drawings), whereas others use a visual display unit. Each system uses a different input language, although most are simple variations of either BASIC or FORTRAN. Plotters can draw in different colors and produce different styles and types of drawings. Figure 16-30 shows a sample of drawings produced by the Hewlett-Packard 7221A Graphic Plotter.

Two leading manufacturers of graphic plotters and systems are Hewlett-Packard (see Figure 16-31) and McDonnell Douglas's Onigraphics System (see Figure 16-32). Each is very versatile.

All computer graphic systems are available with user guides, and some manufacturers offer courses on how to use their systems.

At present, computer graphics are limited to line drawings with some simple shading. Some illustrators supplement the computer graphic drawing by adding shading with pen and ink, screens, and so on, to improve the visual quality of the drawings.

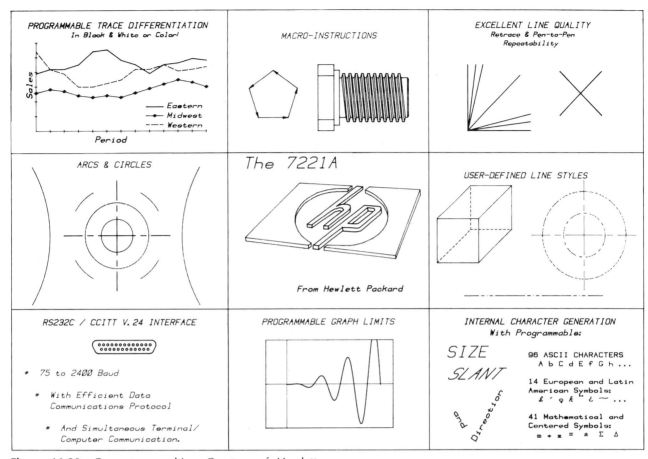

Figure 16-30 Computer graphics. Courtesy of Hewlett-Packard.

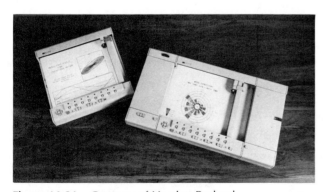

Figure 16-31 Courtesy of Hewlett-Packard.

16-7 OTHER TYPES OF RENDERINGS

There are many other types of rendering techniques that use charcoal, chalks, paints, pen and ink, pencil, magic markers, stippling, and photograph retouching. Figures 16-33 to 16-36 are further examples of renderings. Figure 16-37 shows a set of artist's magic markers.

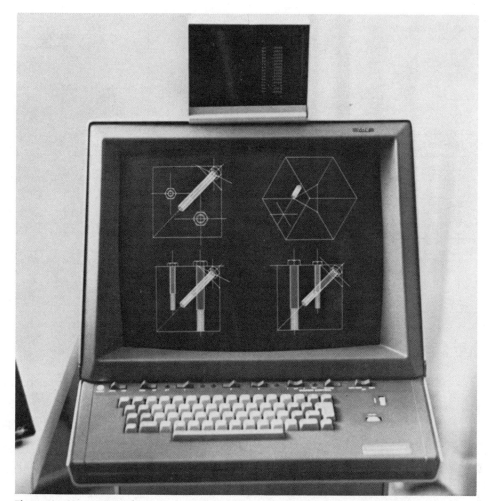

Figure 16-32 Unigraphics. Courtesy of McDonnell Douglas Automation Co.

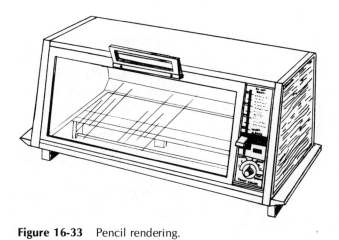

Figure 16-33 Pencil rendering.

Figure 16-34 Rendering in pen and ink.

Figure 16-35 Rendering in pen and ink. Courtesy of Robert J. Berry, Architectural Delineator.)

Figure 16-36 Stippling.

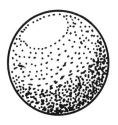

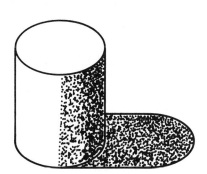

Figure 16-37 A set of magic markers.

CHAPTER 17

GRAPHS AND CHARTS

17-1 INTRODUCTION

Technical illustrators are often asked to prepare graphs and charts for sales presentations, company reports, service manuals, and so on. The three most common types of graphs are pie charts, bar charts, and curve plots. Pie and bar charts are used to present relatively technical data in pictorial form so the reader can quickly assess the data. Curve plotting is often done by computers except when a high-quality presentation is required, such as would be used for an overhead projection or when color is involved.

This chapter will explain how to prepare pie charts, bar charts, and curve plots.

17-2 PIE CHARTS

Pie charts are circular diagrams with various sectors drawn in proportion to their relative values. For example, a company wishes to show its investors how it is spending its money, and the expenditures are as follows: $3.8 million = wages and salaries; $1.2 million = raw materials; $.8 million = factory overhead; $.6 million = capital equipment and

debt; and $.3 million = taxes. To convert these data into a pie chart, first total the data and find the percentage of the total each part represents.

3.8	Wages and salaries
1.2	Raw material
.8	Factory overhead
.6	Capital equipment, Debt
.3	Taxes
6.7	

$$\frac{3.8}{6.7} = .57, \quad \frac{.6}{6.7} = .09, \quad \frac{1.2}{6.7} = .18,$$

$$\frac{.8}{6.7} = .12, \quad \frac{.3}{6.7} = .04$$

The percentages are then multiplied by 360° to find the angular value. For example, .57 (360) = 205°, .09 (360) = 32°, .18 (360) = 65°, .12 (360) = 43°, .04 (360) = 15°. The angular values are then drawn on a circle, as shown in Figure 17-1.

Figure 17-1 is a two-dimensional presentation—width and height, but no depth. A three-dimensional presentation can be created by converting the drawing to either axonometric or perspective form. Figure 17-2 shows the same data drawn as an isometric drawing. An isometric pro-

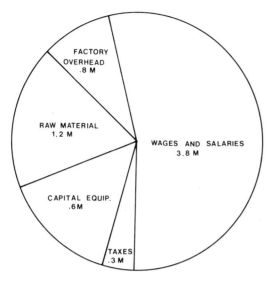

Figure 17-1 A pie chart.

Figure 17-2 An isometric pie chart.

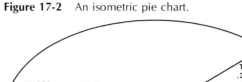

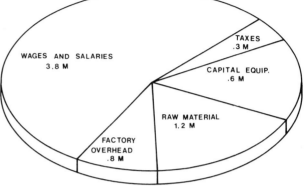

COMPANY EXPENSES

COMPANY EXPENSES

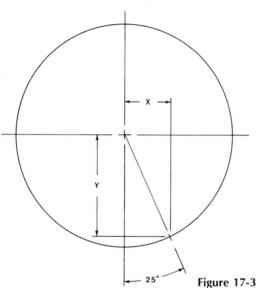

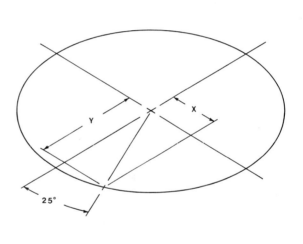

Figure 17-3 Converting an angular dimension to an isometric axis.

tractor was used to lay out the angular measurements in the isometric diagram. If an isometric protractor is unavailable, linear components may be used to transfer the angles, as shown in Figure 17-3. The two-dimensional drawing of Figure 17-1 may be skipped if an isometric protractor is available.

The presentation may be improved by the use of shading, and emphasis can be called to a particular piece by drawing it as if it is protruding from the pie, as shown in Figure 17-4. The same layout used for Figure 17-3 can be used for Figure 17-4. The tracing is shifted before drawing the protruding slice.

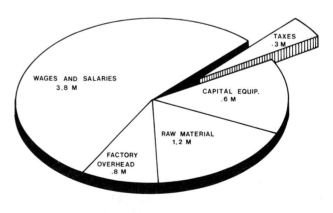

COMPANY EXPENSES

Figure 17-4 A pie chart.

17-3 BAR CHARTS

A bar chart is a chart that shows relative and absolute values by a group of thick lines or rectangular shapes. Figure 17-5 shows the same data presented for the development of a pie chart and a bar chart.

To create a bar chart, locate the fixed categories or values along the horizontal axis and the variable values along the vertical axis. Always use a vertical axis that is easy to interpret, and if the actual values are important, include them with the appropriate bar.

the same axis. For example, Figure 17-7 shows HP versus RPM for three separate engines. Ideally, the curves would be distinguished by using different colors, but if only black and white reproduction is available, curves may be distinguished by different line patterns. Each curve should be clearly labeled.

Figure 17-8 shows three curves distinguished by shading. The shading used is the dry transfer type.

Figure 17-9 illustrates two curves distinguished not only by different line patterns, but by differently shaped data points. The actual data values are located by a small centered dot (not always visible in the finished work) and then outlined by a shape

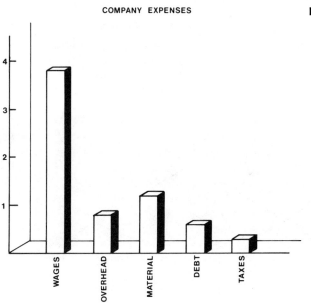

COMPANY EXPENSES

Figure 17-5 A bar chart.

Figure 17-6 A technical curve.

17-4 CURVE PLOTTING

Curve plotting is a graphic presentation showing the relationship between two or more variables. Figure 17-6 illustrates the relationship between horsepower (HP) and revolutions per minute (RPM) for a reciprocating gas engine.

Mathematical convention calls for the independent variable to be plotted on the horizontal axis and the dependent variable along the vertical axis. In Figure 17-6, HP is dependent on RPM and is, therefore, the dependent variable.

A family of curves is a group of curves plotted on

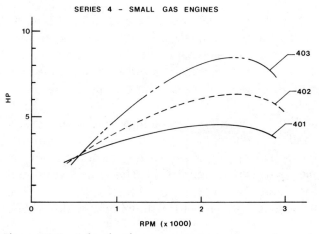

Figure 17-7 A family of curves.

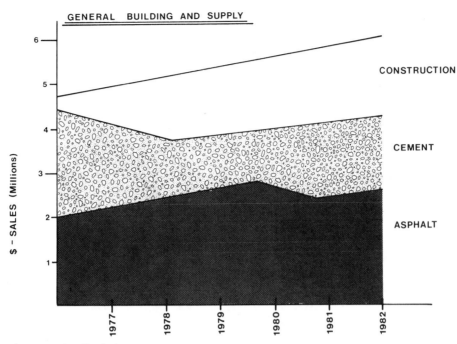

Figure 17-8 Shaded curves.

such as a circle, square, star, and so on. If two or more data points coincide, the shapes are drawn over each other.

All curve plots should have their axes clearly marked and must have titles.

Figure 17-10 depicts a template cut with different shapes that are helpful when showing different data points.

Figure 17-11 exhibits a set of curves drawn by computer.

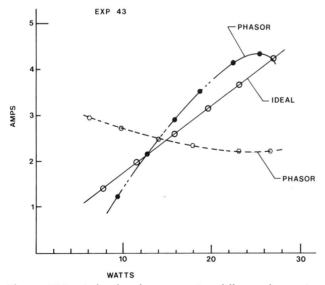

Figure 17-9 A family of curves using different data point symbols.

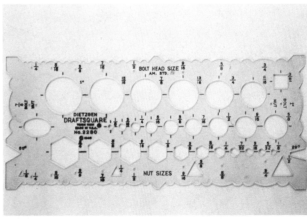

Figure 17-10 A template for drawing different types of data point symbols.

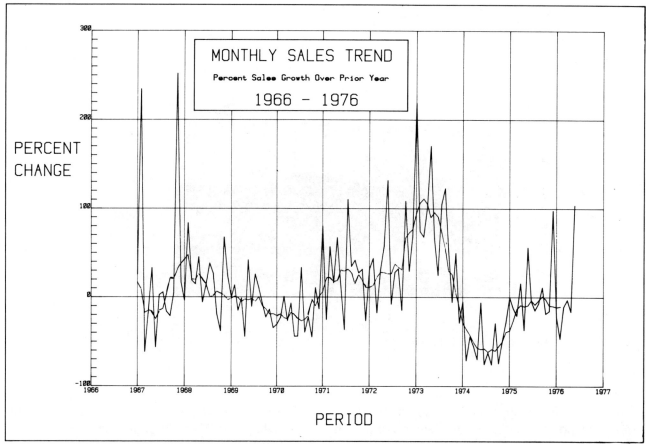

Figure 17-11   An example of a computer curve plot.

PART THREE

PERSPECTIVE DRAWINGS

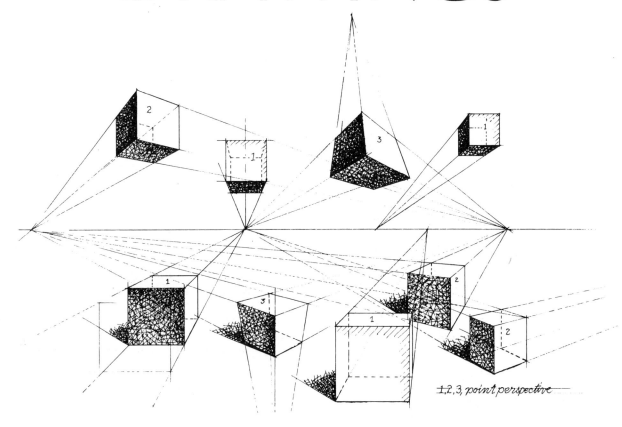

1,2,3, point perspective

This part of the book explains one-, two-, and three-point perspective drawings.

Perspective drawings have receding axes that converge as they approach a vanishing point. They are more lifelike than axonometric drawings, but can be more difficult to draw. When combined with shading and shadows, they are artistically pleasing and are ideal for large objects such as houses, buildings, and so on.

CHAPTER 18

ONE-POINT PERSPECTIVES

18-1 GENERAL LAYOUT

A one-point perspective drawing is a drawing based on one vanishing point. It is similar to an oblique drawing in that its frontal plane is drawn "true shape." However, unlike oblique drawings, planes parallel to the frontal plane become decreasingly smaller as they approach the vanishing point. This means that circles can be drawn with a compass in the frontal plane or any plane parallel to it but must diminish in radius as the plane approaches the vanishing point.

To prepare a one-point perspective, the following procedure is used. Figure 18-1 illustrates.

1. Lay out three parallel horizontal lines: a picture plane line, a horizon line, and a ground line. The distance between these lines is arbitrary and can be varied. Mark off two points: a vanishing point (VP) and a station point (SP). The vanishing point MUST be located on the horizon line and the station point MUST be located directly below or below (on a vertical line) the VP. More will be said later about the relationship between the lines, the points, and their effect on the shape of the final drawing. See Figure 18-1-1.

2. Draw a side orthographic view on the ground line and a top orthographic view on the picture plane line, as shown in Figure 18-1-2. (A numbered isometric view of the object has been included for reference.) Project a vertical line from 4,1 and 2,3 on the PP line to the G line. These lines define the maximum width. Project the heights from the side view parallel to the G line as shown. Project the intersections of the horizontal and vertical lines onto the VP. See Figure 18-1-2.

3. To establish the depth of the object, project the back surface (9, 10, 12—the other point, 11, is not seen) onto the SP. Where the projection line crosses the PP line, draw a vertical line downward until it crosses the projection line drawn to the VP in step 2. See Figure 18-1-3.

4. The remaining points are projected in the same manner. For each point, the height and width are first located on the frontal plane and then are projected onto the VP; the depth is then projected from the top view, as defined in step 3. See Figure 18-1-4.

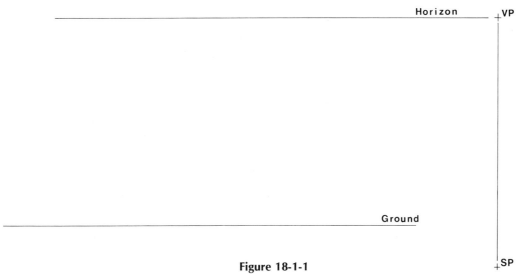

Picture Plane

Horizon   VP

Ground

SP

Figure 18-1-1

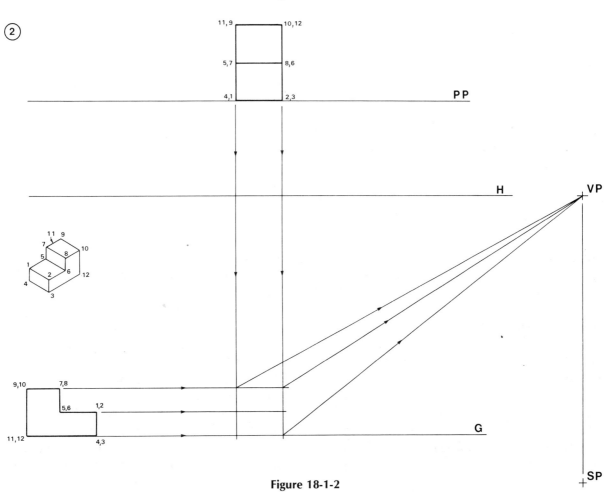

Figure 18-1-2

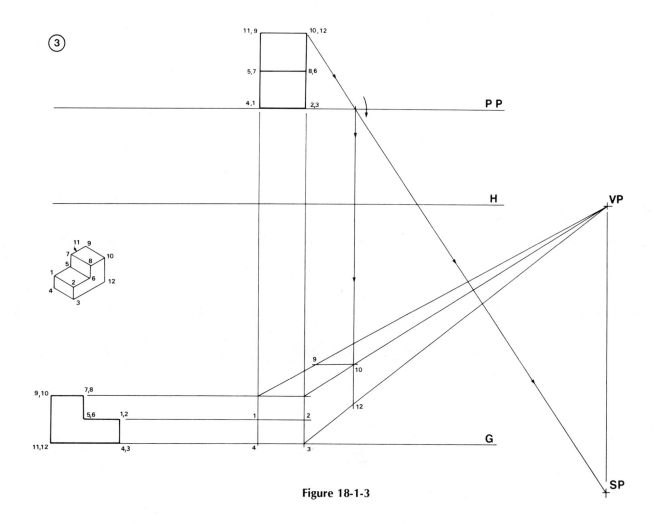

Figure 18-1-3

18-2 LAYOUT VARIATIONS

The distance between the PP line, the H and G lines, as well as the location of VP and SP will affect the final drawing of the object. In Figures 18-2, 18-3, 18-4, and 18-5, the relationship between these points and lines has been changed so that you may study the results. In general, the distance between the lines will affect the appearance of the final object.

The greatest change in the shape of the object can be obtained by moving the VP and SP. If the VP is to the right, the object will recede to the right, and vice versa. Figures 18-2 and 18-3 are identical except that the SP is closer to the VP in Figure 18-3. Note how this slight change moves the back sur-

face of the object to the right. The closer the SP is to the VP, the sharper the angle of the projection lines from the top view, which results in wider vertical projection lines and finally a wider final drawing.

Figures 18-4 and 18-5 show two other variations: the VP and SP as the same point; and the SP above the VP. The points could also have been placed within the object, as shown in Figure 18-6, which gives the effect of looking into the object.

All the different variations use the same basic principles outlined in Section 18-1. The application depends on the desired final results. For example, a greatly elongated object may help create a more dramatic effect and could serve to call attention to an object.

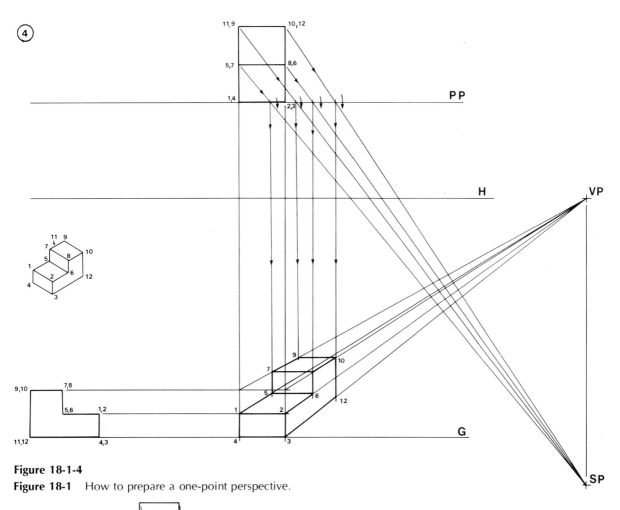

Figure 18-1-4

Figure 18-1   How to prepare a one-point perspective.

Figure 18-2   One-point perspective.

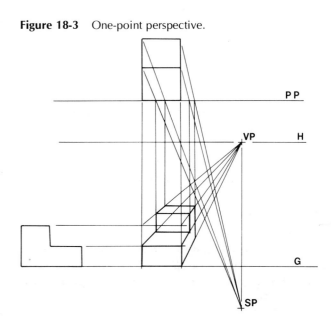

Figure 18-3   One-point perspective.

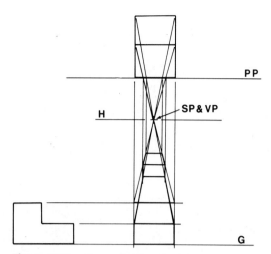

Figure 18-4 One-point perspective.

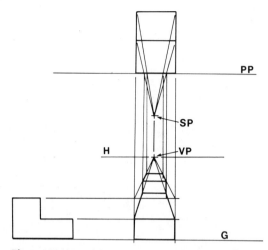

Figure 18-5 One-point perspective.

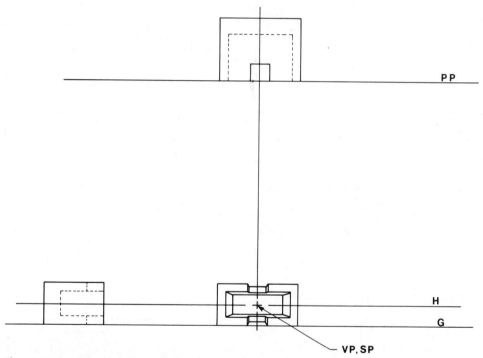

Figure 18-6 One-point perspective.

18-3 CIRCLES AND ROUNDED SURFACES

Circles and rounded surfaces are drawn using different techniques depending on which surface they are located. The three surfaces are front, top, and right side. See Figure 18-7.

Circles and rounded surfaces in the frontal plane may be drawn using a compass or circle template; that is, they are true circles of constant radius. This is the chief advantage of one-point perspectives,

because it permits much greater speed in preparing drawings.

Figure 18-8 shows a cylinder drawn in one-point perspective. It was created using the procedure outlined in Section 18-1. In this example, the centerpoint of the circle is the key. We need only determine the location of the frontal centerpoint and project it back to locate all the centerpoints. The circle size is determined by projecting the intersection of the frontal circle and the horizontal

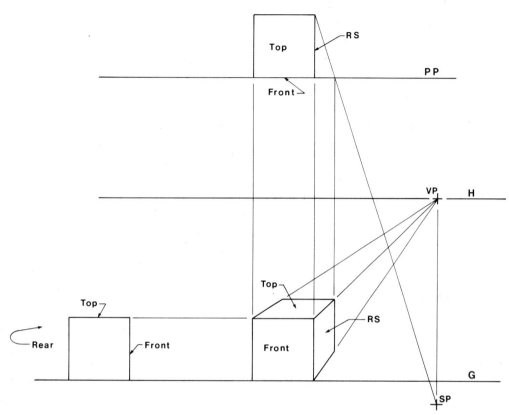

Figure 18-7 Surfaces of a one-point perspective drawing.

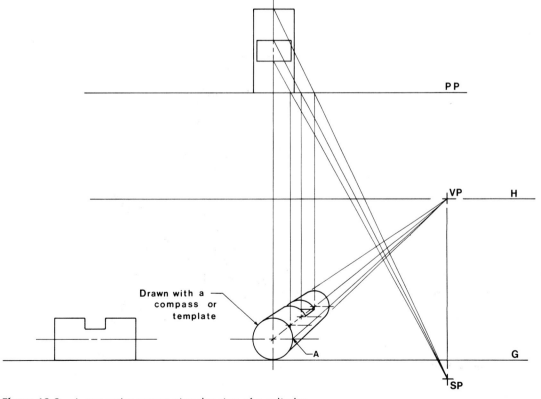

Figure 18-8 A one-point perspective drawing of a cylinder.

centerline (point 1 in Figure 18-8) onto the VP. The depth is determined by projection onto the SP and then vertical projection as outlined in Section 18-1, step 3.

Figure 18-9 illustrates how to draw circles and rounded surfaces located in the top surface. The resultant shape in the one-point perspective is not a circle or an ellipse, but an elongated ellipse with the front end larger than the back.

To project a circle or rounded surfaces into the top surface of a one-point perspective drawing, proceed as follows.

1. Project the intersection of the circle with the centerlines (points 1, 2, 3, 4). See Figure 18-9-1.

2. As with all rounded surfaces, construction is difficult because there are no edge lines or points to work from as there are with rectangular-shaped surfaces. This problem is overcome by adding points to the surfaces and then projecting these theoretical points. In Figure 18-9-2, two 45° lines were drawn. Their intersections with the circle are labeled 5, 6, 7, and 8. These points do not really exist on the circle, but serve as projection points

and help define the final shape in the top surface.

Figure 18-9-2 shows the projection of point 5. First the point is projected directly into the frontal plane by drawing a vertical line from the top view to the frontal plane. If a height is needed, it may be projected from the side view. Once the point is located on the frontal plane, it is projected to the VP. The actual location of the point on the top surface is found by the intersection of the projection line from the frontal plane and another projection line from the top view, which gives the depth of the point from the frontal plane. This projection line is determined by using the SP as outlined in Section 18-1, step 3.

3. Figure 18-9-3 shows the projection of points 5, 6, 7, and 8. The procedure is the same as outlined for point 4 in step 2.

4. Figure 18-9-4 shows the final object drawn in one-point perspective. The points for the bottom surface (not shown) were defined using the same procedure outlined for the top surface points.

NOTE: The top and bottom surfaces of the object are not the same shape and must be defined separately.

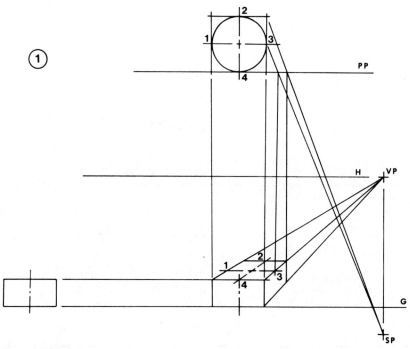

Figure 18-9-1

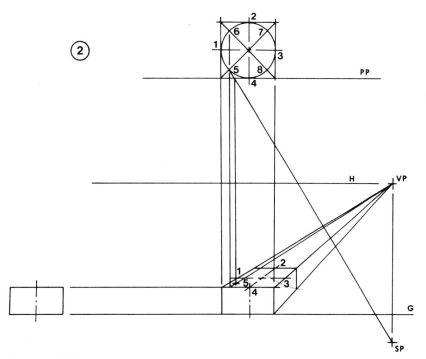

Figure 18-9-2

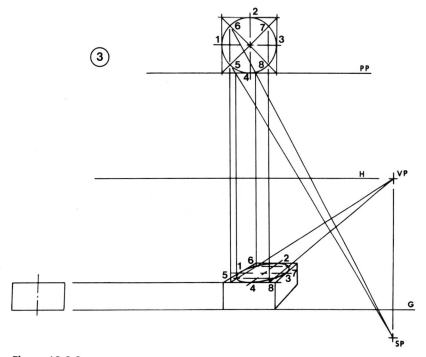

Figure 18-9-3

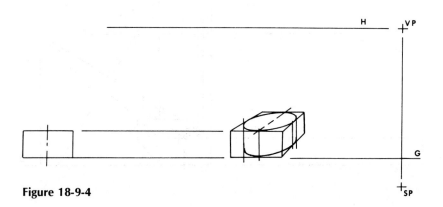

Figure 18-9-4

5. The final step is connecting the projected points with a smooth continuous curve. This can be accomplished by using either a French curve or a flexible curve as a guide. If the object is sufficiently small, an ellipse template may be used. The template will not be exactly correct, but will, if offset and carefully aligned, give a very good approximation. The choice of ellipse size and angle must be by trial and error.

Figure 18-10 shows a circular shape projected into the right-hand plane of a one-point perspective drawing. The procedure is almost identical to that described for projecting circles to the top surface. The only difference is in using the side view to add the needed additional points (Figure 18-10-2) and the projection of these points to the top view by orthographic projection (Figure 18-10-3).

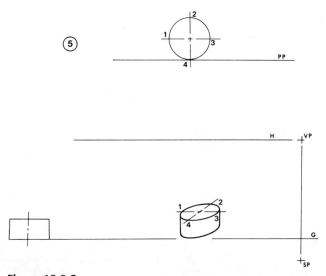

Figure 18-9-5

Figure 18-9 Circles in the top surface of a one-point perspective drawing.

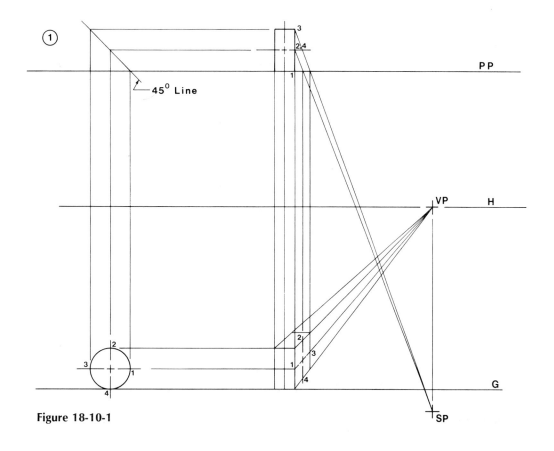

Figure 18-10-1

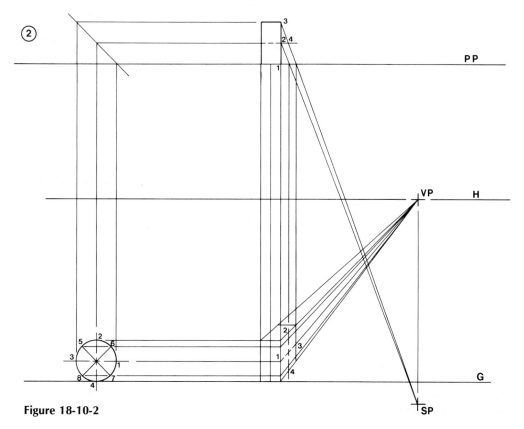

Figure 18-10-2

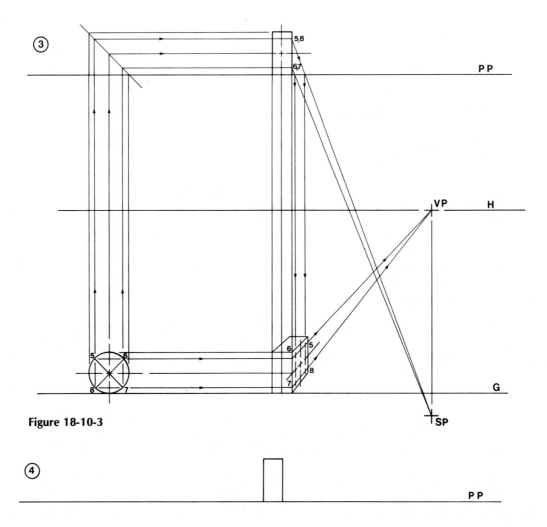

Figure 18-10-3

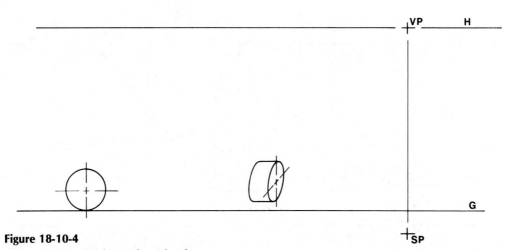

Figure 18-10-4
Figure 18-10 Circles in the right plane.

18-4 CASTING SHADOWS

Casting shadows on a one-point perspective requires the introduction of two more reference points: light source bottom (LSB) and light source top (LST). Figure 18-11-1 illustrates. The object is first drawn, as outlined previously, and points LSB and LST are added. LSB is usually located on the H line, but need not be. LST is located directly (a vertical line) above LSB at an arbitrary distance: the greater the distance above LSB, the shorter the shadow. Lines are then projected from LSB through the corners of the bottom surface of the object and, similarly, lines are projected from LST through the top surface of the object.

In the example shown in Figure 18-11-1, the front corners of the top surface (points 1 and 2) have been added for demonstrative purposes. The resultant shadow, outlined by points 3, 4, and 5, is the shadow the object would cast if the object were a cube. Points 3, 4, and 5 are defined by the intersection of the projection lines from LSB and LST.

Figure 18-11-2 illustrates the finished projection lines. Note how a short vertical line was added under the base of the step to define the bottom of the step (point 6) and, in turn, was used to help define the shadow of the step portion of the object (points 7 and 8).

The right side of Figure 18-11-2 exhibits how the defined shadow area could be used. There are many other variations.

Figure 18-12 illustrates another projection technique for casting shadows. This system locates the LSB on the horizon line and the LST directly (on a vertical line) BELOW the LSB. The resulting shadow points toward the light source. A sample of how the derived shadow area could be used has been included.

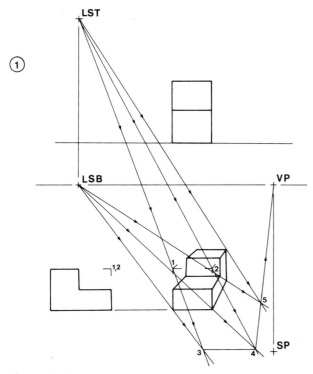

Figure 18-11-1

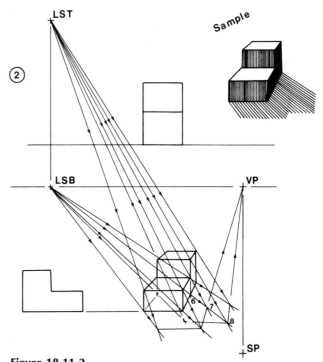

Figure 18-11-2

Figure 18-11 Casting a shadow.

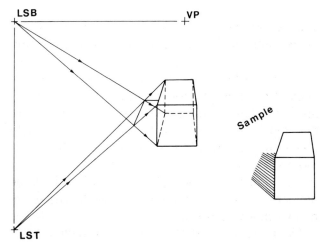

Figure 18-12   A variation of shadow casting.

18-5 ONE-POINT PERSPECTIVE GRIDS

One-point perspective grids are grid patterns drawn to match the proportions of a one-point perspective drawing. They enable the illustrator to work more quickly than when using the projection system outlined in Section 18-1, but they are not as exact. See Figure 18-13.

One-point perspective grids can be thought of as a floor or wall that has equal-sized tiles and whose sizes diminish as the floor approaches the VP. The grid system can be used to closely approximate the diminishing proportions required in one-point perspective drawings and can eliminate the need for measuring. For example, the object shown in Figure 18-13 has overall dimensions of $2 \times 2 \times 3$. These dimensions can be laid out on the grid pattern by letting each unit on the grid represent one unit (1 inch) on the object. The half-units for the step portion can be estimated as halfway between grid lines.

The disadvantage of grid patterns is their inaccuracy. They are excellent for objects that contain mostly whole numbered proportions, but for objects with many fractional proportions, or with much detail, they can be difficult to use. The approximations tend to accumulate and become confusing, resulting in incorrectly proportioned final drawings.

To prepare a one-point perspective grid, use the following procedure. See Figure 18-14.

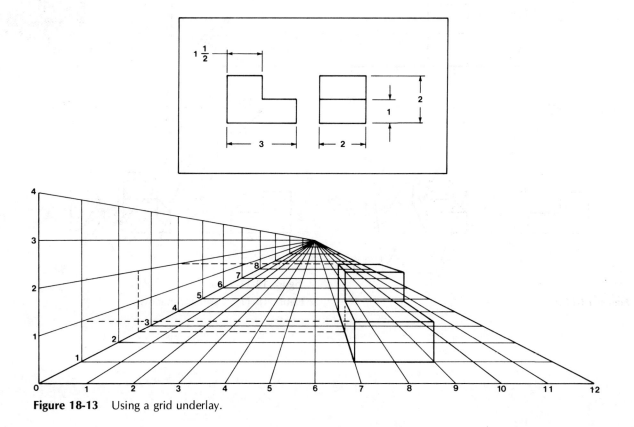

Figure 18-13   Using a grid underlay.

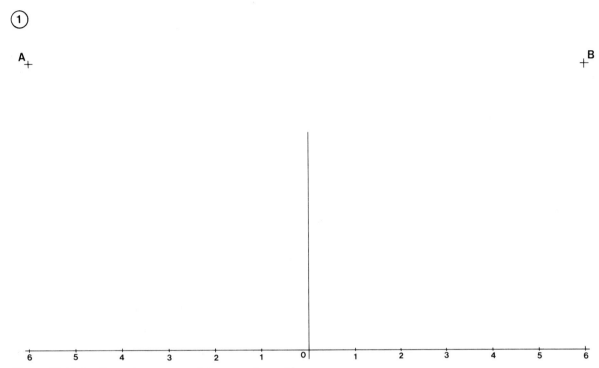

Figure 18-14-1 Preparing a one point perspective grid.

1. Draw a horizontal line and mark off equal-sized units. In the example shown in Figure 18-14-1, the centerline was labeled 0 and the other units labeled in sequence away from this point. The grid in Figure 18-13 was labeled from the left corner.

In addition, draw two points (A and B) above the horizontal line that are located equidistant from the grid centerline. The points only need to be equidistant if a symmetrical grid is desired.

2. Draw lines from points A and B to each of the points on the horizontal line. Label the intersection of lines 6-B, and 6-A, the VP. See Figure 18-14-2.

3. Draw horizontal lines through the intersection of line 6-B and each of the lines drawn from point A. The lines should run from line 6-B to line 6-A. For example, see line S-T in Figure 18-14-3.

In addition, draw lines between each of the points on the initial horizontal line to the VP. For example, line 5-VP.

4. Darken the appropriate lines, as shown in Figure 18-14-4.

Grid patterns may be varied for different effects by moving points A and B. Figure 18-15 illustrates this by showing three different grid patterns, each based on the same horizontal line, divided into the same number and equal-sized parts, whose points A and B have been varied. The further apart points A and B are located from the initial horizontal line, the more the grid appears to rise, and, conversely, the closer the points are located to the initial horizontal line the flatter the grid. In each case, points A and B must be located along the same horizontal line.

②

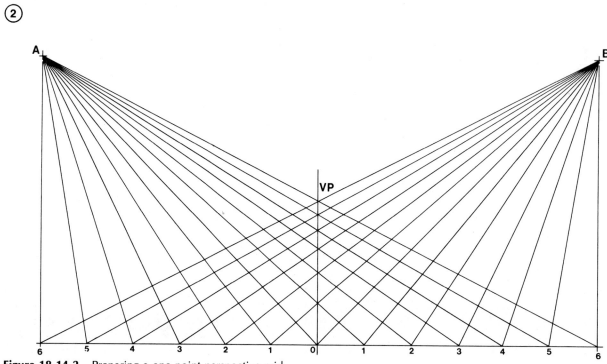

Figure 18-14-2 Preparing a one point perspective grid.

③

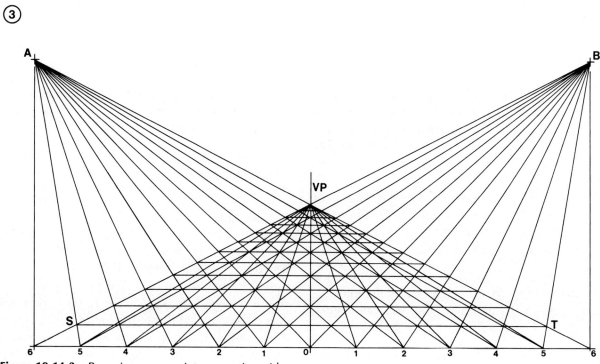

Figure 18-14-3 Preparing a one point perspective grid.

④

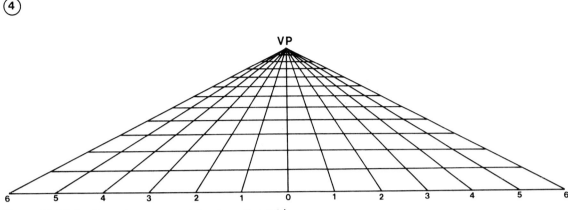

Figure 18-14-4 Preparing a one point perspective grid.

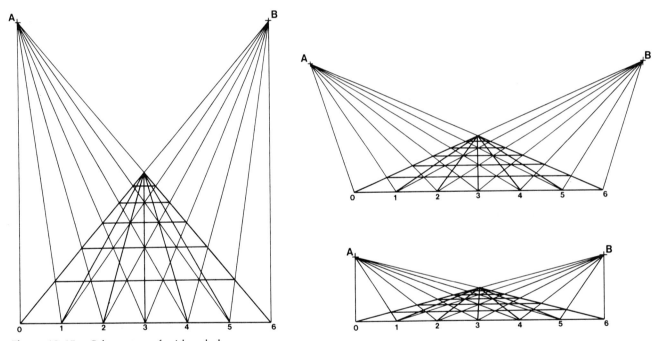

Figure 18-15 Other types of grid underlays.

Figure 18-16 shows a grid pattern with points A and B offset. The result is an eccentric grid.

Figure 18-17 illustrates another grid variation. It is actually a composite of four grid patterns joined to form a box. The result is as if we were looking into a room or corridor. The grid was created as follows:

1. Draw a rectangle of desired proportions. (A square could also be used.) Mark off equal spaces all around the rectangle and draw in the center-lines. See Figure 18-17-1.

Different scales may be used on the vertical lines than those used on the horizontal. For example, the vertical scales may be marked in half scale and the horizontal in full scale.

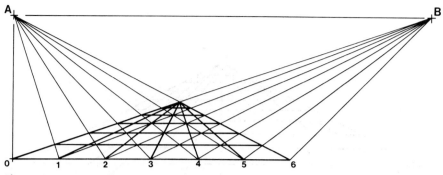

Figure 18-16　An offset grid underlay.

①

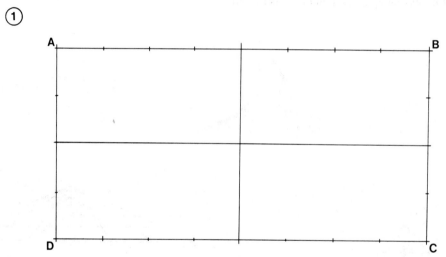

Figure 18-17-1　Preparing a center point one point perspective grid.

②

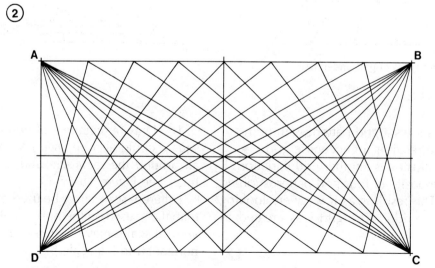

Figure 18-17-2　Preparing a center point one point perspective grid.

2. Draw lines from the four corner points A, B, C, and D, to each of the points on the horizontal lines (A-B and D-C). See Figure 18-17-2.

3. Draw lines, horizontal and vertical, to form a series of decreasing rectangles, through the inter-

section of the lines drawn for step 2, as shown in Figure 18-17-3.

4. Darken the appropriate lines. The center-point of the rectangle is the VP of the grid. Draw lines from each point on the original rectangle to the VP. See Figure 18-17-4.

③

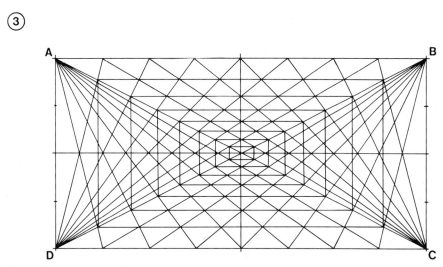

Figure 18-17-3 Preparing a center point one point perspective grid.

④

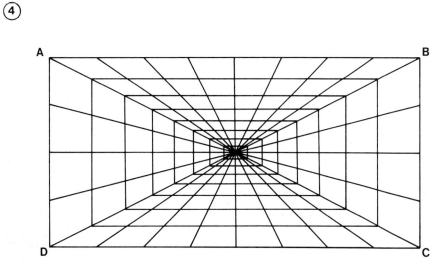

Figure 18-17-4 Preparing a center point one point perspective grid.

HOW TO USE ONE-POINT PERSPECTIVE GRIDS

Grids are generally used by illustrators as "underlays." An *underlay* is a predrawn pattern that is placed under a transparent sheet of drawing paper or mylar. It may be purchased commercially at art stores, or you may prepare your own. Figure 18-18 illustrates one type of commercially available grid.

It is strongly urged that you prepare several different one-point perspective grids for use as underlays. They will save valuable time when preparing drawings. For purposes of durability, prepare the grid in ink on mylar.

Figure 18-13 illustrates how to use a grid when preparing a drawing. Basically, all that is required

is to match the number of grid units to the dimensions of the object involved and approximate the fractional distances. However, if done properly and with imagination, this simple process can lead to some spectacular results. For example, Leonardo da Vinci's masterpiece, *The Last Supper*, started with a one-point perspective grid system, with the head of Christ as the VP.

Figure 18-19 is another example of how a one-point perspective grid system can be used. The figure is inspired by a work done by Jan Vredeman de Vries around 1600.* Figure 18-20 shows how

---

*Perspective, Jan Vredeman de Vries, was originally published in 1604. Reprints are available from Dover Publications, Inc., New York.

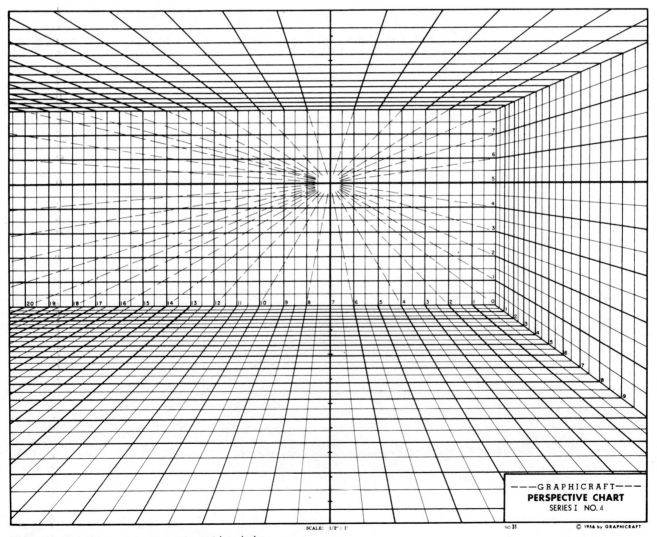

Figure 18-18   One point perspective grid underlay.

the original grid was developed. It is a symmetrical grid, but was made to appear offset in the final drawing by locating the grid VP left of center. The stairs were first located in the frontal plane; then later projected into the drawing. The columns and wall positions were derived from the grid pattern, and the shading was added in alignment with the grid pattern. The spacing for the shading and shadows was done freehand.

Figure 18-19 An example of a one point perspective drawing.

Figure 18-20 The layout for Fig. 18-19.

Figure 18-21   Preparing Fig. 18-19.

Figure 18-22   Preparing Fig. 18-19.

Figures 18-21 and 18-22 are photographs taken as the drawing was being prepared. The original grid was done in pencil and then used as an underlay. The final drawing was traced in ink.

One other point of interest is the use of a pin at the VP. This is an old trick used by illustrators to permit fast, accurate location of the VP (you literally don't have to look). In this example, a spare compass point was inserted at the VP (a straight pin could also have been used); then the straightedges were abutted to it when drawing all receding lines. See Figures 18-21 and 18-22.

3. The depth of the object is found by projecting lines from the back corners of the object in the top view to the SP, as shown in Figure 19-1-3. Where the projection lines cross the PP line, draw vertical lines perpendicular to the PP line downward until they cross the two axis lines drawn in step 2.

It should be noted that only the front edge of the object—that is, the edge aligned with line C-C—is the true length. All other lines and surfaces are foreshortened.

4. Project the rest of the corners and edges of the object, as shown in Figure 19-1-4. In each case, the corner is projected toward the SP. Where the projection line crosses the PP line, vertical lines are drawn downward until they cross the appropriate height lines. The height lines are found by projecting the height from the side orthographic views to line CC and then to either the VPR or VPL as required.

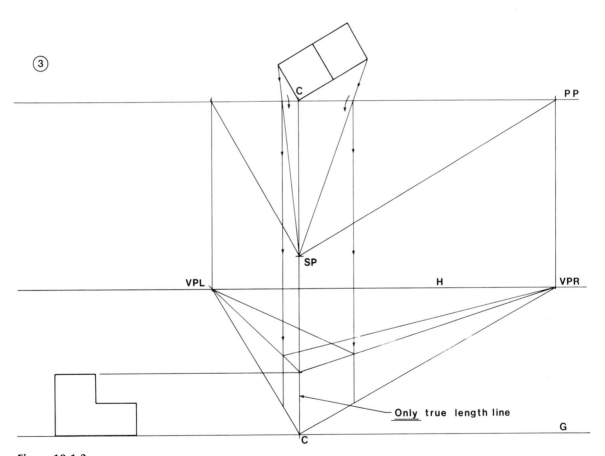

Figure 19-1-3

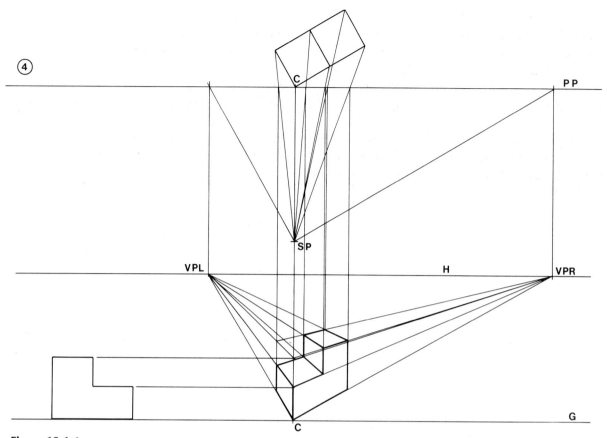

Figure 19-1-4

Figure 19-1 Preparing a two-point perspective drawing.

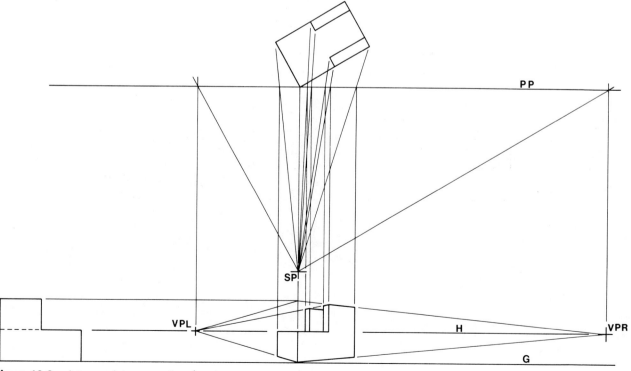

Figure 19-2 A two-point perspective drawing.

19-2 LAYOUT VARIATIONS

The proportions on the final drawing can be varied by changing the distance between the PP, H, and G lines and the SP. In general, the object will appear flatter if either line H is located closer to line G, or if the SP is located further from line PP. The movement of SP from line PP will locate VPR and VPL further apart, resulting in a flatter, more stretched-out drawing.

Figure 19-2 illustrates one of many possible variations that can be created by changing the locations of the PP, H, and G lines and point SP.

19-3 CIRCLES AND ROUNDED SURFACES

Circles and rounded surfaces are drawn in two-point perspective drawings by first projecting the points from the orthographic views into the drawing where the centerlines intersect the edge of the circle or surface, and then by adding points to the circle, for better shape definition, and in turn projecting these points. It is easier when working with circles and rounded surfaces to think of them as square surfaces. The square surfaces are much easier to project using the procedures outlined in Section 19-1; they can then serve as reference surfaces for the projection of the circles and round surfaces.

We will only deal with circles in the examples presented, because the techniques involved are identical to those used for rounded surfaces. Rounded surfaces are, in fact, usually just part of a circle. However, even for irregularly shaped surfaces, the projection techniques are the same.

Figure 19-3 illustrates how to project a circle onto the three faces of a cube drawn in two-point perspective. The procedure is as follows.

1. Draw the cube in two-point perspective using the procedure outlined in Section 19-1. Project the centerlines onto the cube using the same procedure. See Figure 19-3-1. Note that only one end of the centerline need be projected onto the two-point drawing. The length and direction of the centerline can then be determined by projection onto the vanishing points.

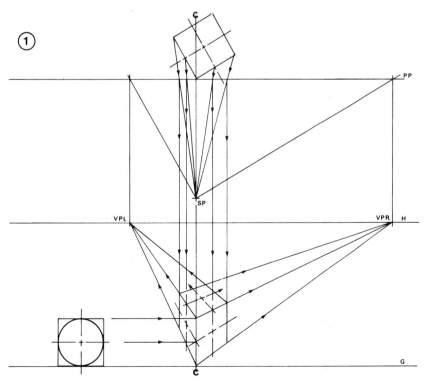

Figure 19-3-1

2. Circles can be projected onto the right-hand surface by first projecting the centerlines as outlined in step 1, and then drawing two 45° lines in the side orthographic view, as shown in Figure 19-3-2. Label the intersection points of the 45° lines with the circle 1, 2, 3, and 4.

Points 1, 2, 3, and 4 are then projected from the side orthographic view onto the top orthographic view. A 45° mitre line is required for the between view projection. The mitre line is drawn through the intersection of the PP line and a vertical line drawn from the furthest right point of the circle (in this example, the intersection of the horizontal centerline and the right side of the circle). Points 1, 2, 3, and 4 are projected by drawing vertical lines from the side orthographic views until they intersect the 45° mitre line, and then by drawing lines until they intersect the centerline C-C. From line C-C, the projection lines are pivoted to the right to about point 5 (the intersection of C-C and line PP) until they intersect the front, right-hand surface of the top orthographic view. These final points are also labeled 1, 2, 3, and 4 appropriately.

After points 1, 2, 3, and 4 have been projected from the side orthographic view to the top orthographic, they can be projected into the right side of the two-point perspective using the procedure outlined above. This will give the proper depth location of the points.

To get the heights of points 1, 2, 3, and 4, project the points from the side orthographic to the right surface of the two-point perspective by drawing horizontal lines from the points to line C-C and projecting these intersections onto the VPR. The exact locations of points 1, 2, 3, and 4 are the intersections of the vertical lines and these converging projection lines.

The final elliptical shape is drawn by using an elliptical template as a guide. This is an approximate method. To draw the exact shape, a French curve would be used to piece together an irregular shape. This is not only time consuming, but very difficult to form into a smooth curve. For this reason the ellipse template is almost always used.

The proper ellipse is selected by trial and error. Match different angle ellipses until you find one

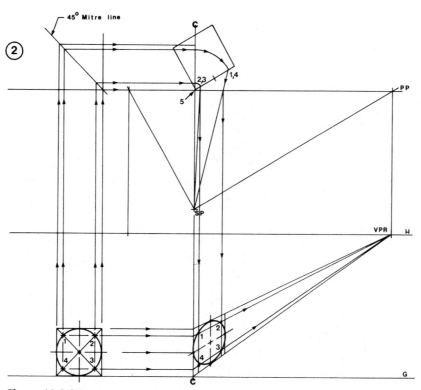

Figure 19-3-2

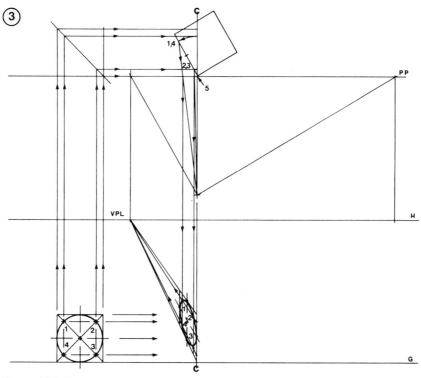

Figure 19-3-3

that comes closest to matching the eight points (1, 2, 3, 4, and the four centerline points) and draw in the ellipse. Because the actual shape of the hole is diminishing toward the VP, the ellipse template will have to be offset—that is, rotated and not aligned with any centerlines to give good visual results. Note that, in Figure 19-3-2, points 2 and 4 were not intersected; yet the final ellipse is visually acceptable. A 40° ellipse template was used as a guide for the final drawing.

3. The procedure used to draw a circle in the left-hand surface of a two-point perspective is almost exactly the same as outlined in step 2 for drawing a circle in a right-hand surface. The differences are: first, to rotate the projection lines of points 1, 2, 3, and 4, from the side orthographic views to the line C-C, to the left about to point 5 until they intersect the top view of the left-hand surface. Second, the projection of points 1, 2, 3, and 4, by drawing the horizontal lines to line C-C, is toward the VPL. See Figure 19-3-3.

The horizontal projection lines are incomplete in Figure 19-3-3 for clarity. These lines should extend to line C-C, then converge to the VPL.

4. Drawing a circle in the top surface of a two-point perspective requires a different procedure from that used for the right and left surfaces. Points 1, 2, 3, and 4 are added to the top view, as shown in Figure 19-3-4. Lines are then drawn through the points and continued until they intersect the top orthographic views of the left- and right-hand surfaces. For example, a line is drawn through points 2 and 3 and extended until it intersects the top orthographic view of the right-hand surface, labeled point d. Points a, b, and c are the other point line projections.

Points a, b, c, and d are projected to the top surface of the two-point perspective by using the procedure outlined in Section 19-1. The points are thus located on the outer edges of the cube and then are projected toward the appropriate VPs. The intersections of these lines define the positions of points 1, 2, 3, and 4. The final elliptical shape is drawn by using an ellipse template as a guide and matching the eight defined points (1, 2, 3, 4, and four centerline points) by trial and error. In the example shown in Figure 19-3-4, a 40° ellipse template was used.

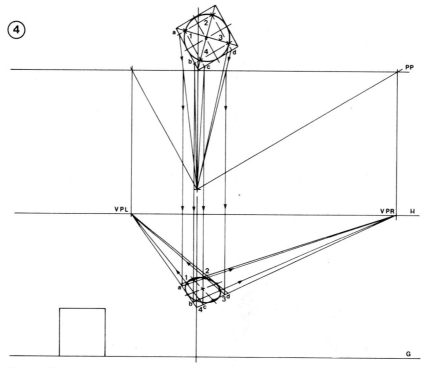

Figure 19-3-4

Figure 19-3 Circles in two-point perspective drawings.

19-4 CASTING SHADOWS

Casting shadows in two-point perspectives is done in a manner similar to that used for one-point perspectives (see Section 19-4). Two additional points—light source bottom (LSB) and light source top (LST)—are added to the layout drawing at arbitrary distances above and below the VPL, respectively, as shown in Figure 19-4-1. Lines are then projected through the various corners of the object from LST and LSB. The intersections of these projection lines define the shape of the cast shadow.

As stated, the distance between LSB and LST is arbitrary. In general, the further the distance between the points, the shorter the shadow, and vice versa.

19-5 TWO-POINT PERSPECTIVE GRIDS

Grid patterns drawn using a two-point perspective axis system are very helpful as underlays. They can be placed under a sheet of drawing paper and used as a reference system to help produce two-point perspective drawings quickly and accurately.

The size and proportions of the grid will depend on the final drawing requirements, but the procedure used to develop any two-point perspective grid is as follows. Figure 19-5 illustrates.

1. Draw, near the bottom of the paper, a horizontal line. Draw a vertical line near the center of the paper. Define, at some arbitrary distance above the horizontal line, a horizon line and mark off two vanishing points: VPR and VPL. See Figure 19-5-1.

The horizontal and vertical lines are then calibrated by marking off equal-length distances. The intersection of the horizontal line is the 0 point, and all distances are measured from this point. In the given example, the distances to the left of the vertical line are marked off with lengths exactly half of that used for the distances to the right of the vertical line. The choice of distance depends on the individual drawing requirements.

2. Draw lines from each of the points labeled 8 to the vanishing points, as shown in Figure 19-5-2.

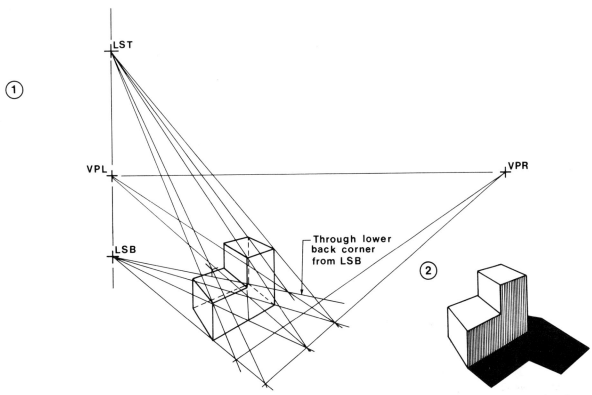

Figure 19-4-1   Casting a shadow.

Figure 19-4-2   The results of Figure 19-4-1.

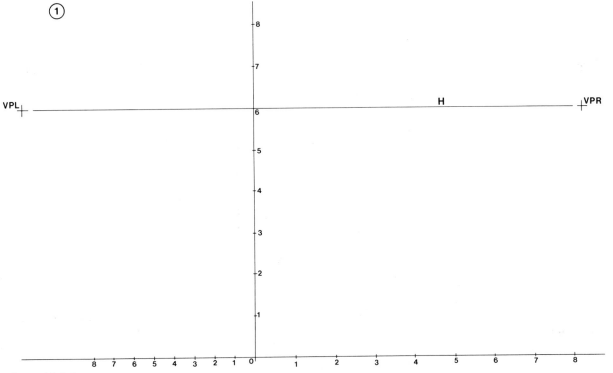

Figure 19-5-1

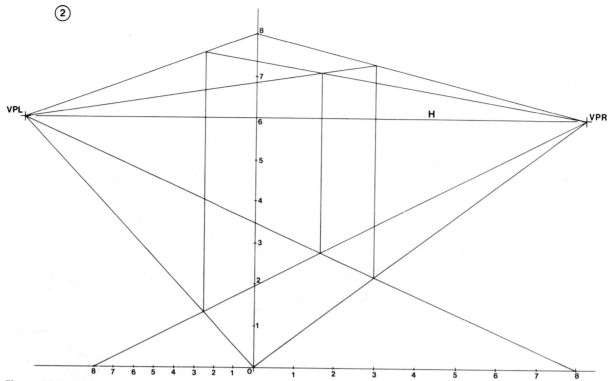

Figure 19-5-2

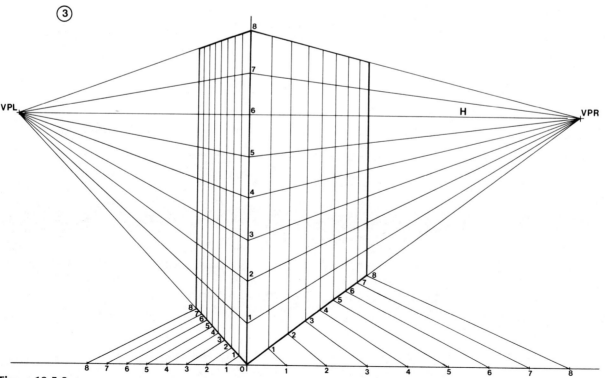

Figure 19-5-3

The choice of 8 units per scale was also arbitrary. Any number of units could be used, and each scale need not contain the same number of units.

3. To create an external two-point perspective grid, project the points 1 through 8 from the right axis toward the VPL, but stop at the line 0-VPR, as shown in Figure 19-5-3. Points 0 through 8 on the left axis are projected toward the VPR, but stop at the line 0-VPL. Draw lines from points 0 through 8 on the vertical line to both the VPR and the VPL. Vertical lines are then drawn from the projected

point, 1 through 8, on line 0-VPL and 0-VPR as shown.

4. To draw an internal two-point perspective grid, draw lines from points 0 through 8 on the right axis to the VPL and from points 0 through 8 on the left axis to the VPR. The height units are calibrated on the back corner line (a vertical line drawn upward from the intersection of lines 8-VPL and 8-VPR). The grid lines are developed by drawing lines from VPL and VPR through points 0 through 8, as shown in Figure 19-5-4.

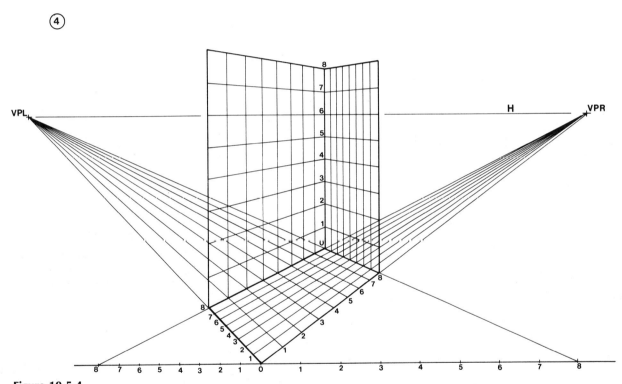

Figure 19-5-4

Figure 19-5   Preparing a two-point perspective grid underlay.

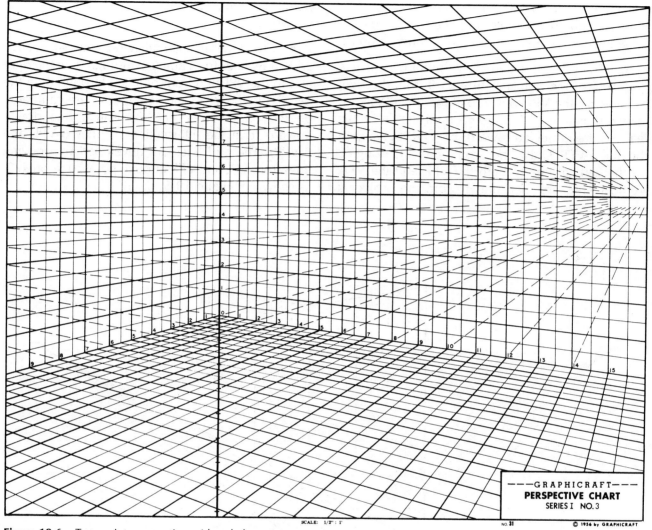

Figure 19-6 Two-point perspective grid underlay.

As a point of interest, the internal grid shown in Figure 19-5-4 was developed from the external grid shown in Figure 19-5-3. The reverse could also be done. However, this could not be done if exact premeasured height distances are required.

Figures 19-6 and 19-7 are samples of two-point perspective grid patterns that are commercially available. Many different patterns are available.

Students are recommended to develop several different grid patterns for future use. Draw the grids with ink on mylar. Do at least one internal and one external pattern.

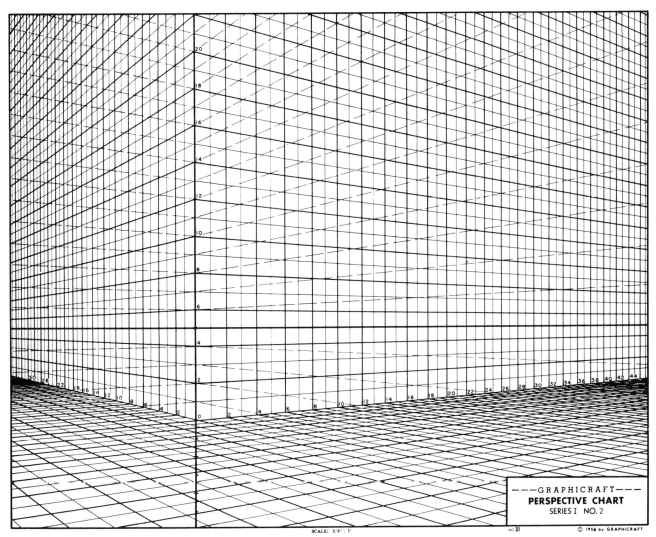

Figure 19-7 Two-point perspective grid underlay.

CHAPTER 20

THREE-POINT PERSPECTIVES

20-1 GENERAL LAYOUT

Three-point perspective drawings are perspective drawings based on three vanishing points. They are difficult and time consuming to draw and are only used for very large objects or when special visual effects are desired.

For most objects, two-point perspectives are sufficient and are therefore used. Three-point perspective layouts require considerable paper to generate a final drawing of reasonable size. Grid underlays help but, in general, three-point perspectives are rarely drawn.

Figure 20-1 shows one of several methods that can be used to layout a three-point perspective. It is the most compact (uses the least amount of paper area) of all the methods. The method is outlined here, and it is suggested that the student try at least one three-point layout.

1. Draw a large (as large as will fit on the paper) equilateral triangle labeled ABC, as shown in Figure 20-1-1. Construct perpendicular bisects along each side of the triangle. Label the perpendicular bisects D, E, F, and label their central intersection point O.

2. Draw a horizontal line through point O. Mark off equally spaced units to the left and right of point O. The spacing to the left of point O need not equal the spacing to the right, but in most cases it is better to keep them equal. If, for example, the object is very wide, smaller spacing could be used to the right of point O, but this will alter the visual proportions of the final drawing.

In addition to the horizontal line, draw a line GH perpendicular to line AD through point O. Mark off equal spaces along GH below point O. Again, the distances used should be equal to those used along the horizontal line.

3. Draw lines from points 1 and 2 on the horizontal line left of point O to corner B. Likewise, draw lines from points 1 and 2 on line GH to corner B. Draw a line from point 1 on the horizontal line to corner A.

Where the line drawn from point 2 on line GH to corner B intersects line EC, label the intersection K. Point K represents the front lower corner of the object. From point K, draw a line to corner A and to corner B.

Label the intersection of the line from point 2, on the horizontal line, to the left of point O with the

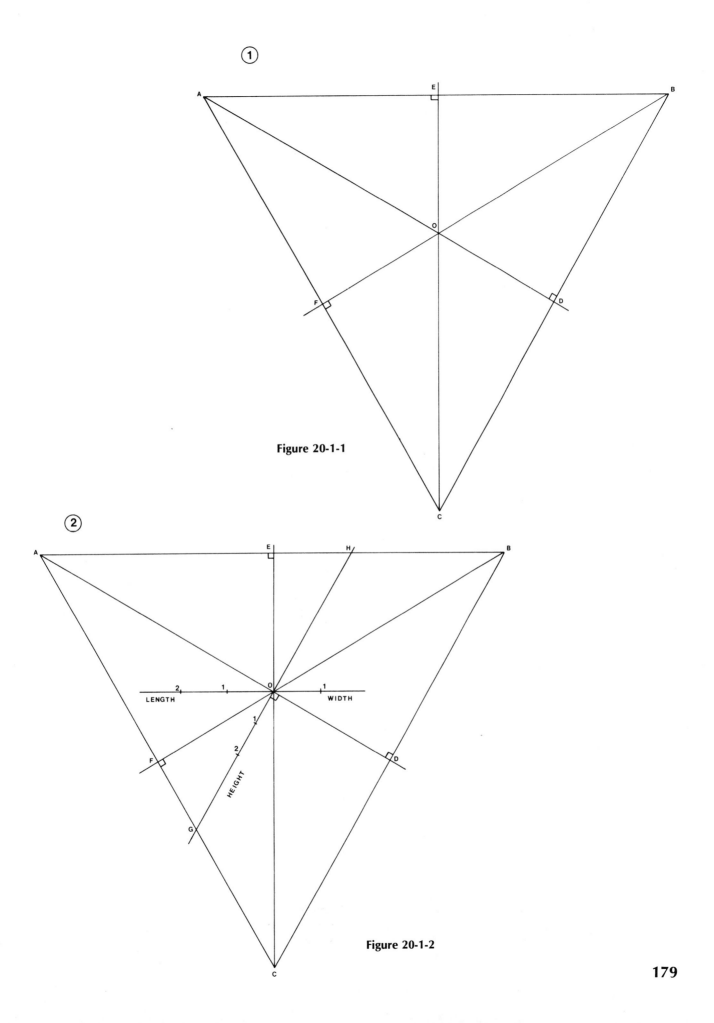

Figure 20-1-1

Figure 20-1-2

179

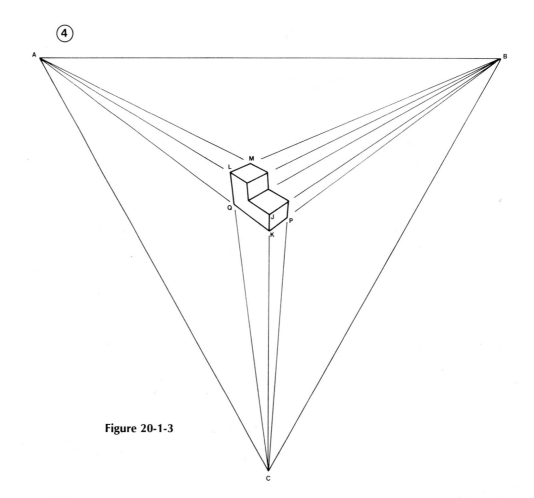

④

Figure 20-1-3

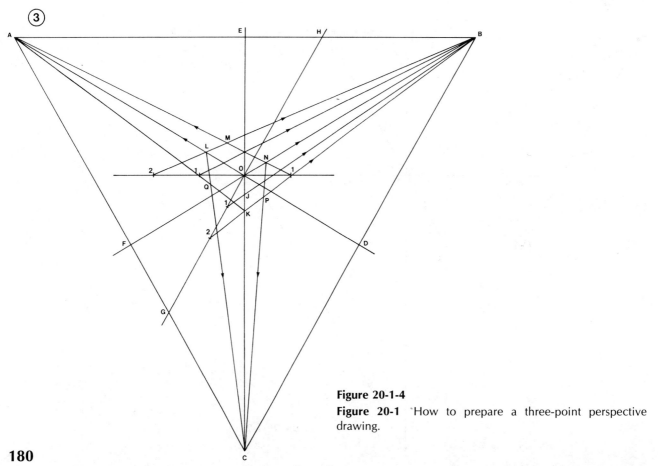

③

Figure 20-1-4
Figure 20-1 How to prepare a three-point perspective drawing.

line AD as point L. Point L represents the upper back corner of the object. From point L, draw a line to corner C. Label the intersection with KA point Q.

Label the intersection of the line from point 1, on the horizontal line, to the right of point O to corner A with line FB as point N. Point N represents the front, top right corner of the object. Label the object L, M, O, N, J, K, and P as shown.

4. Darken the final shape of the object as shown. Note that all edges of the object that were parallel to one of the principal plane lines in the orthographic views now recede to one of the three vanishing points A, B, or C.

Circles and inclined lines are handled as they were in one- and two-point perspectives.

20-2 THREE-POINT PERSPECTIVE GRIDS

Figure 20-21 shows the basic layout pattern for an external (seen from the outside) three-point perspective grid. The location of the three vanishing points as well as the choice of 30° and 15° is arbitrary and may be varied according to the final results desired. The spacing distance is also arbitrary, but in this example the spacing is equal on the vertical and on the 15° line. The 30° line used space half that used on the vertical and 30° lines.

Figure 20-2-2 shows the completed grid pattern.

Figure 20-3 depicts an object drawn using the grid developed in Figure 20-2 as an underlay. The use of grid patterns enables us to draw objects much larger in the final size than those drawn by

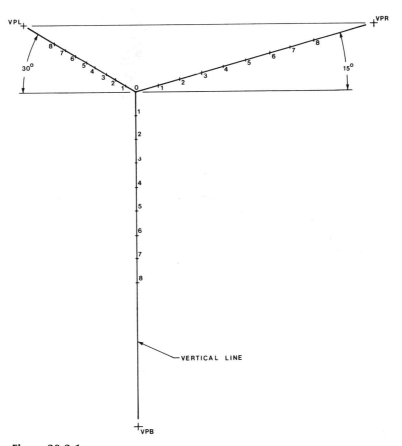

Figure 20-2-1

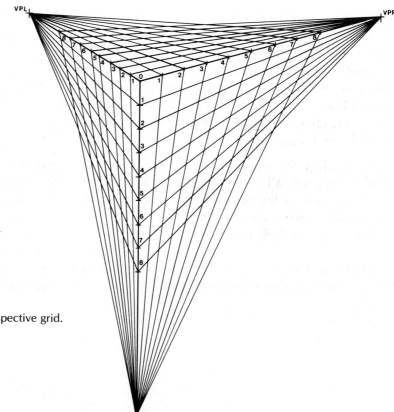

Figure 20-2-2
Figure 20-2   Preparing a three-point perspective grid.

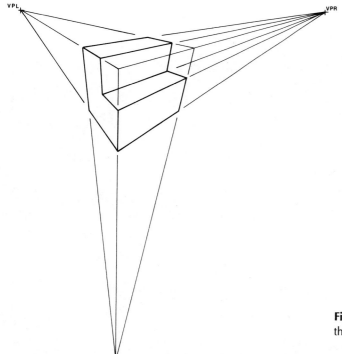

Figure 20-3   A three-point perspective drawing made using the grid shown in Figure 20-2.

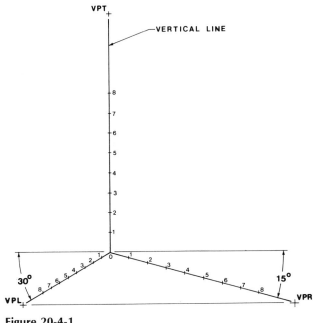

Figure 20-4-1

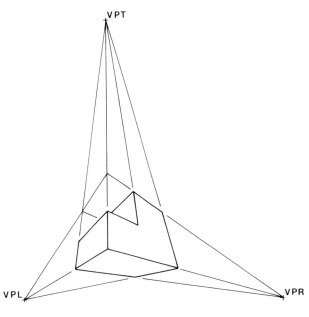

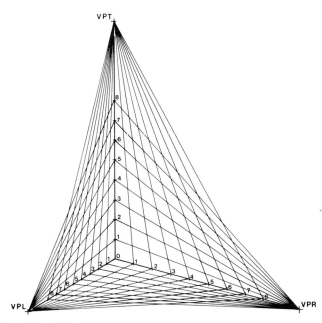

Figure 20-4-2

Figure 20-4 A variation of three-point perspective grid pattern.

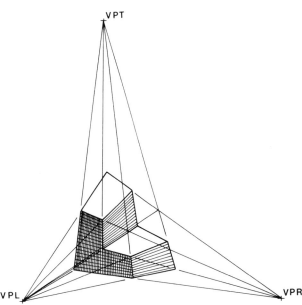

Figure 20-5 Examples of three-point perspective drawings.

the development layout method explained in Section 20-1.

Figure 20-4-1 illustrates how to develop an internal (seen from the inside) three-point perspective grid. It is essentially an inversion of the external grid shown in Figure 20-2. Figure 20-4-2 shows the finished pattern, and Figure 20-5 exhibits two examples of objects drawn using the grid developed in Figure 20-4 as an underlay. Note that care must be taken when using a grid underlay to correctly position the object. The lower example in Figure 20-5 is very difficult to visualize and is badly distorted. The position of the upper example is much clearer.

PART FOUR

EXERCISE PROBLEMS

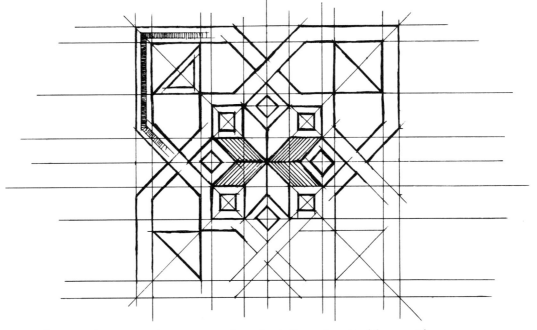

This section contains over a hundred Exercise Problems. There are no specific instructions as to what type of drawing (isometric, perspective, etc.) is to be prepared, although some Exercise Problems do use a specific format and therefore tend to lend themselves to that particular format. For example, the thread-fastener problems are presented in isometric form, but could be done as perspectives. In some cases, it may be interesting to do the same problem in several formats and compare the results.

An effort has been made to keep the presentation of the problems true to industrial situations. For this reason, orthographic views and pictorial drawings as well as photographs, freehand sketches, and general word problems have been included. Some problems have dimensions and some do not. In the case of the photographs, "by eye" proportions may be used.

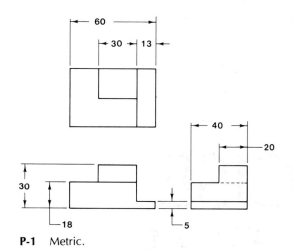

P-1 Metric.

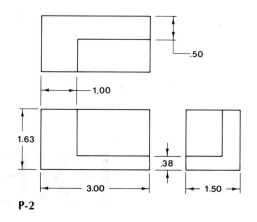

P-2

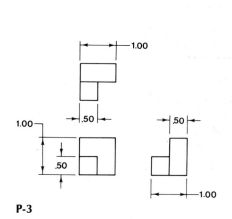

P-3

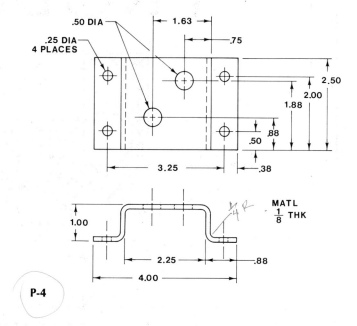

P-4

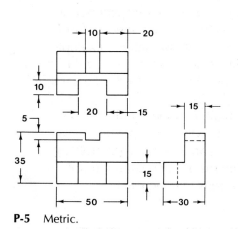

P-5 Metric.

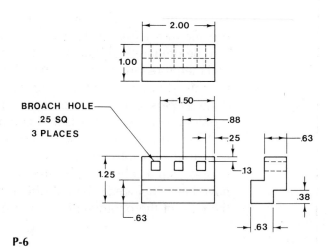

P-6

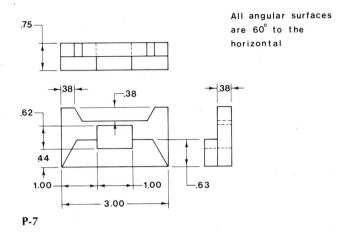

.75

All angular surfaces
are 60° to the
horizontal

P-7

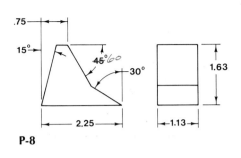

P-8

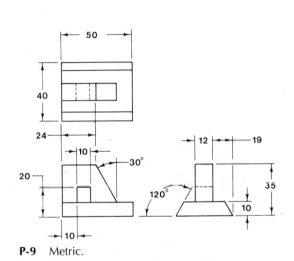

P-9   Metric.

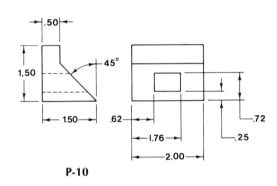

P-10

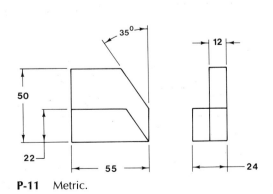

P-11   Metric.

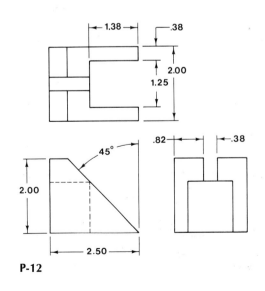

P-12

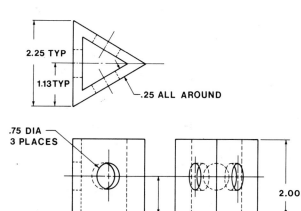

2.25 TYP

1.13 TYP

.25 ALL AROUND

.75 DIA
3 PLACES

2.00

1.00

P-13

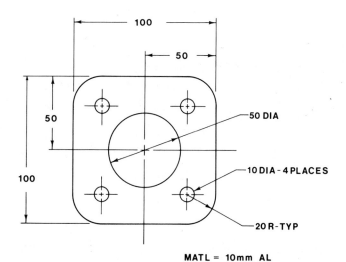

100

50

50

100

50 DIA

10 DIA - 4 PLACES

20 R - TYP

MATL = 10mm AL

P-15 Metric.

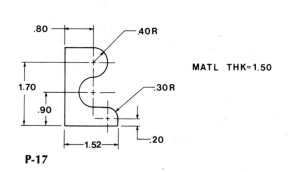

.80

.40 R

1.70

.90

.30 R

MATL THK = 1.50

1.52

.20

P-17

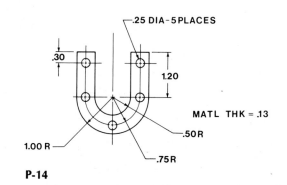

.25 DIA - 5 PLACES

.30

1.20

MATL THK = .13

.50 R

1.00 R

.75 R

P-14

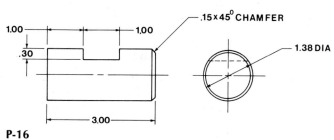

.15 × 45° CHAMFER

1.00

1.00

.30

1.38 DIA

3.00

P-16

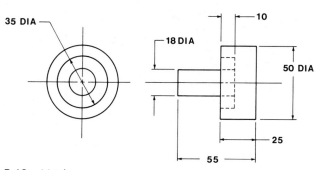

35 DIA

10

18 DIA

50 DIA

25

55

P-18 Metric.

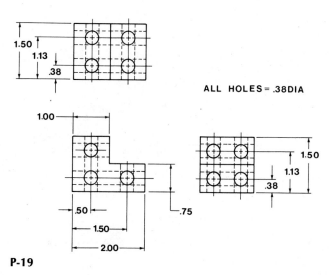

1.50

1.13

.38

ALL HOLES = .38 DIA

1.00

1.50

1.13

.50

.38

.75

1.50

2.00

P-19

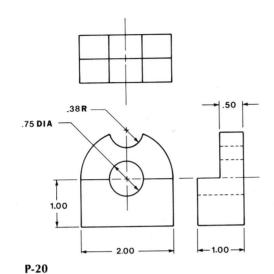

P-20

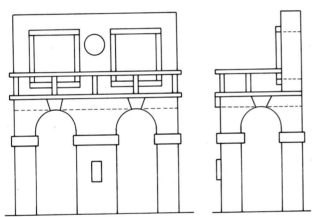

P-22   Scale the drawing.

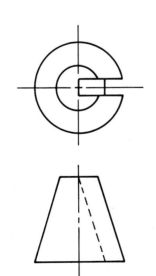

P-24   Scale the drawing.

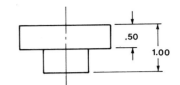

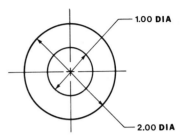

P-21

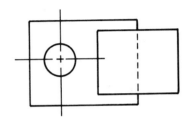

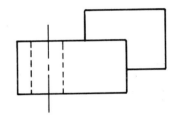

P-23   Scale the drawing.

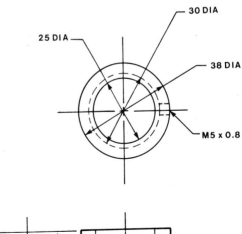

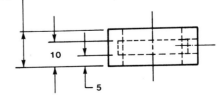

P-25   Metric.

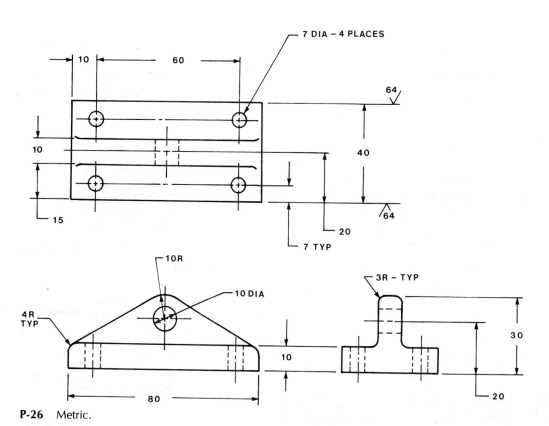

P-26 Metric.

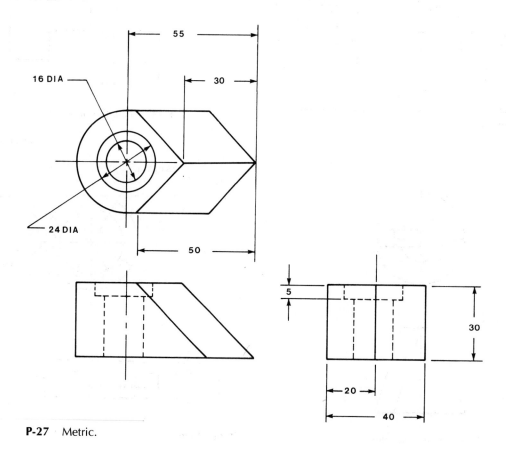

P-27 Metric.

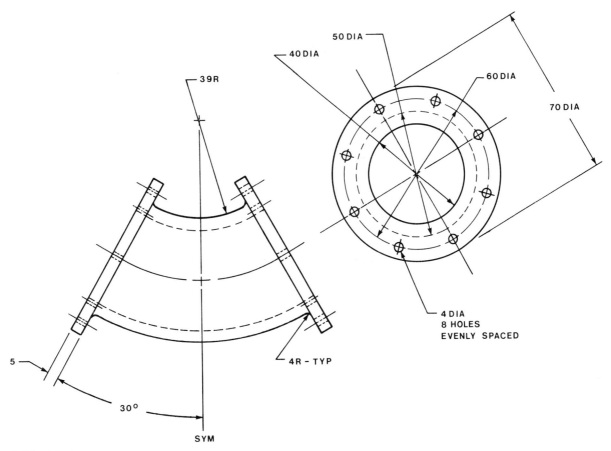

P-28 Metric.

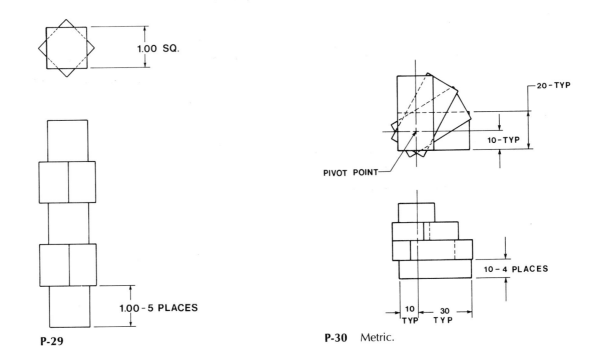

P-29

P-30 Metric.

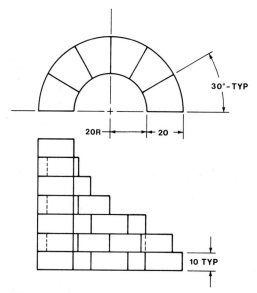

P-31 Metric.

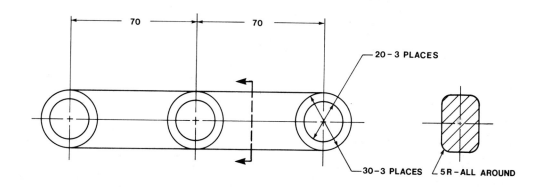

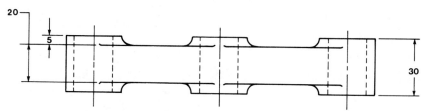

P-32 Metric.

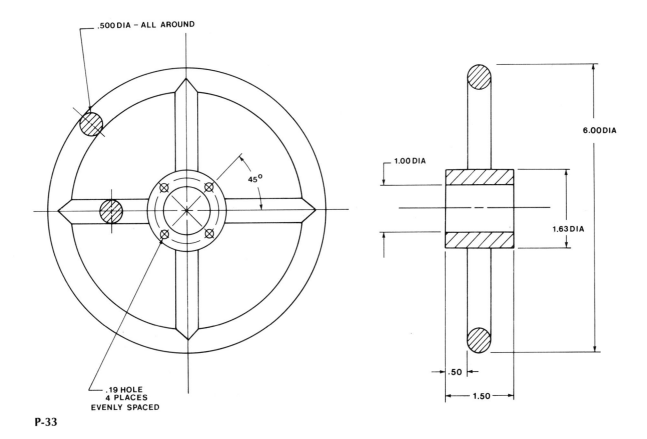

.500 DIA – ALL AROUND

45°

1.00 DIA

6.00 DIA

1.63 DIA

.50

1.50

.19 HOLE
4 PLACES
EVENLY SPACED

P-33

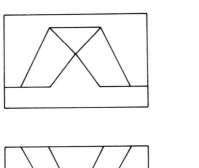

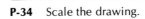

P-34 Scale the drawing.

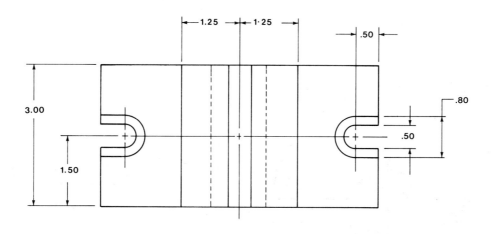

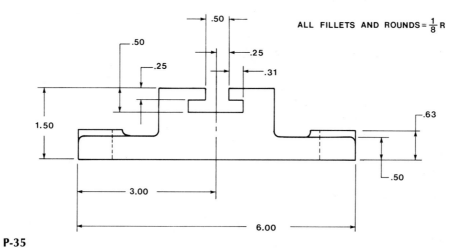

ALL FILLETS AND ROUNDS = $\frac{1}{8}$ R

P-35

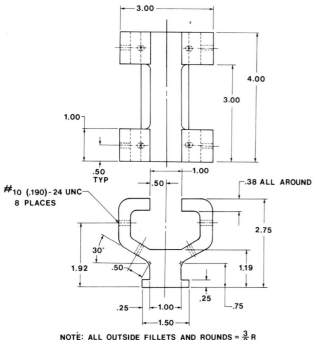

#10 (.190)-24 UNC
8 PLACES

NOTE: ALL OUTSIDE FILLETS AND ROUNDS = $\frac{3}{8}$ R
ALL INSIDE FILLETS AND ROUNDS = $\frac{3}{16}$ R

P-36

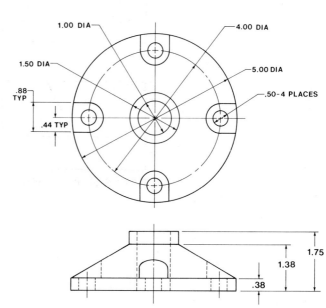

P-37

Compression Spring

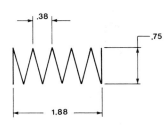

P-38

Tension Spring

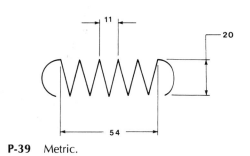

P-39 Metric.

Illustrators are sometimes asked to work from photographs. Problems **P40** to **P43** are photographs of various electronic devices. Redraw them as inked drawings. Approximate the dimensions from the given photographs. (Photographs courtesy of Tandy Corporation.)

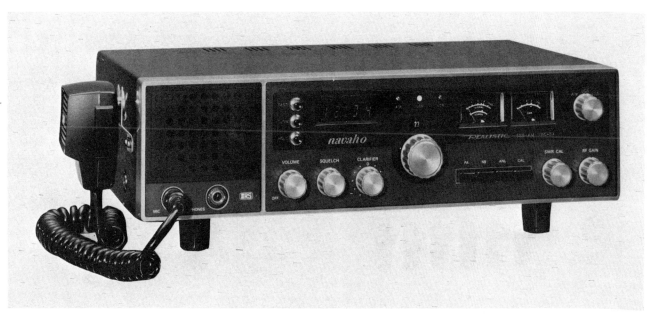

P-40

P-41

P-42

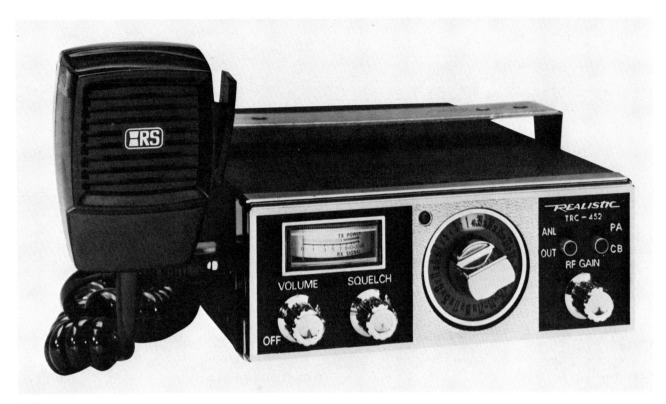

P-43

Prepare ink underlays for the following types of drawings (**P-44** to **P-51**).

P-44   Isometric.   **P-45**   Dimetric.

P-46 Trimetric.

P-47 Oblique, cavalier.

P-48 Oblique, cabinet.

P-49 One-point perspective.

P-50   Two-point perspective.

P-51   Three-point perspective.

P-52   This is an inking exercise. It is comprised entirely of straight lines. Part
1 shows how to set up the drawing.

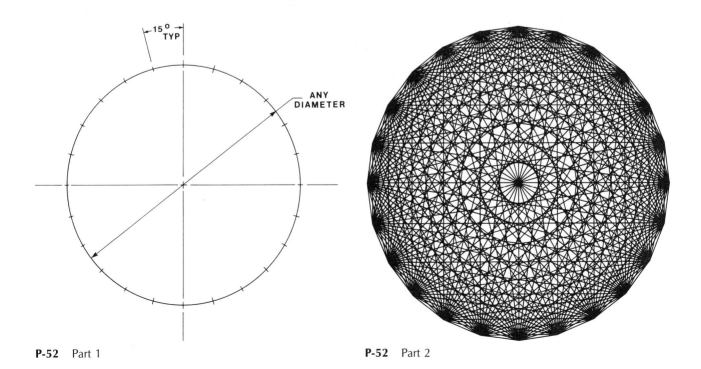

P-52   Part 1

P-52   Part 2

P-53   This is an isometric drawing that only has surface shading. Redraw the drawing by eye and add shadows. Modify the drawing as necessary.

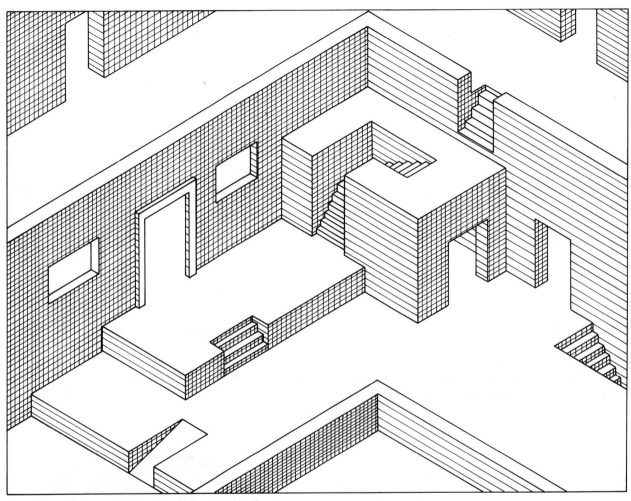

P-53

Illustrators are sometimes asked to prepare charts and forms. For example, **P-54** is a form designed for hockey coaches on which they can make notes and work out plays. These charts and forms are done in ink, using good quality lettering techniques, so that they can be reproduced clearly in quantity.

Prepare a drawing for each of the following assignments.

P-54   The original for this diagram has been lost. Prepare a new one based on the information shown.

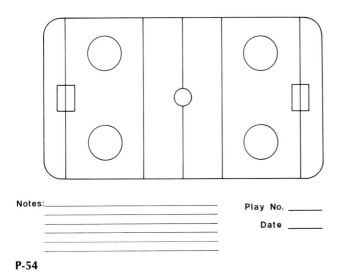

Notes:_____   Play No. _____
_____   Date _____
_____
_____
_____

P-54

P-55   Prepare a diagram of a basketball court. Include a space for NOTES, GAME, and DATE.

P-56   A football coach has asked you to prepare a general form that can be used to design, record, and teach plays. You have been given a rough sketch of the coach's idea. Working from this sketch, prepare a form of "camera ready" quality that includes the offensive lineup and lines for play numbers, defenses, and comments.

PLAY No: _____   DEFENSE: _____

O O O ⊗ O O   O
O   O
O   O

PLAY NAME: _____   DATE: _____
P-56

P-57   Prepare a calendar of the upcoming academic year (September 1 to June 30). Show all important activities. Work in ink and LEROY lettering.

P-58   Prepare a table for the following Standard Lumber Sizes.

Nominal Size	Actual Size	Nominal Size	Actual Size
1 × 2	¾ × 1½	2 × 4	1½ × 3½
1 × 3	¾ × 2½	2 × 5	1½ × 5½
1 × 4	¾ × 3½	2 × 8	1½ × 7¼
1 × 5	¾ × 4½	2 × 10	1½ × 9¼
1 × 6	¾ × 5½	2 × 12	1½ × 11¼
1 × 8	¾ × 7¼	3 × 4	2½ × 3½
1 × 10	¾ × 9¼	4 × 4	3½ × 3½
1 × 12	¾ × 11¼	4 × 6	3½ × 5½
2 × 2	1½ × 1½	6 × 6	5½ × 5½
2 × 3	1½ × 2½		

Plywood (all sizes are true):
  Standard sheet size 4′ × 8′
  Standard thickness ¼″, ⅜″, ½″, ⅝″, ¾″, 1″

P-58   Standard Lumber Sizes (inches).

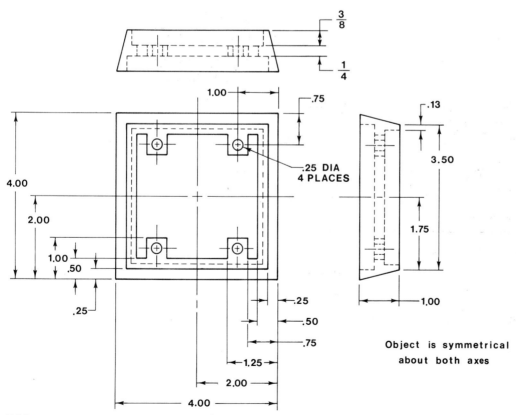

Object is symmetrical about both axes

P-59

P-60 Assume the part shown has a thickness of .26 inches.

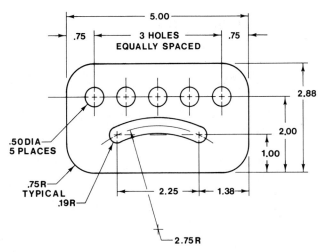

P-60

P-61 The holes in this figure are dimensional using a coordinate system. The lower left corner is the O,O point. All hole dimensions are given in the table.

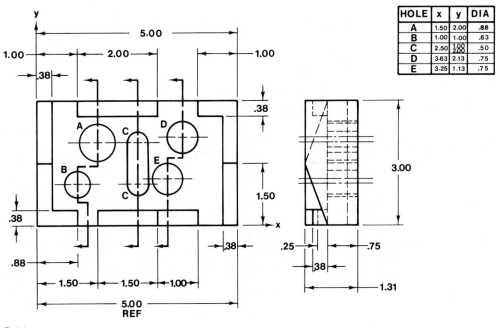

HOLE	x	y	DIA
A	1.50	2.00	.88
B	1.00	1.00	.63
C	2.50	1.00 / 2.00	.50
D	3.63	2.13	.75
E	3.25	1.13	.75

P-61

Using the format shown in **P-62,** draw the following bolts with appropriate nuts. Draw each bolt and nut in both indicated positions.

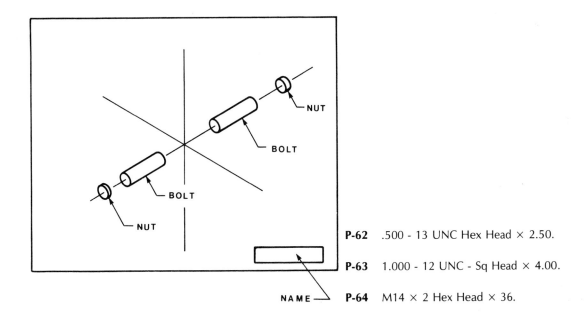

P-62 .500 - 13 UNC Hex Head × 2.50.

P-63 1.000 - 12 UNC - Sq Head × 4.00.

P-64 M14 × 2 Hex Head × 36.

Using the format shown in **P-65,** add the following information at the indicated letter.

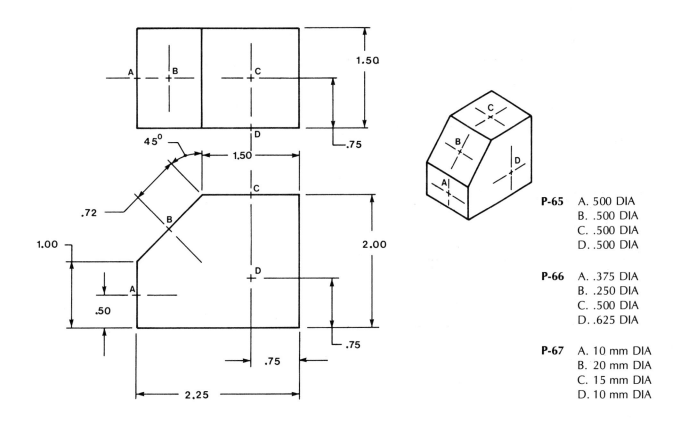

P-65 A. 500 DIA
B. .500 DIA
C. .500 DIA
D. .500 DIA

P-66 A. .375 DIA
B. .250 DIA
C. .500 DIA
D. .625 DIA

P-67 A. 10 mm DIA
B. 20 mm DIA
C. 15 mm DIA
D. 10 mm DIA

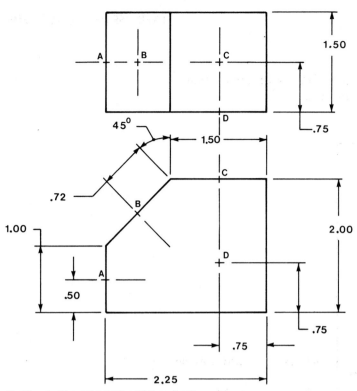
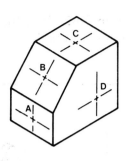

P-68   A. ¼ - 20 UNC - 2BX × 1.00
      B. ⅜ - 16 UNC - 2BX × .75
      C. .250 Drill - .75 Cbore, .375 deep
      D. .375 drill - 82° csk, .750 DIA

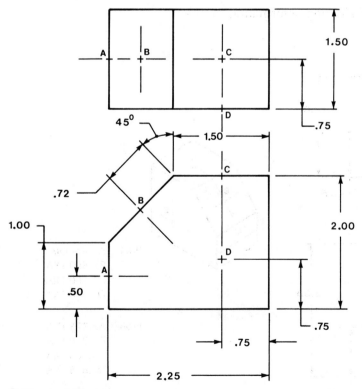
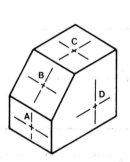

P-69   A. ⌀ 16 mm
      B. .500 drill - 1.000 sface
      C. M20 × 2.5
      D. .44 drill - .62 cbore, .125 deep

Using the format shown in **P65**, add the following fasteners. Show the fasteners in the exploded position—that is, not in the block but outside the block, and along a centerline that aligns with the centerline of the block.

P-70   A. ¼ - 20 UNC × 2.00 round head
       B. ⁷⁄₁₆ - 14 UNC × 1.50 flat head
       C. 10 (190) - 32 UNF × 1.25 fillister head
       D. .500 - 20 UNF × 1.50 headless - (blade type) screw

P-71   A. M10 × 1.5 - 20 long flat head
       B. M36 × 4 - 100 round head
       C. M8 × 1.25 - 24 fillister head
       D. M16 × 2 - 30 headless - (allen type) screw

Prepare an exploded drawing for the following objects; each object has five or more pieces.

P-72   Lead holder.

P-73   Lead sharpener.

P-74   Technical pen.

P-75   Compass.

P-76   Your choice.

Prepare an exploded drawing of the following assemblies.

HANDLE ASSEMBLY

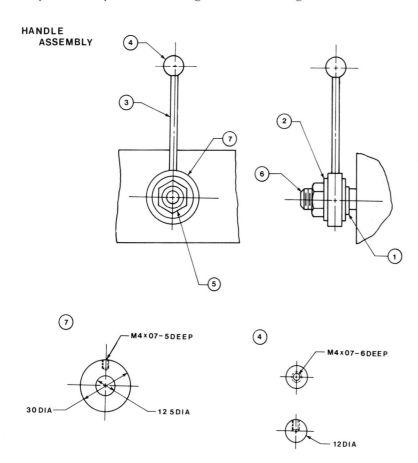

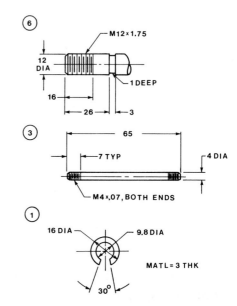

P-77

7	HOLDER	1
6	SHAFT, DRIVE	1
5	M12×1.75 NUT	1
4	BALL, HANDLE	1
3	SHAFT, HANDLE	1
2	2×12 ID×24 OD	2
1	SNAP RING	1
NO	NAME	QTY

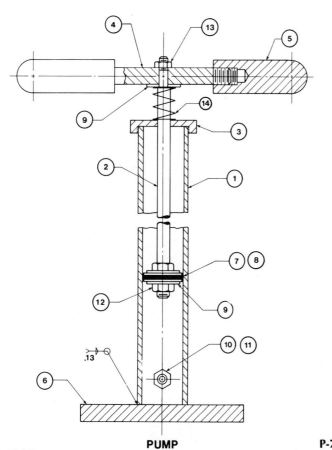

PUMP

P-78-(I)   Details for the P78 assembly are on pages 211 and 212.

① BODY

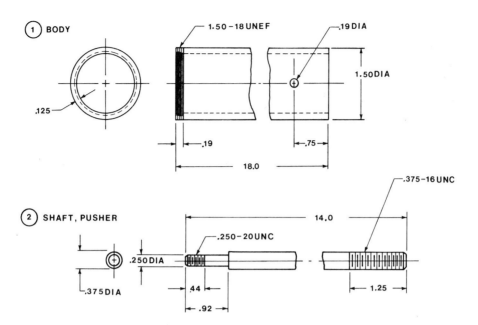

② SHAFT, PUSHER

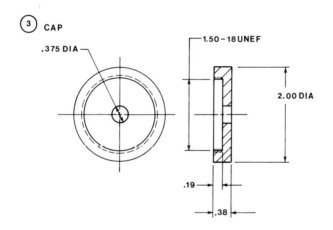

③ CAP

④ SHAFT, HANDLE

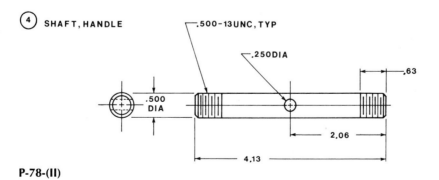

P-78-(II)

(5) HANDLE

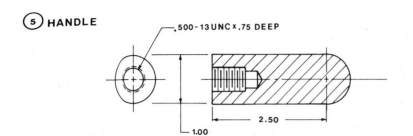

.500-13UNC x .75 DEEP

2.50

1.00

(6) PLATE, BASE

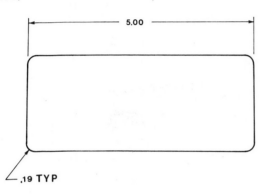

5.00

2.00

.50

.19 TYP

(7) HOLDER, GASKET

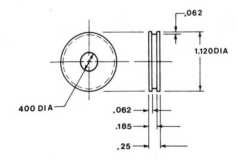

.062

1.120 DIA

400 DIA

.062

.185

.25

(8) GASKET

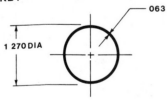

063

1 270 DIA

(9) WASHER

.063 x .38 ID x 1.00 OD

P-78-(III)

(10) NOZZLE (VENDOR ITEM)

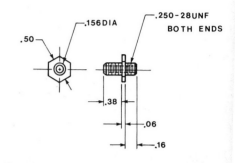

.156 DIA

.250-28UNF
BOTH ENDS

.50

.38

.06

.16

(11) NUT, CROWN

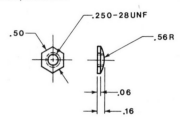

.250-28UNF

.50

.56 R

.06

.16

(12) NUT

.375-16 UNC

(13) NUT

.250-20 UNC

(14) SPRING

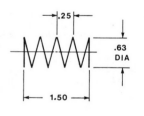

.25

.63
DIA

1.50

WIRE GAGE = 14(064)

P-78-(IV)

P-79 The seven objects shown in P-79 are all made from $20 \times 20 \times 20$ cubes. When combined properly, they will form a single $60 \times 60 \times 60$ cube. Using the given information, create a series of pictorial instructions that shows how the seven objects fit together to form the larger cube.

PUZZLE PROBLEM

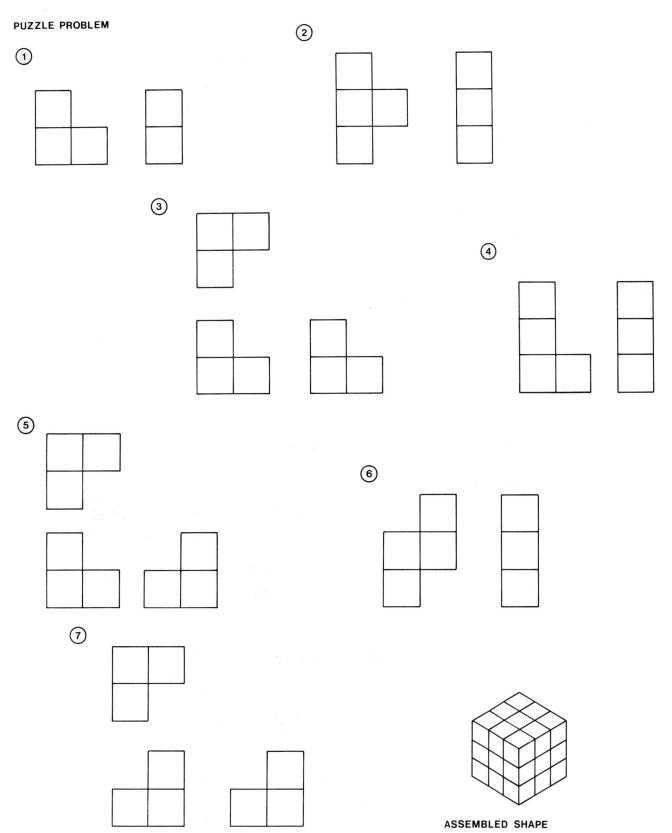

ASSEMBLED SHAPE

P-80   Prepare an exploded drawing of the following assembly.

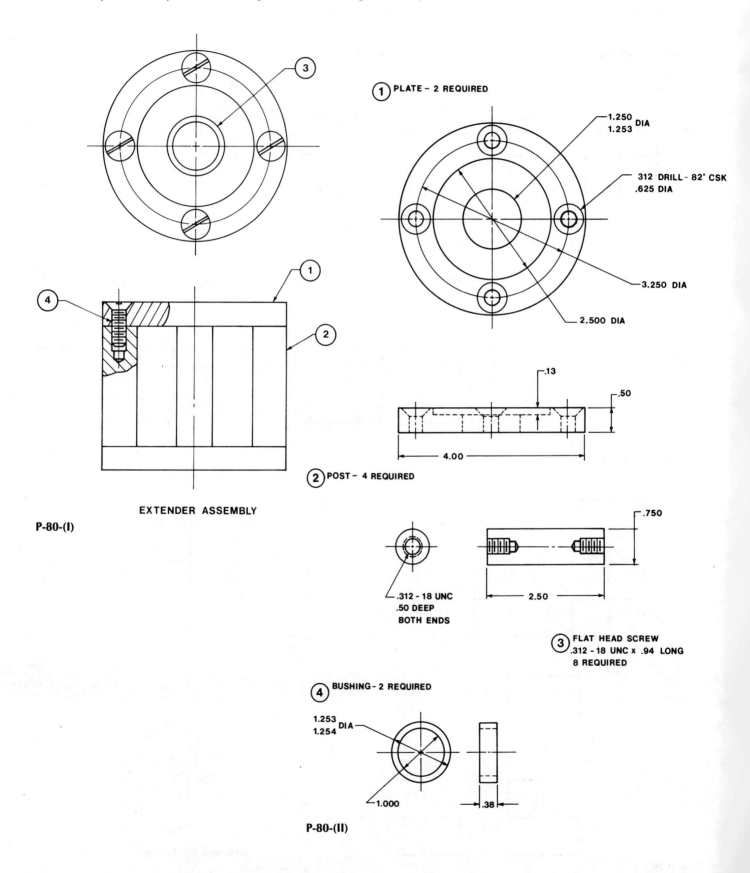

EXTENDER ASSEMBLY

P-80-(I)

① PLATE – 2 REQUIRED

1.250 / 1.253 DIA

312 DRILL - 82° CSK .625 DIA

3.250 DIA

2.500 DIA

.13

.50

4.00

② POST – 4 REQUIRED

.312 - 18 UNC .50 DEEP BOTH ENDS

.750

2.50

③ FLAT HEAD SCREW .312 - 18 UNC x .94 LONG 8 REQUIRED

④ BUSHING - 2 REQUIRED

1.253 / 1.254 DIA

1.000

.38

P-80-(II)

P-81   A chemistry instructor has asked for help in preparing some diagrams for a publication. The current diagrams are two dimensional. You are asked to redraw the diagrams using instruments to make them three dimensional. The center is to be drawn as a sphere, with the atomic number located next to it. The electrons (small spheres) on the circles should be evenly spaced, and the circles should each be oriented at a different angle. All electrons should be clearly visible.

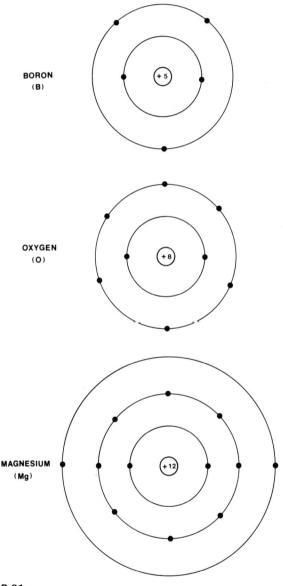

BORON
(B)

OXYGEN
(O)

MAGNESIUM
(Mg)

P-81

Prepare exploded drawings of the following assemblies (**P-82** to **P-86**).

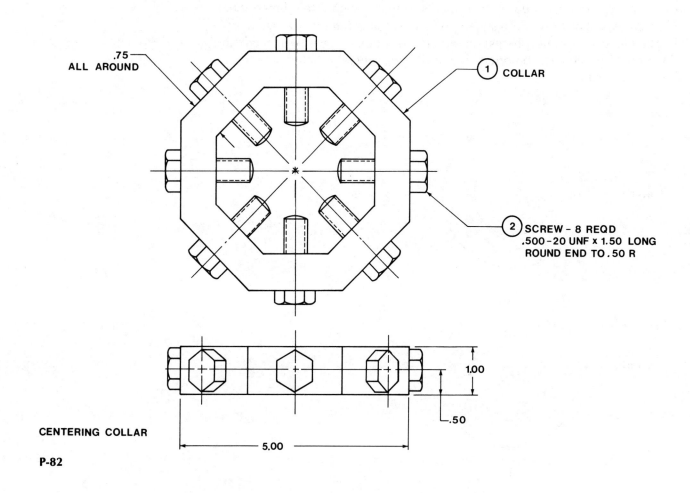

.75
ALL AROUND

① COLLAR

② SCREW - 8 REQD
.500 - 20 UNF x 1.50 LONG
ROUND END TO .50 R

1.00

.50

5.00

CENTERING COLLAR

P-82

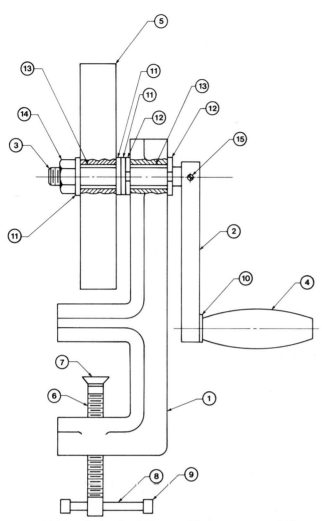

P-83-(I)   Details for the P83 assembly are on pages 218 and 219.

P-83-(II)

15	#10-24 UNC x .13 LONG HEADLESS SET SCREW	1
14	.50-13 UNC NUT	1
13	BUSHING	2
12	SNAP RING	2
11	.06 x .50 ID x 1.00 OD WASHER	3
10	.06 x .50 ID x .75 OD WASHER	1
9	END CAP	2
8	SHAFT, TWIST	1
7	PIVOT	1
6	SHAFT, HOLDING	1
5	GRINDING WHEEL	1
4	HANDLE ASSEMBLY	1
3	SHAFT, GUIDE	1
2	LINKAGE	1
1	BODY	1
NO	NAME	

BODY

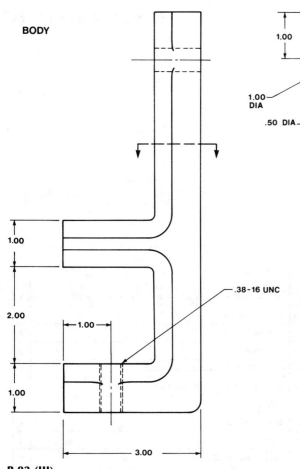

P-83-(III)

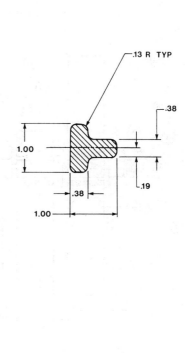

TWIST SHAFT

HOLDING SHAFT

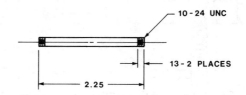

GUIDE SHAFT

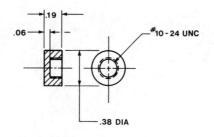

P-83-(IV)

END CAP   Scale: 2 = I

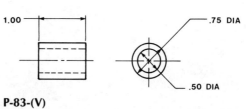

BUSHING

P-83-(V)

218

HANDLE ASSEMBLY

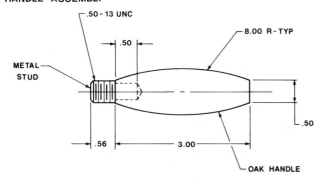

.50 - 13 UNC

8.00 R - TYP

METAL
STUD

.50

.50

.56

3.00

OAK HANDLE

GRINDING WHEEL
SCALE: 1/2 = 1

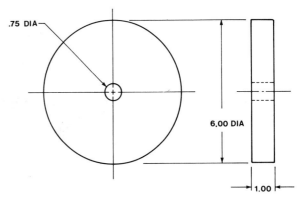

.75 DIA

6.00 DIA

1.00

SNAP RING
SCALE: 2 = 1

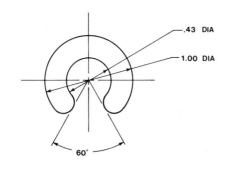

.43 DIA

1.00 DIA

60°

P-83-(VI)

END CAP
SCALE: 2 = 1

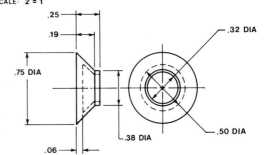

.25

.19

.75 DIA

.06

.32 DIA

.38 DIA

.50 DIA

P-83-(VII)

LINKAGE

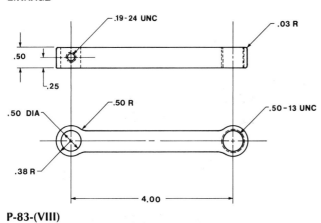

.19 - 24 UNC

.03 R

.50

.25

.50 DIA

.50 R

.50 - 13 UNC

.38 R

4.00

P-83-(VIII)

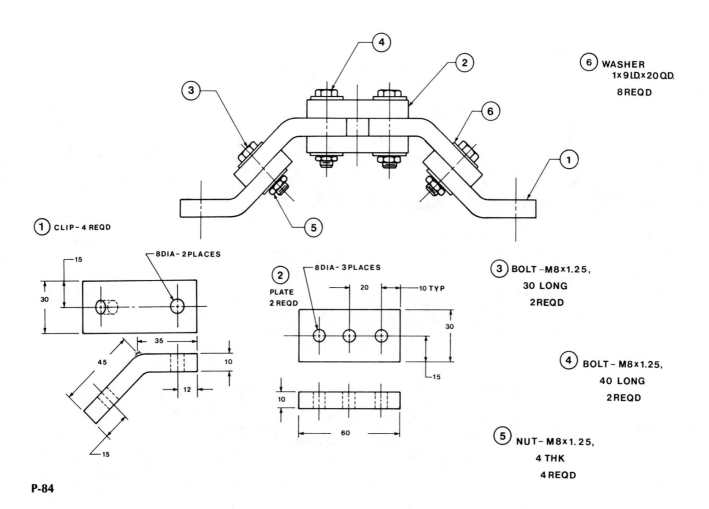

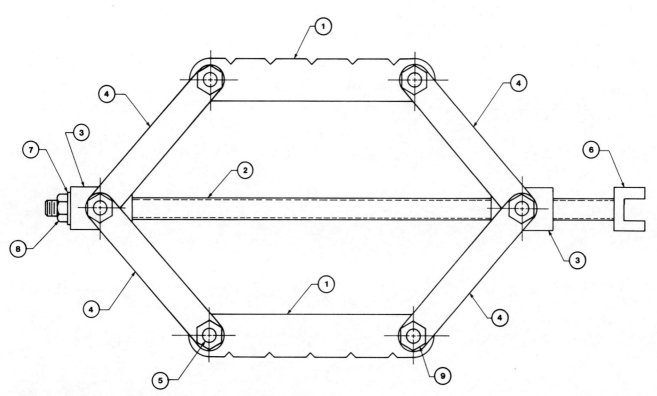

P-85-(I) Details for the P85 assembly are on page 221 and 222.

NO	NAME	QTY
9	.31-18 UNC NUT	24
8	.38-16 UNC NUT	1
7	.06 x .38 ID x .75 OD NYLON WASHER	1
6	END PIECE	1
5	HOLDER STUD	12
4	SUPPORT CLIPS	8
3	SLIDER BLOCK	2
2	DRIVE SCREW	1
1	BASE PLATE	2

P-85-(II)

BASE
PLATE

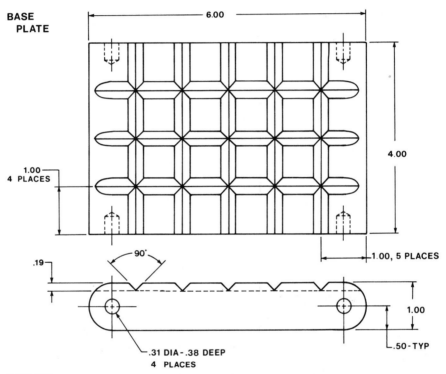

P-85-(III)

SLIDER BLOCK

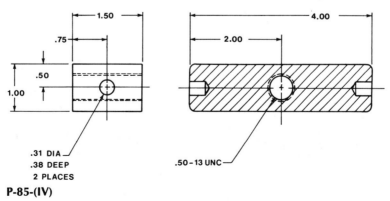

P-85-(IV)

DRIVE SCREW

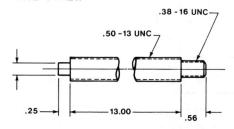

.50 –13 UNC

.38 - 16 UNC

.25

13.00

.56

END PIECE

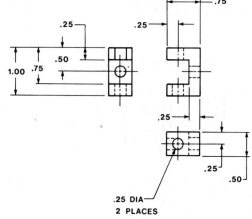

.75

.25

.25

.25

.50

1.00 .75

.25

.25

.50

.25 DIA
2 PLACES

P-85-(V)

HOLDER STUD

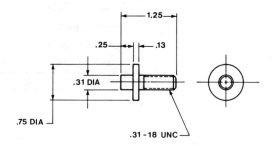

1.25

.25

.13

.31 DIA

.75 DIA

.31 - 18 UNC

SUPPORT CLIP

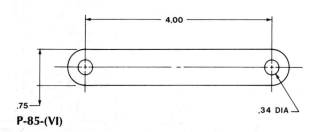

4.00

.75

.34 DIA

P-85-(VI)

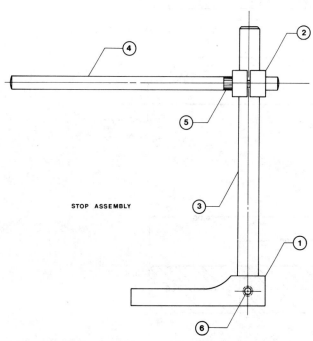

STOP ASSEMBLY

P-86 Details for the P86 assembly are on page 223.

(1) BASE

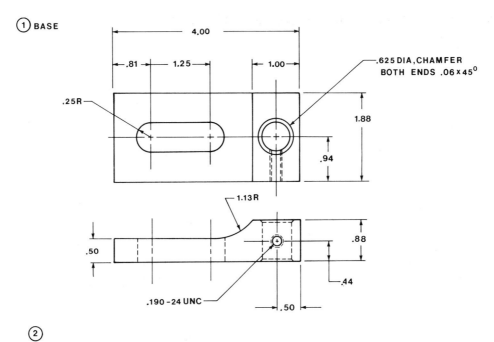

(2)

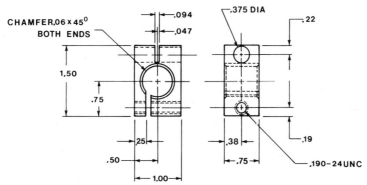

(3) POST, CENTER

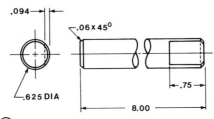

(5) SCREW
.190–24 UNC x .625 LONG
FILLISTER HEAD

(6) SCREW
.190 24 UNC x .50 LONG
HEADLESS

(4) POST, STOP

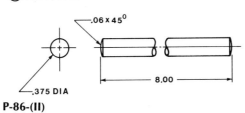

P-86-(II)

Prepare pictorial drawings of the following objects (**P-87** to **P-90**).

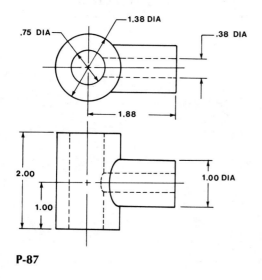

P-87

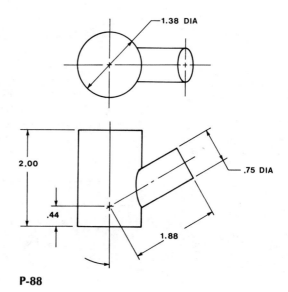

P-88

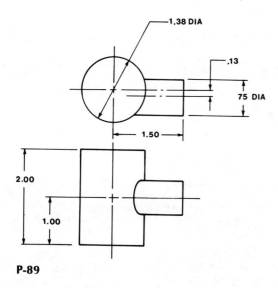

P-89

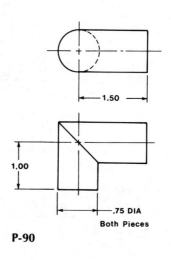

P-90

P-91   Prepare an exploded drawing for this assembly.

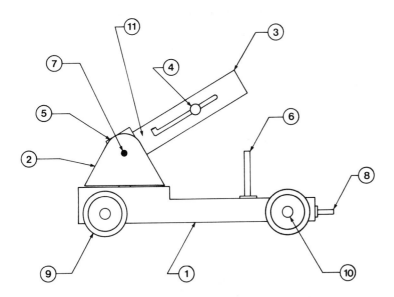

No.	NAME	PART No.	QTY
11	SPRING, COMP.	VENDOR	1
10	AXLE	80-406	2
9	WHEEL	72-620	4
8	COUPLING	72-202	1
7	PIVOT PIN	80-405	1
6	FWD SUPPORT	80-454	1
5	COLLAR	78-363	1
4	LAUNCH SUB ASSY	78-364	1
3	BARREL	85-454	1
2	YOKE	85-767	1
1	BODY	86-787	1
No.	NAME	PART No.	QTY

TOY CANNON TRUCK

P-91-1   Details for the P91 assembly are on page 225, 226 and 227.

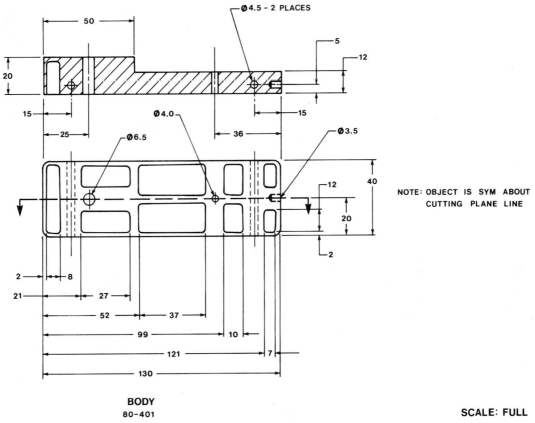

BODY
80-401

NOTE: OBJECT IS SYM ABOUT
CUTTING PLANE LINE

SCALE: FULL

P-91-2

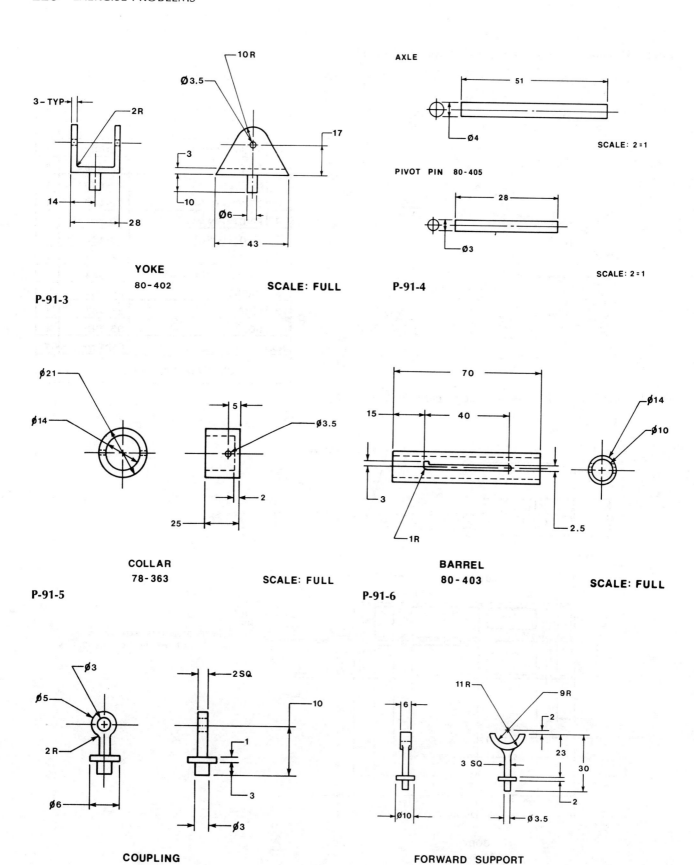

10R

Ø3.5

3 - TYP

2R

17

3

14

10

Ø6

28

43

YOKE
80-402

SCALE: FULL

P-91-3

AXLE

51

Ø4

SCALE: 2 = 1

PIVOT PIN 80-405

28

Ø3

SCALE: 2 = 1

P-91-4

Ø21

Ø14

5

Ø3.5

2

25

COLLAR
78-363

SCALE: FULL

P-91-5

70

15

40

3

1R

2.5

Ø14

Ø10

BARREL
80-403

SCALE: FULL

P-91-6

Ø3

Ø5

2R

Ø6

2SQ

10

1

3

Ø3

COUPLING
72-202

SCALE: 2 = 1

P-91-7

11R

9R

6

2

23

30

3 SQ

2

Ø10

Ø3.5

FORWARD SUPPORT
80-404

SCALE: FULL

P-91-8

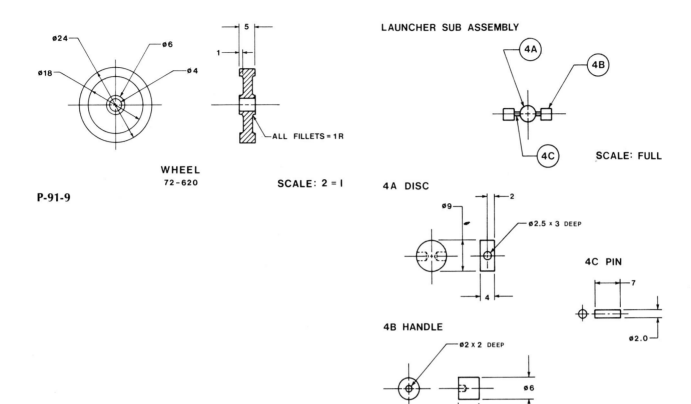

ø24 ø6
ø18 ø4

5
1
ALL FILLETS = 1R

WHEEL
72-620

SCALE: 2 = 1

P-91-9

LAUNCHER SUB ASSEMBLY

4A
4B
4C

SCALE: FULL

4A DISC

ø9
2
ø2.5 x 3 DEEP
4

4B HANDLE

ø2 x 2 DEEP
ø6
6

4C PIN

7
ø2.0

SCALE: 2 = 1

P-91-10

Prepare pictorial drawings of the following objects (P-72 to P-97).

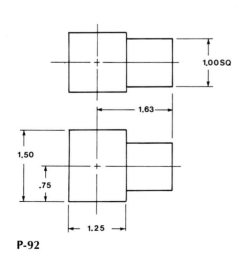

1.00SQ
1.63
1.50
.75
1.25

P-92

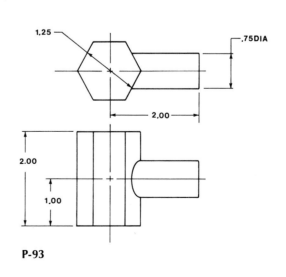

1.25
.75DIA
2.00
2.00
1.00

P-93

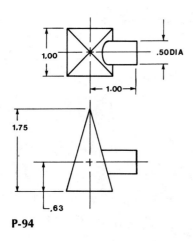

P-94

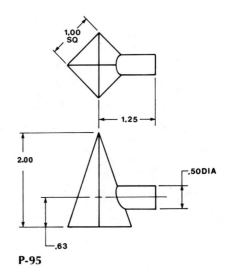

P-95

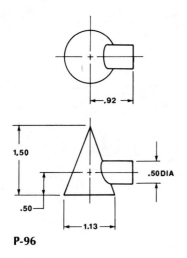

P-96

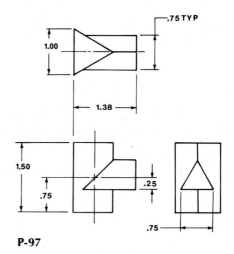

P-97

P-98   Using a LEROY lettering set, letter the entire alphabet and the numbers 1 to 26 as follows: 1.A, 2.B, 3.C, etc.

P-99 Using a LEROY lettering set, create a title block for your school. Include the school's name and address, plus illustrator's name, date, scale, title, and so on.

P-100 Using a LEROY lettering set, create your own business card. Include your name, address, telephone number, and profession.

P-101 Use your initials and create two personal logos; one freehand and one using drawing instruments.

P-102 Create three geometric designs; use those shown here as examples. Start with a square, a circle, or some other geometric shape.

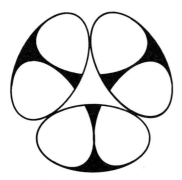

P-102-1

P-102-2

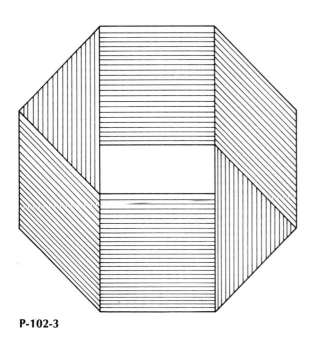

P-102-3

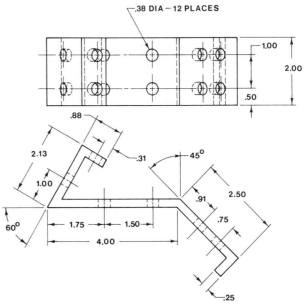

P-103

P-104   Metric—an example of a first angle projection drawing.

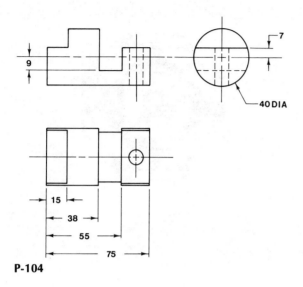

P-104

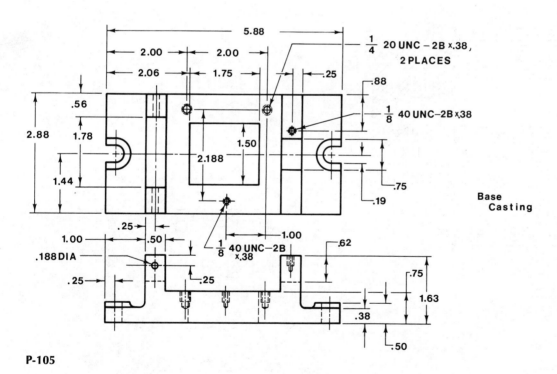

P-105

An example of pen-and-ink rendering by Robert J. Berry, architectural delineator.

233

INDEX